WHY YOU'RE HERE

WHY YOU'RE HERE

Ethics for the Real World

JOHN G. STACKHOUSE, JR.

OXFORD
UNIVERSITY PRESS

OXFORD

UNIVERSITY PRESS

Oxford University Press is a department of the University of Oxford. It furthers
the University's objective of excellence in research, scholarship, and education
by publishing worldwide. Oxford is a registered trade mark of Oxford University
Press in the UK and certain other countries.

Published in the United States of America by Oxford University Press
198 Madison Avenue, New York, NY 10016, United States of America.

CIP data is on file at the Library of Congress
ISBN 978-0-19-063674-6

9 8 7 6 5 4 3 2 1

Printed by WebCom, Inc., Canada

To M. E. M.

Before I became a Christian, I do not think I fully realized that one's life, after conversion, would inevitably consist in doing most of the same things one had been doing before: one hopes, in a new spirit, but still the same things. . . . Christianity does not exclude any of the ordinary human activities. St. Paul tells people to get on with their jobs. He even assumes that Christians may go to dinner parties, and, what is more, dinner parties given by pagans. Our Lord attends a wedding and provides miraculous wine. Under the aegis of His Church, and in the most Christian ages, learning and the arts flourish. The solution of this paradox is, of course, well known to you. "Whether ye eat or drink or whatsoever ye do, do all to the glory of God."

—C. S. LEWIS

Those who wish to focus on the problem of a Christian ethic are faced with an outrageous demand—from the outset they must give up, as inappropriate to this topic, the very two questions that led them to deal with the ethical problem: "How can I be good?" and "How can I do something good?" Instead they must ask the wholly other, completely different question, "What is the will of God?"

—DIETRICH BONHOEFFER

CONTENTS

PART III: RESPONDING TO THE CALL OF JESUS

INTRODUCTION

"GOD GAVE ME A LIFEBOAT and said, 'Moody, save all you can!'" So declared the great Chicago evangelist Dwight L. Moody a century ago.[1]

Is that why Christians are in the world? To rescue people out of it?

Lots of Christians think so. Others, however, claim that the task of Christians is to conquer the world—as gently as possible—in order to bring it under the beneficial sway of Christian principles and, ideally, to bring everyone to the worship of Jesus as Lord.

Is that why Christians are in the world? To take it over for Jesus?

Still other Christians, of course, find the first group annoying and the second group alarming. They simply want to do a good day's work, raise a family, volunteer in worthy causes, go to church, enjoy good friends, and, if someone really wants to know, say a little bit about their faith.

Is that why Christians are in the world? To be decent citizens?

To many of us, one of these options seems right, not least because important Christian teachers and even whole movements commend one or another of these visions of Christian presence in the world.

For others of us, however, these options leave us cold—or at least wanting more. Saving people sounds admirable, of course, but abandoning the planet and all the good that we experience here seems awfully radical. Offering the benefits of Christian culture to a confused and complicated world sounds generous, but trying to convert or coerce everyone else seems awfully imperialistic. As for quietly going about one's affairs and contributing to the world just as one can sounds both sensible and humble, but going through life much like everyone else seems perhaps unworthy of the name "Christian"—or any name at all. Did Jesus really die on a cross merely to inspire honorable, but otherwise unremarkable, lives?

This book is about how to live as God intended us to live. It actually, and without irony, offers an answer to the question: What is the meaning of life? We all want to know how a person should live well. What does genuine success look like, measured according to what standard? Can my life, and our lives together, have lasting significance?

As such, this is a book of ethics. But it is not merely about "right and wrong." The Greek word *ethos* means the *character* or *nature* of something or someone. Ethics does include questions of morality, but it derives from a more fundamental concept, the concept of *essence*, of what it is to *be* this or that. Thus medical ethics, at least traditionally, goes beyond bioethics to questions even of dress (whether to wear a lab coat), etiquette (whether to introduce oneself as "Dr. Smith" or "Margaret"), and advertising services (whether to do so and, if so, how to do so properly). The issue in these cases, and many more, is not just "right or wrong" but what is *proper* or *seemly* or *appropriate* to the profession of medicine in its several modes, given what it *is*. Christian ethics, likewise, is not only about what is right or wrong but fundamentally also about what it is to *be Christian* in the world, what is proper to the profession and practice of Christian faith.

In sum, this book explores these questions:

Why are we here?

Who are we, *what* are we, and what are we supposed to do?

What, in short, is our *vocation*?

The word "vocation" comes from the Latin word *vocare* and basically means "calling." When we hear the word "vocation" or "calling," we tend to think of religious work—like becoming a priest or a nun. But a Christian view of vocation is much, much bigger than that. How big? This big: *everyone, everything, everywhere, in every moment.*

True, some Christians have indeed equated vocation with work, particularly what they understand to be religious work. Especially in Roman Catholic and Orthodox Christianity, for someone to have a "vocation" means for him or her to have a sense of divine calling to a religious career and, indeed, to a whole life pattern of religious service. This use of "vocation" has been Protestantized (so to speak) so that pastors and missionaries in those traditions often speak this way about what they do and who they are. Seminary and missionary training often begins with the sharing of testimonies about "receiving the call" to the pastorate or the mission field. This use of "vocation" also has been secularized to apply to other traditional professions—to what some would call "secular priesthoods" or "helping professions." Thus one still hears people say that they "have a calling" to a career in medicine, the law, or education.

Other Christians, however, have understood vocation to be the call of Christ to *every* Christian, not just the full-time clergy or a particular range of professionals. The divine call, they say, is for everyone to participate in specific, definably *Christian* activities. Thus one's actual job is not one's vocation or even an important part of it. Jobs provide for our physical needs and are thus a necessity in the world as it is, but they are not actually part of one's divine calling. Instead, the call of Christ is to undertake evangelism, or charity, or some other work that goes beyond and is quite clearly different from the regular work—indeed, beyond the ordinary life—of any normal human being.

This is the view in which I was raised. The only guidance my church tradition offered me about how to live as a Christian was to tell me to do two things: (1) avoid sin (such as lying or gossiping, stealing office supplies, cheating on taxes, having sex outside of marriage, and so on); and (2) evangelize my co-workers and customers as often as possible. In other church traditions, I would have been told that my Christian vocation was to care for the poor, so I ought to volunteer in the church food bank or in the severe weather shelter. In still others, I would have been told that my Christian vocation was to seek justice, so I ought to write letters for Amnesty International or protest discrimination against whatever local group was currently being oppressed. In each of these varieties, however, I would have been given no serious Biblical and theological framework in which to understand and undertake *most* of what I did *most* of the time. School, work, sports, art, romance, financial planning, childrearing—none of these would ever be addressed from the pulpit or Sunday school lectern.

Some Christians, therefore, have seen *vocation* as a particular *job*. Others have seen vocation as *not a job*, but specifically religious service.

A third view is the one I recommend and will trace here, namely, that our job is a *part* of our vocation, and so are whatever specifically Christian activities in which we engage, but our vocation stretches out to encompass everything we are and do. Vocation is about *everyone, everything, everywhere, in every moment.*

In most religions, there is an inclination to distinguish between what we might call "heroes" on the one hand and "ordinaries" on the other, between what are sometimes termed "religious" and "secular" individuals. Buddhist monks, for example, hope to achieve nirvana through their rigorous ascetic practices, while the vast majority of Buddhists live much less demanding lives. Buddhist laypeople provide practical support to the monks in their spiritually superior labors and otherwise try to live properly according to their station in life, hoping to acquire enough positive karma to be reincarnated as a superior sort of person who might, in fact, take up monasticism and thus achieve nirvana and liberation from the cycle of rebirth. One sees similar patterns throughout Indian religions and, indeed, around the globe.

Christianity also has manifested this two-tiered system through the ages, although different traditions and times have lionized different elites. We might (somewhat irreverently) summarize the upper Christian tier as, progressively, martyrs, monks, mystics, magisteria, missionaries—and megachurch leaders.

One of the key revisions of Christian life that emerged from the sixteenth-century Protestant Reformation was centered in this zone. The Reformers declared that the Bible knows nothing of "super-Christians" versus "regular Christians." There are just *Christians.* There are not some believers who are saints and others who are non-saints. The

New Testament says that *all* Christians are saints, because the root of that word is simply "to be set apart for special use," and each Christian is truly set apart by God for divine service.

With this Reformation eradication of what we might call a two-tiered system of seriousness came two positive teachings: (1) all (legitimate) work is blessed by God, not just religious work; and (2) vocation is more than work and encompasses one's entire life. The Old Testament law seems to cover all sorts of topics we modern Westerners don't typically think of as being of divine interest (from diet to hygiene, and from how to farm to how to dress), demonstrating that God really does care about everything in human life. Vocation, therefore, is the divine calling to every person to do God's will in every mode and form of human life: public as well as private, secular as well as religious, juvenile as well as adult, corporate as well as individual, female as well as male.

As this last sentence implies, however, God does not call only Christians. In fact, long before we encounter any Christians in the Bible, we encounter human beings—right on the first page, in fact. And by the time we get to the end of the Bible, the term "Christian" has fallen away as no longer useful. For at the beginning and at the end, there is no need for the label "Christian" to pick out those human beings who are loyal to God, who are connected properly to God and live in partnership with God. There are just human beings, doing what humans are supposed to do.

In the first part of this book, then, we will look at what it is that human beings are supposed to do—in this life, and in the next. We will examine what I term the *permanent* call of God on *every* human life and society, what we literally were made for.

In the next part, we will look at the peculiar work God gives to the peculiar people who are indeed currently (temporarily) marked by the label "Christian." We Christians are indeed people (!), so we are supposed to do everything the first chapter says we are supposed to do as human beings. But Christians also have a distinct mission in the world, and we'll see what that is in due course. Then we will conclude this discussion of vocation by seeing how these two vocations are interwoven and reinforcing, rather than two starkly different modes of life between which we somehow switch in various circumstances.

The third part will set out some basic, but vital, implications for living as human beings engaged in both our own rehabilitation and in the restoration and cultivation of a damaged world. Indeed, the world is very much what Jesus called it, a "mixed field" in which good and bad are not only present but often also intertwined such that it is difficult and sometimes even destructive to try to eliminate the evil because the good might also be harmed in the process.

Worse, many of us—maybe all of us—live in a world in which it is simply impossible to be and act in a way that does not implicate us in some kind of evil and perhaps even requires us to do things that normally would be wrong, but in this situation are, in fact, right. Does this line of thinking disquiet you? It should. But it may be the most sensible, useful, and Biblical way of living in the time between the Fall and the return of Jesus.

"Useful" is a high value for the Christian life—or it ought to be. Many Christians today, alas, comfort themselves with the assurance that God does not call his people to produce results but instead to remain faithful and pure. We will see that this idea of vocation is both self-serving and self-deluding. God instead calls his people, and all people, to action that produces important results. *Faithfulness*, that is, includes the requirement of *effectiveness* or, perhaps better, *fruitfulness* (John 15:16).

We are called to live and work in situations charged with meaning, therefore, but also fraught with dysfunction and danger. *Compromise* is therefore a word we need to consider: Is it a pathetic and even seductive word drawing us away from heroic Christian idealism? Or is it a realistic word that ought to be one of the prudent Christian's tactical options? When we engage in public life, at what ought we to aim? Some say, "All or nothing." Others recommend a "faithful presence."[2] I recommend *maximizing shalom*.

Let's see, then, what case I can make for that recommendation.

This book is adapted from a larger, more academic volume in which I first set out my thoughts on these matters: *Making the Best of It: Following Christ in the Real World*.[3] Readers looking for more extensive considerations of most of the following issues, as well as detailed studies of crucial figures in my thinking (the Niebuhr brothers, C. S. Lewis, and Dietrich Bonhoeffer), can consult that book. There are also a number of substantive developments in my thought that show up in the present volume, both structurally and materially. The present volume also takes into better account than did my previous writing the dark truth that it isn't just "on occasion" or "somewhere else" that people face ethical borderline situations. We all live in deeply compromised moral environments. Having to make the best decision among regrettably impure options is a far more common experience than I had earlier acknowledged, and I have wrestled with the implications of that recognition in what follows. And years of lecturing on these questions have prompted me to rearrange the material in what I hope will be a pattern that makes more sense, especially to non-specialists.

One important difference between this book and *Making the Best of It* is that I have not included a chapter on "method in ethics" in the present volume. I have developed my thinking about that question substantially in subsequent years; the crucial question of how Christians can listen for the voice of their Lord can be referred to an entire book on that subject: *Need to Know: Vocation as the Heart of Christian Epistemology*.[4] It reflects significant changes from the scheme presented in *Making the Best of It*, and I hope readers follow up this book with that one.

To Cynthia Read and her colleagues at Oxford University Press's New York offices I am thus grateful for the opportunity to write a book that not only makes more accessible what I previously published but also, I think, improves conceptually upon it in some key ways. This is my fifth project with Ms. Read, and I remain quietly giddy that she has wanted to produce any of these books, let alone all of them.

The acknowledgement section of *Making the Best of It* lists debts incurred in the writing of that book that necessarily carry over to this one as well. I am ashamed to note, however, that I did not therein acknowledge the cumulative impact of teaching these ideas over almost two decades to many fine students at Regent College, Vancouver, and then to some more at Crandall University, Moncton. I likewise ought to have thanked the many churches and other organizations that let me present intermediate versions of these ideas across North America, in the UK, and in Korea, Malaysia, India, Australia, and New Zealand. I remain abashed that so many opportunities to get things right have resulted in work that nonetheless remains all too flawed.

Crandall University has proven to be a most congenial community in which to work. Their welcome to this scholar "from away" has been warm and thorough. I am particularly grateful for the affirmation and facilitation of my work I have received from President Bruce Fawcett, administrator extraordinaire Janet Williston, and my old friend and brilliant colleague Keith Bodner.

Throughout the writing of this book, as she always has, my fair spouse remained an utterly reliable source of wisdom, comfort, provocation, and affection. She needs no such instruction from the likes of me to know why she's here. During this odd season of bicoastal living according to God's mysterious calling, I have badly missed also our beloved sons and daughter-in-law, and I would be delighted if they and their friends benefit from this book.

I wrote in *Making the Best of It* that no one has influenced my thinking in this sphere more than my doctoral supervisor and mentor, Professor Martin E. Marty. It thus is obvious to whom this book ought to be dedicated, and is.

Feast of St. Teresa of Calcutta 2016

PART I

OUR (PERMANENT) HUMAN CALLING

Make Shalom

THE BASIC CALLING

OF HUMANITY

ANYONE WHO OPENS A BIBLE notices, perhaps with disappointment, that it does not present us with a convenient set of questions and answers. It is not a catechism, not a dictionary, not an owner's manual—at least, not in the forms we're used to. The Bible instead is fundamentally a story. While it does contain a wide range of other genres—including poems, laws, prophecies, lyrics, proverbs, letters, apocalypses, and more—at base the Bible is a narrative with a beginning, a middle, and an end.

Most cultures in the world have understood human life to be lived within a cyclical pattern: birth, growth, decline, death—with rebirth or at least procreation to perpetuate the cycle. The ancient Israelites innovated in human cultural history by understanding the world as a line, not a circle. Yes, they acknowledged the obvious cycles of nature. But they understood the world to be moving from one condition to another along a timeline of development. Indeed, the line was not merely linear, so to speak, but *intentional* and *purposeful*—what the Greeks would call *teleological*: destined toward an End that was also an Outcome, a goal.[1]

We will better understand who we are and what we are to do according to the Bible if we take the Bible's own shape seriously and look for our answers in the Story. So let's start at the beginning.

THE CULTURAL MANDATE: MAKE SHALOM

What is the very first commandment in the Bible? You might think it would be "Worship God" or at least the Golden Rule ("Treat others as you would want them to treat you"), but it isn't. In fact, it's something called "the cultural mandate."

"In the beginning, God created the heavens and the earth" (Gen. 1:1). In this primeval narrative, we encounter theological truths entailed by God's words and deeds. And most of those truths bear directly on human life in the world. (Happily, I do not need to pause here to detail my views of precisely how to understand the literature, science, history, and so on of the Genesis creation accounts. These are important matters, of course, but for our purposes—which are theological and ethical—Christians can and should take the story on its own terms: this is the authoritative picture of God creating the world.)

God creates the world and it is pronounced "very good" (1:31). The world is very good in all its materiality, temporality, and finitude. In some philosophies and cultures, those characteristics are exactly what make creation *not* good, but instead something to be merely lived in, or endured, or "seen through" to spiritual realities beyond. In certain outlooks, the world is even to be despised as distracting or harmful. (Even some Christians can sound like this about creation—but they're badly wrong.) Christianity revels in the goodness of the world. Animals matter; plants matter; the oceans and rivers and lakes matter; the hills and the valleys and the mountains and the pebbles matter; the air matters. God intended them all to exist, and God made them very good.

We might pause for a moment here amid all this goodness to note a serious ethical error quite common in our time. Nowadays many people argue about ethics as if we were still in Eden. Few actually speak as if we were truly in the Garden, of course. What I mean is that some people argue that the world in its natural state, untouched by human interference, is simply and unqualifiedly good. And anything natural—that is, anything unaffected by and not a product of human action—is pronounced good.

This outlook shows up in the phrasing, "God made me/it this way," as if that settles the issue. "God doesn't make mistakes" and "God doesn't make junk" are more slogans of this sort. The most common use of this argument in current ethical controversy, of course, is in the realm of gender and sexuality. If some form of sexual or gender difference can be shown to be the direct result of, say, fetal brain development, and thus is perfectly natural (note how loaded both of those terms are: "perfectly" and "natural"), then such difference ought to be validated as being just as good as the heterosexual norm.

This type of argument should be recognized as simply a contemporary form of "What is, is good." Christians, however, should be the first to recognize that we haven't lived in Eden for a long, long time. Much has happened since then, and some of it has been pretty bad. Dispositions toward alcoholism and other forms of chemical addiction, toward violence, and toward schizophrenia—all can be shown now to have organic roots. To argue directly from "is" to "ought" is not immediately wrong from the Christian point of view, but it certainly isn't automatically right, either. Each case depends on whether the matter in question has to do with God's original creation or with what has happened to that creation since the Fall.

With this caution in mind, let's proceed to the climax of the creation story:

> Then God said, "Let us make humankind in our image, according to our likeness; and let them have dominion over the fish of the sea, and over the birds of the air, and over the cattle, and over all the wild animals of the earth, and over every creeping thing that creeps upon the earth."
>
> So God created humankind in his image, in the image of God he created them; male and female he created them. God blessed them, and God said to them, "Be fruitful and multiply, and fill the earth and subdue it; and have dominion over the fish of the sea and over the birds of the air and over every living thing that moves upon the earth." (Gen. 1:26–28)

Having created everything else, God then creates human beings specifically in his "image" and "likeness"—the exact words the author of Genesis uses to describe Seth, the third child of Adam and Eve (Gen. 5:3). We human beings were created to resemble God and to act like God.

The phrase "image of God" gets my vote as the most plastic in the history of Christian thought. It seems that every writer or speaker who wants to say anything about the nature of humanity focuses our attention on his or her special theme—human rationality, or human spirituality, or human relationality, or whatever—and then definitively pronounces this particular feature *the* image of God.

The actual text of Genesis, however, does not ascribe any particular, let alone peculiar, abilities to the humans God creates in God's image. Rather than having something *attributed* to the first human pair, God *assigns* something to them: a role, not a particular talent or trait. And this role is known as the *cultural mandate*.

For what has God been doing for the first twenty-some verses of the Bible? Creating. And if God now decides to make a creature who resembles God, surely the most natural reading of the text leads us to conclude that this will be a *creative* creature. And this is exactly what we find as God issues a commandment to these new beings.

Strangely, this very first commandment God gives the first human beings seems comically superfluous. God doesn't normally waste time telling us to do things we're going to do anyway: "Enjoy the taste of a good meal!" or "Remember to keep breathing—in, out, in, out . . . " But here in Genesis God seems to command, even to over-command, something most of us don't need much prodding to do: have sex.

Why do I say "over-command"? Because God actually repeats the command to procreate, and then repeats it again! "Be fruitful and multiply, and fill the earth."

> *"Be fruitful"*—have a kid.
> *"And multiply"*—have lots of kids.
> *"And fill the earth"*—that's a lot of kids . . .

Why is God saying all this? God tells human beings to reproduce—and to reproduce *a lot*—so as to fulfill our fundamental calling as "images of God": to bring the whole earth under our creativity, under our cultivation.[2] These three verbs of reproduction lead to two verbs of cultivation: "and subdue it; and have dominion."

These latter verbs ("subdue" and "have dominion") are quite strong: the sort of actions that elsewhere in the Old Testament have to do with the Conquest of Canaan (e.g., Num. 32:29; Josh. 18:1). And why would human beings have to engage in such strenuous actions? After all, God just made the world and pronounced it "very good"!

"Very good" it was, yes—but not *perfect*. (There are terms in Hebrew for "perfect," and they aren't used here.) The world is created with massive potential to be turned by us creative creatures into reality. We are not to simply observe the world, nor even merely to enjoy it. We are to make something of it. That's what *culture* is. The world is a giant studio, filled with paints and canvases and brushes and easels into which God invites the human beings as artists. The world is very good, yes, but it is *wild*—and therefore needs to be subdued, to be ruled, to be cultivated so that it becomes everything it can be.

This idea that everything is to become all it can be is the heart of the Hebrew word *shalom*. Usually translated "peace," *shalom* means not only something negative—"no war or conflict of any kind"—but also something wonderfully positive: the *flourishing* of all things. This flourishing is not only of each individual thing—each human being, yes, and also each animal, tree, landscape, and waterway—but also of each *relationship* among individuals, each *group* that individuals form, each *relationship* among groups or between groups and individuals, and the whole of creation in loving harmony with God. Shalom is literally *global flourishing*, and it is the intended outcome of God working with God's "little gods" to cultivate the world.

The burgeoning human family therefore is to move out from the initial Garden, planted by God (Gen. 2:8–15), to make a garden of the whole planet. We are to be "little lords," deputies of God, doing God's kind of work in obedience to God's basic commission. God calls us to be creative: to *pro-create* in order to *co-create*.

Caring for the earth and making the best of what God has given to us to cultivate is thus our primary duty under God. Yes, of course we are to love God above all and love our neighbors as ourselves. I take those for granted, as surely the Israelite author and Israelite readers of this ancient text would have taken them for granted as well. And to these great commandments we will presently turn. Nonetheless, it is striking that the very first commandment God gives to humanity in the Bible is this one: garden the world.

(We can pause here in passing to note that some Christian writers have said that among the benefits wrought by the Incarnation of our Lord was its "sanctifying of the ordinary," its validation of everyday work. But this well-intentioned claim is a mistake. Jesus came as the Son of Man *reminding* us of, as well as *showing* us flawlessly, what God had *already* revealed to us at the creation of the world: the dignity of human beings and our divinely commissioned work in God's world. We didn't need the Incarnation to know that God wants us to make shalom. We possessed our original instructions from our very genesis.)

God has never rescinded this commandment, never set it aside for something else, never indicated that it is temporary and we will one day outgrow it. Instead, we are to carry on this permanent human calling day by day, and we will carry on this vocation in the world to come.

Lots of us don't think we will, whether we are Christians or otherwise. We envision the next life as an eternal day at the beach. We wake up in our heavenly cabana, put on our heavenly sandals and swimsuit, pull some heavenly fruit off a branch for breakfast, and head out to see if the heavenly surf's up today.

But our happy, human task forever will instead be tending the world and acting creatively to make it better and better. And we will do so right alongside Jesus who, as the Human One ("the Son of Man"), models for us what we humans are to do: "If we endure," Paul promises, "we will reign with him" (2 Tim. 2:12). And in the Revelation to John, the Christian faithful are several times described as reigning with Christ (Rev. 5:10; 20:6; 22:5).

Did you ever wonder: Over what or whom will resurrected humanity *reign* with Christ, since all of Christ's enemies have been removed from the scene forever? The answer is this: we will reign with Christ over a renewed earth, as we human beings continue to be, and "have dominion" as, the "image of God."

Dallas Willard properly sets aside the old notion of the "beatific vision"—that mistaken Christian teaching, down through the ages, that we will spend eternity in blissful contemplation of God. The end of Dante's *Divine Comedy, Paradiso,* powerfully depicts us all sitting in a giant Rose Bowl (look it up: I'm not kidding) gazing forever at the interesting geometric patterns of the Trinity. And thus we shall ever be with the Lord? No, Willard writes,

> We will not sit around looking at one another or at God for
> eternity but will join the eternal Logos, "reign with him," in
> the endlessly ongoing creative work of God. . . .

Thus, our faithfulness over a "few things" in the present phase of our life develops the kind of character that can be entrusted with "many things." . . . His plan is for us to develop, as apprentices to Jesus, to the point where we can take our place in the ongoing creativity of the universe.[3]

And how wonderful it will be to engage in work in that context: the consequences of the Fall removed (more about that dark subject in chapter 3), with everyone fully cooperating, including nature itself, and in constant communion with God. We can scarcely imagine what scholarship would be like in that situation, or engineering, or music, or architecture, or (my personal favorite) cuisine . . .

TWO IMPLICATIONS OF THE CULTURAL MANDATE

An important ethical error in our day stems from the failure to see the hierarchy instituted in both of the Genesis accounts of creation (chapters 1 and 2). Human beings are given dominion over the rest of the world. Despite the assertions of "deep ecology" and similar ideologies that place human beings on the same level as all other animals (in the striking phrase of PETA founder Ingrid Newkirk, "A rat is a pig is a dog is a boy"), the Bible says that human beings are literally the lords (*domini*) of creation. Such a term in our society resonates negatively with words such as "dominate" and with ugly ideas such as human exploitation and despoliation of the rest of creation. Christianity is then charged with facilitating modern technology and its selfish use by humans on the rest of the world. Does Genesis provide a rationale for such rapacity?[4]

Quite the contrary. Human beings are created in the image of God, and therefore are literally to look like and act like God in regard to the rest of creation. Indeed, we are "lords" under the express authority of God, who is *the* Lord: "'The world is mine,' declares the Lord, 'and all that is in it'" (Ps. 50:12).

The formal name of my native country, the Dominion of Canada, helps us here, for in this case, "dominion" means "a self-governing nation of the Commonwealth of Nations other than the United Kingdom that acknowledges the British monarch as chief of state."[5] "Dominion" has nothing to do with the act of domination but rather with authority that is wielded under the authority of another, as the Canadian Parliament governs Canada under the authority of the Queen.[6] So human beings are "lords" in the feudal sense, we might say, under the authority of the Great King who gives us our lands and our authority to govern them, and to whom we owe fealty and obedience in all we do. Pope John Paul II warns us well:

> Humankind, which discovers its capacity to transform and in a certain sense create the world through its own work, forgets that this is always based on God's prior and original gift of things that are. People think that they can make arbitrary use of the earth, subjecting it without restraint to their wills, as though the earth did not have its own requisites and a prior God-given purpose, which human beings can indeed develop but must not betray.[7]

If God therefore is our patron and our example, how does God, this Great King, act toward the world he made? With care; with sustenance and creativity. Human beings are the gardeners under God's commission.

We differ strikingly from God, to be sure, in that we have a symbiotic relationship with our fellow creatures. Unlike God, we cannot exist without them. That basic fact also governs how we treat our fellow creatures. Who benefits when the gardener does her work well, the gardener or the garden? Clearly they both do. The gardener is "in charge" in both senses of that term: she decides what is to be done with the garden because she has been charged by God to make those decisions, precisely to benefit both herself and the garden under her care.

Andy Crouch thus observes that radical ecological activists, such as biologist David Suzuki, philosopher Peter Singer, and the like, miss a fundamental point when they accuse human beings of "speciesism." Yes, we humans think we are special. But this dominion we Christians believe we have from God is an oversight *on behalf of others*:

> In the whole known universe we are the only species that takes responsibility for the others; the only species that demonstrates the slightest interest in naming, tending, and conserving the others; [the only species] that indeed is accountable for the stewardship of the others; and the only species that feels guilt (however fitfully and hypocritically) when its stewardship fails.[8]

We are the only species that is to care *for* everything else because we are the only species that, at our best, cares *about* everything else. If instead we should act just like any other species, then we would stop regarding the interests of other species and exploit them at will. We therefore must not let ourselves be driven to guilty consciences, let alone self-loathing, by those ecological extremists who, understandably horrified by how we have harmed the earth, condemn human dominion, if not humanity itself, as a curse. We all should bewail the mistakes we have made in our stewardship of creation. Of course we must repent of mistreatment of our fellow creatures. But we must do so as responsible lords who have acted irresponsibly and who now intend to make things right, not as usurpers who ought to slink away from the throne room and leave the world to fend for itself. God made us to bless the earth by exercising dominion. God did not want us to leave as few footprints as possible, leaving the earth alone as much as we can. God commanded us instead to spread out, over the whole globe, and bring it all under our influence, to subdue it for its own good, to make it even more fruitful, beautiful, and sustainable, under God's guidance and by the resources he invested in the whole globe. We dare not be shamed into relinquishing this role because we have performed it badly up to now. We must take it up afresh, do the best we can, and look forward to the shalom that our administration will bring, in concert with Christ's rule, in the world to come.

A second fundamental affirmation emerging from the cultural mandate is that all human beings share the dignity and responsibility of this commandment. More pointedly, all human beings who are making shalom, whether they intend to honor God or not, are thereby doing his will. God continues to bless all humanity with both a certain inclination toward this task and the resources to undertake it.[9] And inasmuch as any of our neighbors are indeed cultivating the earth in whatever might be their work, art, leisure, and so on, we can recognize it, approve it, and cooperate with it—again, whether or not the name of God or of Jesus is invoked in the enterprise.

Example? Let's use Richard Dawkins—I'm sure he wouldn't mind. When Professor Dawkins was undertaking science, as he used to do, he was making shalom—blessing the world by skillfully investigating and describing it. Thus he was fulfilling the cultural mandate, and thus he was doing the will of the God he has spent so very much energy trying to disprove.

I admit that it is pleasant to think of Richard Dawkins as willy-nilly obedient to the purposes of God. The fun only increases when we consider how his more recent work, that of Professional Atheist, also has made shalom in at least two respects. First, it has brought forward a number of valid concerns with which Christians ought to deal. Second, the controversy he has fomented has provided occasions for thousands of people to talk about religion publicly and intellectually, instead of in the typical ways of referring to religion as either a benign private pursuit or as a fanatical political threat. So Richard Dawkins has been doing the will of God, and in several respects.[10]

Some might see the definition of "doing the will of God" as too expansive here. An arch-atheist doing the will of God because he is doing competent science or engaging in ideological provocation? But we must avoid too restricted a definition of what it means to be engaged in the work of *shalom*. We can have too narrow a sense of what may count as worthy work, art, and so on. Advertising, cosmetics, and fashion, for example, are readily denounced by Christians (and others) for their obvious excesses and evils. But we usually fail to credit their virtues: advertising can help us make good decisions amid the welter of choices we must make in a wealthy and complex society; cosmetics can beautify the body in the same way in which we innocently feel we ought to beautify our homes or churches; and fashion can give vent to our creativity even as it also testifies to our limitations, as we cannot and do not entertain all design possibilities at once, but instead formulate, improvise upon, and enjoy creative works within the terms set by the current trends.

In sum, God's original creation commandment motivates and governs all we do. In any situation, we are to cultivate shalom: take what we're given and make the best of it.

THE GREAT COMMANDMENTS: LOVE GOD AND LOVE YOUR NEIGHBOR

> When the Pharisees heard that he had silenced the Sadducees, they gathered together, and one of them, a lawyer, asked him a question to test him. "Teacher, which commandment in the law is the greatest?"
>
> He said to him, "You shall love the Lord your God with all your heart, and with all your soul, and with all your mind." This is the greatest and first commandment. And a second is like it: "You shall love your neighbor as yourself." On these two commandments hang all the law and the prophets. (Matt. 22:34–40)

This story comes from the life of Jesus. In answer to what a clever chap thinks is a clever challenge—out of the 613 laws of the Hebrew Scriptures, pick the most important—Jesus draws together two commandments that would have been as familiar to his audience as the Ten Commandments: love God thoroughly and above everything else, and love your neighbor as yourself. Any Jewish kid with a decent religious education would have been able to cite these verses from the Book of Moses (Deut. 6:5; Lev. 19:18).

Yet, as usual, there is more than one level to Jesus' retort. It is more than a mildly sarcastic humbling of the scholar by making him recite his ethical ABCs. Jesus draws together these commandments from different parts of the Torah, welds them together, and then sets them down in front of Israel and, indeed, the whole world. Everything else God has to say, Jesus claims, hangs on these two commandments.

These two commandments form a unit that I will call the second of the *creation commandments*. For surely these commandments do not begin to operate only with the giving of the Law to Moses but also from the very creation of Adam and Eve. Implicit in the Garden of Eden is the expectation that the first humans will love God above all else—obeying God particularly in God's command not to eat the forbidden fruit. And they will love each other as him- or herself, a commandment that is particularly graphic given Eve's origin out of Adam's body in Genesis 2 and their marriage that symbolically reunites them into that "one flesh" of primordial humanity.

We are to love God and love our neighbors as ourselves. There is nothing we can justify doing if it means not loving God above all else and with all that we are. There is nothing we can justify doing if it means not loving our neighbors as ourselves. Whatever other factors there may be in an ethical choice, these two abide as the framework on which everything else hangs.

We have seen that shalom denotes an all-embracing sphere of mutual contribution and benefit. Within it, individuals and groups are never presented with a stark choice between benefiting themselves and others, never forced to honor God over their own well-being.

Much Christian piety and preaching have been importantly misguided and misleading on this account. In fact, frequently a doctrine of "unselfishness" has been commended.

This rather negative virtue is often connected with the positive virtue of *agapē* as the highest and best form of love, and
it has been depicted as utterly other-focused and self-giving.
"Loving as God loves," so this mistaken idea runs, "means
loving another person with no regard for yourself." A related
theme, particularly in certain Lutheran and Calvinist circles,
has been to celebrate the supreme importance of "the glory
of God" as if the pinnacle of piety is to seek God's glory at the
expense of one's own utter loss.

This psychological absurdity is not, thank God, actually
taught in Scripture. The amazing paradox in more accurate
Christian teaching is that losing one's life *is the way to save it*
(Matt. 16:24–27). Spending one's goods on others is the way
to pile up treasures of much greater value that will last forever
(Matt. 19:21). One is never faced with a severe necessity of sacrificing one's own interests entirely for the interests of others.

Does this mean that there is really no such thing as
authentic altruism, no noble self-sacrifice? Christianity centers on the greatest self-sacrifice of all—that of God for God's
creatures. But even here, it is not as if one person's interests
are entirely abandoned for another's. There is a wonderful
sense in which altruism can be genuine in Christianity as
in no other religion or philosophy. In most other religions
and philosophies, altruism appears reducible to self-interest.
My ethical duty as a Hindu in India is to "do my dharma" in
order to pile up good karma. Or, as a Confucianist in China,
I am to play my part so that society can be stable and thrive—
but I do so to bring myself maximum benefit. In the contemporary West, morality has been construed as doing all I can
so that my genes can replicate themselves most abundantly.
None of these ethics, it should be clear, is what we mean by
altruism—exerting oneself for the other's sake.

As Martin Luther argued in "The Freedom of a Christian," God has already provided for us in Christ a life and a destiny both abundant and everlasting far in excess of any reward our moral goodness could possibly merit. And since God has freely given us this great gift regardless of our ethical striving, we are free now to love others out of gratitude and obedience to God. "We love, because he first loved us," the Apostle John reminds us (1 John 4:19).

Still, there is *something* to the intuition that as we do good to others, good accrues to us as well. As John writes throughout that same epistle, love for God, for one's neighbor, and for oneself are wonderfully braided together, in what I call a "win-win-win scenario." The Christian paradox is that altruism is both genuine and also in one's own interest—including even the altruism of God. How can this be?

Let us hew closely both to the words of Scripture and to our great example of love. Jesus suffered and sacrificed himself on the Cross "for the joy set before him" (Heb. 12:2). He did not die in a zero-sum game in which he simply had to lose so that we would gain. Yes, of course he did lose so that we would gain: "by his poverty you have become rich" (2 Cor. 8:9). But it was a *temporary* sacrifice, a *temporary* poverty, that was embraced to benefit Jesus *and* us. It was an expenditure that was truly costly—may I not be misunderstood as depreciating the marvelous grace of God in Christ! But that sacrifice was meant to bring joy to God and to bring salvation to us.

For that is the nature of love. It is never the choice of one or the other: "you versus me." The joy of the beloved redounds to the joy of the lover. God's own joy is bound up in our well-being. As Irenaeus put it, "The glory of God is a man fully alive!" and the Westminster Shorter Catechism responds, "Man's chief end is to glorify God, and to enjoy him forever."[11] Our joy, when we are properly oriented to the world, is bound up in the well-being of everything else. The shepherd exerts himself to find the lost sheep because he cares about the sheep, yes, and his worry about the sheep makes him anxious and sad. So once the sheep is rescued, the shepherd returns to the fold with joy (Matt. 18:12–14). It is ridiculous to try to pull apart what is, in the nature of the case, a seamless unit. The lover's well-being depends upon the well-being of the beloved.

Here is the upshot, then, and it is an important and interesting one. It is bad ethics to urge people to care for others at their own expense, as if they must sacrifice their self-interest for others' interests. The Christian view of love is the mutual flourishing of shalom. When you win, I win and God wins. When God wins, you win and I win. And so on, and so on: endlessly around the circle of love.

Christian ethics, therefore, does not ask what is in fact both impossible and irresponsible: "Deny your own self-interest for the sake of others." We should not even urge each other, as many have in Christian history, somehow to love God merely for God's own sake according to God's splendid worthiness. The Scripture never makes such a demand upon us. The Bible does command us to love God supremely as the logical, appropriate thing to do in the light of God's evident greatness and astonishing love toward us (Rom. 12:1). But loving God *supremely* never entails loving God *solely*. In fact, God's whole plan of salvation is to welcome us into a universal circle of love, of mutual care in everyone's interest.

We are made by God for shalom, and that means we automatically seek our own interests as well as the interests of the beloved, since we properly seek the interests of *everyone*.

Sin confuses us, to be sure, and breaks up what ought to be a seamless unity of purpose. But when the gospel appeals to us, it does not ask us to abandon our self-interest. Instead, it tells us that we are deranged by sin and we are seeking what is best in the wrong ways.[12] "There is a way that seems right to a person, but its end is the way to death" (Prov. 14:12). Our true self-interest is precisely that to which the gospel properly appeals: Here is how to be saved! Here is how to have life and have it abundantly! Here is how to prepare for the everlasting joy to come!

We are all in this together. Thus we ought to work hard, truly self-sacrificially and even to the death, for everyone's benefit: God's, the world's, and mine. We do not have to feel conflicted in some "you or me" scenario or even a "God or me" choice. The world God has made is not a grim zero-sum system; it is a world promising abundant life forever and for all.

To be selfish is to act against our own self-interest. God has made the world not only as a circle of life but also as a circle of love. To try to wrench ourselves free of that order to concentrate on what we think is our own welfare is to pull away from the matrix of mutual blessing in which our own interest truly lies. So we, for our own sake as much as anything, should embrace this dual commandment.

A second feature of this great commandment to love God and our neighbor is that the command is positive: "love." It is not negative: "avoid sin." This difference emerges in Jesus' disputes with the Pharisees, the most scrupulous of the Jewish sects of his day. Mark Buchanan writes:

> The Pharisees had an ethic of avoidance, and Jesus had an ethic of involvement. The Pharisee's question was not "How

can I glorify God?" It was "How can I avoid bringing disgrace to God?" This degenerated into a concern not with God, but with self—with image, reputation, procedure. They didn't ask, "How can I make others clean?" They asked, "How can I keep myself from getting dirty?" They did not seek to rescue sinners, only to avoid sinning.[13]

Our mission is to get things done, not to avoid getting dirty, or bloody, in the process—and loving God and one's neighbor in this troubled and troubling world often entails dirt and blood. Faithfulness can rarely oblige fastidiousness. David Martin broadens our view:

> Those who obey that [Christian] vision move from special privilege to special responsibility, from keeping themselves apart to welcoming the stranger within the gate, from the multiplication of Abraham's physical seed to the scattering abroad of a spiritual seed, from a Jerusalem jealously guarded as the citadel of an ethnic faith with a divine land grant, to new Jerusalems which offer a light to the Gentiles and envisage a free city in the spirit, the "mother of us all."[14]

It is worth pausing a moment over this command to love our neighbors. In ethical discussions the point is frequently made that love is expected of individuals, while the lesser standard of justice is applied to governments and other secular institutions. Interestingly, this distinction is typically made both by those who defend a sort of hard-headed "Christian realism" and those who oppose it in the name of an evangelical, Anabaptist, or liberal alternative. I suggest that both sides are mistaken on this crucial point.

As even Reinhold Niebuhr (the very model of a "Christian realist") came to aver in his later writings, love is, in fact, required of states, of governments at every level, of institutions such as hospitals and universities, of businesses, and of every other human group—not just of individuals. Love is crucial to the God-given task of cultivating the world, of making the best of it. Mere justice will not suffice to secure the greatest possible shalom, which is our calling. So love must function here, too.[15]

Let us not stumble at this point over the definition of "love." Some ethicists believe that love can be shared only by individuals and not by groups, and so to call on states or other institutions to "love" is to confuse categories. But this is to misunderstand the nature of love in this context. In the Bible's commandments, love does not mean a sentiment, an affectionate feeling for another, and the like. Love is the act of going beyond the strict requirements of justice, beyond satisfying some standard of correct behavior, to seek the welfare of the other, to do something to benefit the other beyond his or her strictly just deserts. Businesses, schools, hospitals, and governments, among other collectivities, can and should love in this sense.

Consider the outcomes of the First and Second World Wars, particularly the difference between the Treaty of Versailles, in the former instance, and the Marshall Plan, in the latter. Versailles certainly could be criticized for being less than just, even punitive, but no one would characterize the Marshall Plan as mere justice. In fact, many contemporary critics of the Marshall Plan advocated strict justice instead: better to let Germany lie in the wretched bed it had made. Yet it was *not* better to do so—not better not only for Germany, but not better also for the United States or even the European nations who had been victimized by Germany. The Marshall Plan, going well beyond justice to what I would not hesitate to call *love*, made for peace—shalom—in Europe, as did similar efforts in postwar Japan.

One might retort that the Marshall Plan was mere geopolitical calculation, a shrewd move to secure America's own interests. But in a win-win-win scheme, this cynical view is not the only plausible one. Yes, it was truly in America's interests to make peace in Europe and to restore health to war-ravaged societies. So what? To benefit from an act of love doesn't make that act less loving or less shalom-producing. The same goes for the more recent case of American armed forces providing major assistance to areas devastated by the Indian Ocean tsunami in 2004—scoring points with Muslims from Indonesia to Africa who otherwise were inclined to fear and hate America because of its violent involvement in the Middle East and Afghanistan.[16] The way of love, which both includes and supersedes justice, is in everybody's interest.[17]

To be sure, this kind of love must be framed and measured by realism. "Aha!" might come the reply. "God's love isn't like that. God's love is vast, unmeasured, boundless, free. It is that kind of love that is required of individuals, and obviously it cannot be expected of states."

Yet this characterization of God's love is poetically extravagant. God's love is vast, to be sure, but God does dole it out to us according to the divine purposes. God does not make everything lovely. God does not make every day Christmas Day. Instead, as a wise lord and wise parent, God loves us in ways we don't like, and may even fear, according to the actual need of the situation and our capacity to respond well in it. The love that God expects of us—corporately and individually—is very much like the love God shows us.

Thus we are to love our neighbors realistically: according to their need, according to their capacity to receive what we have to offer, and according to our resources, which are not limitless. The wise parent does not simply shower the child with presents, much as he or she would like to do so, because the child would not benefit from this excess and neither would the parent. The same is true of any good supervisor, or executive, or owner, or governor. The truly loving thing to do is not strict distributive justice, to be sure, but it is not a blizzard of indulgence either.

We can now consider the injunctions in the Sermon on the Mount to "turn the other cheek," go the extra mile, and so on. These instances Jesus cites are instances of what I call in this context *love*. It is going beyond what is strictly necessary in the situation, to demonstrate the abundant life of the Kingdom, the generosity of God even to sinners. Please note that none of Jesus' examples are life-and-death situations or even situations of grave harm—bodily, financial, or otherwise. Nor do they feature people (police officers, judges, rulers, etc.) who have the power to fundamentally change the situation—to bring a miscreant to justice or to prevent such bullying in the first place. I think it is a mistake, therefore, to generalize from these examples either to situations of extreme danger to oneself or others or to situations of political and police action. The examples are vivid instances about mundane dealings with people who dislike you and do not seek your best interest—such as a Roman soldier casually mistreating a Jew.

Properly understood, then, these examples do not set some terribly high standard. Instead, this teaching of returning good for evil—"even if someone strikes you, let alone insults or inconveniences you," we should understand Jesus to say—directs us in our particular circumstances to demonstrate the extravagant patience and (more than mere endurance) the love of God.

When someone cuts you off in traffic and then, down the road, wants to be let into your lane, what then? When someone steals your idea at work and then comes to you for help in implementing it, what then? When a neighbor annoys you with loud music late into the night, and then wakes you early one morning, unrepentant, seeking a boost for his dead car battery, what then?

Jesus' words are the ever-living, ever-relevant Word of God. They guide us when we are victims with little power, empowering us as a mark of the Kingdom to go beyond mere compliance to a counterintuitive generosity, and also when we do have power: we still show love. It is love, it is concern and care for the other, that is the common element in the ethics of weakness and oppression in the Sermon on the Mount and in the ethics of power and responsibility we see in all the other Scriptures—from Genesis 1 forward.

The divine call, then, is to love our neighbors as we love ourselves, to treat them the way we would want to be treated, with the guidance and example of God ever before us. Compassion is not a pleasant, occasional ancillary to the responsibility of a state or a business but is commanded by God of everyone all the time—for everyone's benefit. Let us have no more false dichotomies between justice and love.[18]

Third, inasmuch as our neighbors are loving God and loving their neighbors, they are doing the will of God. And once we have recognized this happy fact, we can approve and cooperate with what they are doing. A major challenge for Christians is to discern what is truly genuine love for God and love for the neighbor in the sometimes bewildering and even disquietingly diverse forms in which people claim to be engaged in such love, whether seeking legal rights to terminate a painful life, or to form nontraditional marriages, or to regulate industries. We must be careful not to condemn too quickly what is meant as good. At the same time, we have been given divine revelation, divine guidance by the Holy Spirit, and the divinely oriented Christian community to assist us to expose false loves, or unhelpful initiatives in the name of legitimate loves, and to resist them in the name of shalom. Indeed, part of exercising dominion over the world is to engage in such discernment. Not everything that flies the flag of Love is truly beneficial. We are responsible to cultivate what is actually good and to weed out, or at least avoid, the bad as best we can.

We have these creation commandments to love God and our neighbors as ourselves as we cultivate the world. It is these commandments that guide Christians, as they ought to guide, and someday will guide, all people, in our work.[19]

MAKING SHALOM IN THE WORLD TO COME

The history of Christian art is full of examples of the longing to return to the Garden of Eden, a "peaceable kingdom" of pastoral tranquility in which wolves lie down with lambs in a verdant paradise. Yet drawing as it does on certain Old Testament prophecies (e.g., Isa. 11:6–9), this vision turns out to be more central to Islam than to Christianity. It is the Qur'an, more than the Bible, that speaks of heaven in terms a Bedouin might especially appreciate: tall trees providing cool shade, endless water, lovely fruits, soothing greenery, and the like (including my personal favorite: wine that "will not hurt the head" [37:47]).

To be sure, this garden imagery is truer to the Bible than the common Christian view of the afterlife: floating in celestial spiritual heights, replete with robes, harps, clouds, and haloes. This "church myth" must be demolished as the quasi-Platonic fantasy it is—a hyperspiritual vision that not only condemns us to everlasting boredom in the next life but also undercuts Christian concern in this life for justice, peacemaking, and environmental responsibility. Such a view of heavenly reward renders us literally too heavenly-minded to be of any earthly good. Wendell Berry is scathing on this point:

> Despite protests to the contrary, modern Christianity has become willy-nilly the religion of the state and the economic status quo. Because it has been so exclusively dedicated to incanting anemic souls into Heaven, it has been made the tool of much earthly villainy. It has, for the most part, stood silently by while a predatory economy has ravaged the world, destroyed its natural beauty and health, divided and plundered its human communities and households. It has flown the flag and chanted the slogans of empire. It has assumed with the economists that "economic forces" automatically work for good and has assumed with the industrialists and militarists that technology determines history. It has assumed with almost everybody that "progress" is good.[20]

(Lest I be misunderstood as carrying a brief for the economic left, what Berry writes can be applied to every economic system we humans have devised, including modern options as diverse as mercantilism, authoritarian "managed" economies, socialism, and communism.)

Let's be clear. We are not going *back* to Eden. And we are not going *up* to heaven. We are going *forward* to the

New Jerusalem on a new earth. Heaven is the abode of God, far "above" (= "different from") the earth in a spiritual realm reserved for spiritual beings (such as angels). We human beings are of the earth, and the earth is our home, upon which God has been graciously pleased to dwell with us.[21] The apocalyptic vision in both Testaments is decidedly earthy and earthly. It is also *urban*: a kingdom, with its capital in Jerusalem, that unites all the peoples of the earth around the worship of God. The Bible sets before us an astonishingly rich vision of purification, judgment, health, security, harmony, plenty, celebration, diversity, and fellowship. Let me say it again: We are not going *back* to Eden, and we are not going *up* to heaven. We are going *forward* to the garden city of the New Jerusalem, as the last two chapters of the Bible tell us:

> Then I saw a new heaven and a new earth; for the first heaven and the first earth had passed away, and the sea was no more.
>
> And I saw the holy city, the New Jerusalem, coming down out of heaven from God, prepared as a bride adorned for her husband. And I heard a loud voice from the throne saying, "See, the home of God is among mortals. He will dwell with them as their God; they will be his peoples, and God himself will be with them; he will wipe every tear from their eyes. Death will be no more; mourning and crying and pain will be no more, for the first things have passed away."
>
> And the one who was seated on the throne said, "See, I am making all things new." Also he said, "Write this, for these words are trustworthy and true."
>
> Then he said to me, "It is done! I am the Alpha and the Omega, the beginning and the end. To the thirsty I will give water as a gift from the spring of the water of life. Those who conquer will inherit these things, and I will be their God and

they will be my children. But as for the cowardly, the faithless, the polluted, the murderers, the fornicators, the sorcerers, the idolaters, and all liars, their place will be in the lake that burns with fire and sulfur, which is the second death."

Then one of the seven angels who had the seven bowls full of the seven last plagues came and said to me, "Come, I will show you the bride, the wife of the Lamb."

And in the spirit he carried me away to a great, high mountain and showed me the holy city Jerusalem coming down out of heaven from God. It has the glory of God and a radiance like a very rare jewel, like jasper, clear as crystal. It has a great, high wall with twelve gates, and at the gates twelve angels, and on the gates are inscribed the names of the twelve tribes of the Israelites; on the east three gates, on the north three gates, on the south three gates, and on the west three gates. And the wall of the city has twelve foundations, and on them are the twelve names of the twelve apostles of the Lamb.

The angel who talked to me had a measuring rod of gold to measure the city and its gates and walls. The city lies four-square, its length the same as its width; and he measured the city with his rod, fifteen hundred miles; its length and width and height are equal. He also measured its wall, one hundred forty-four cubits by human measurement, which the angel was using.

The wall is built of jasper, while the city is pure gold, clear as glass. The foundations of the wall of the city are adorned with every jewel; the first was jasper, the second sapphire, the third agate, the fourth emerald, the fifth onyx, the sixth carnelian, the seventh chrysolite, the eighth beryl, the ninth topaz, the tenth chrysoprase, the eleventh jacinth, the twelfth amethyst. And the twelve gates are twelve pearls, each of the gates is a single pearl, and the street of the city is pure gold, transparent as glass.

I saw no temple in the city, for its temple is the Lord God the Almighty and the Lamb. And the city has no need of sun or moon to shine on it, for the glory of God is its light, and its lamp is the Lamb. The nations will walk by its light, and the kings of the earth will bring their glory into it. Its gates will never be shut by day—and there will be no night there. People will bring into it the glory and the honor of the nations. But nothing unclean will enter it, nor anyone who practices abomination or falsehood, but only those who are written in the Lamb's book of life.

Then the angel showed me the river of the water of life, bright as crystal, flowing from the throne of God and of the Lamb through the middle of the street of the city. On either side of the river is the tree of life with its twelve kinds of fruit, producing its fruit each month; and the leaves of the tree are for the healing of the nations. Nothing accursed will be found there any more. But the throne of God and of the Lamb will be in it, and his servants will worship him; they will see his face, and his name will be on their foreheads. And there will be no more night; they need no light of lamp or sun, for the Lord God will be their light, and they will reign forever and ever. (Rev. 21:1–22:5)

The earth suffers throughout the Book of Revelation. But, like its human inhabitants who also suffer, it is renewed and made fit for this final, eternal cohabitation of God, humanity, and the rest of earthly creation. Let's understand that it is indeed *re-newed*. The "new earth" is not "brand new," just as its human lords are not brand new: there is no second *creatio ex nihilo* (creation out of nothing). God doesn't start all over again. In that case, we would all vanish. Instead of *replacing* us all, and our world, God *resurrects* humanity and, so to speak, resurrects the earth as well into a resplendent ecology of vitality and beauty in which everyone and everything lives in mutually beneficial relationships with each other.

This vision is God's gift to us of an "imagined future." We need a vivid sense of the age to come—of what we can look forward to, of what we live and make our choices in the light of. Otherwise we will succumb to the relentless conformist pressures of our culture.[22] Without an exciting sense of what we have in store in the next world, we will spend our resources entirely to advantage ourselves in this one. This glorious vision is the hope of shalom.[23] Shalom is literally global, universal, cosmic flourishing. And *that* is a vision worth holding up to ourselves and to each other to guide us through each day's challenges.

This vision implies a number of vital principles for Christian life. Let's consider several of them in turn.

1. The individual matters and so does the social. Individuality is maintained in the world to come, as is community. Likewise, the distinction between each of these and God remains as well. This Biblical view therefore repudiates any sort of "blending," "melding," or other process—typical of "union" language in mysticism—that means that each of us somehow disappears into God, or "the Church," or some other Big Generality. Christians should champion neither the individual only (as if one's own spiritual development is all that matters, as many people seem to think) nor only society or "community" or the Church only (as if the welfare of the group is the focus of the Christian religion and the sum of human life).

2. The physical matters and so does the spiritual. The Bible depicts the New Jerusalem as truly physical,

with an architecture of superabundance. It uses the most precious materials of our age as mere *construction* materials: gold common enough to pave roads and pearls large enough to bore through for city gates. The city stands in mind-boggling dimensions: a cubic city, fifteen hundred miles on a side. It enjoys a river winding through it: common enough in North America and Britain but truly exceptional in the water-starved Middle East. And along the river is a garden full of trees bearing fruit (with fruit as the one source of sugar and dessert in that part of the world) and medicine—and doing so *all year* (a once-astonishing luxury we take for granted in the modern world of global transportation). A secure and bountifully supplied garden city? This was a phenomenon ancient Jews had encountered only in the imperial centers of Egypt and Mesopotamia.

More than all these extravagances, however, this New Jerusalem enjoys the light of God's own presence—as if the *shekinah* of God in the Old Testament, which shone occasionally in the tabernacle or temple, now suffuses the entire city, and so completely that the city needs no other illumination! This city is no pale and simple "beatific vision" of the mystic endlessly gazing at the beloved in splendid isolation, but an impossibly rich complex of all that is good in human life on earth with God.

3. Unity matters, and so does diversity. It is one city, with one Lord. The New Jerusalem is the single capital of a single world and a single world order. But the nations enter, and they enter *as such*, in their

evident differences, bringing the best of their cultures in tribute to the one King of all and in contribution to the mutual benefit of all. This vision causes us to exclaim, "Ah! *This* is what we long for in all of our disappointed multicultural efforts!" Diversity, inclusion, particularity, difference—all are blessed by God in a single system of focused worship and mutual giving and receiving.

4. The world to come is in continuity with this world, and fulfills the noble aspirations of this world, even as it clearly transcends this world. Again, the use of precious metals as paving material and gigantic precious stones as masonry symbolizes that the very best of this world corresponds with the very bottom of the next, just as our earthly bodies resemble and are the seeds of the gloriously superior resurrection bodies to which we look forward; just as our current relationships in the church and in human society more generally enjoy occasional flashes of that joyful, easy, and loving companionship of that new era; and just as our periodic worship of God blossoms into constant delight in and praise of God as we dwell together in unity forever.

The extravagant language of the vision also reminds us, as does the very image of a city descending from heaven to earth, that the New Jerusalem is fundamentally and finally God's gift from above. It is not our accomplishment from below. It is the *fulfillment* of our work, yes, just as the New Jerusalem looks something like the original one and the cultural contributions of the kings of the earth are not scorned but welcomed into the civilization to come. But whatever we contribute, whatever we have worked for and worked toward, is fulfilled by the surpassing power, wisdom, creativity, and generosity of God.

What, then, about making shalom in this fabulous place? It seems perfect, with nothing left for us to do but enjoy it. Does the life to come turn out to be, in fact, simply an endless vacation?

We have seen that the commands God gave to our first human parents last into this new age as well. Indeed, the quotation from Revelation above concludes, "They will reign forever and ever," continuing the work of shalom-making, of cultivating the world, as co-creators with God forever. For in the world to come we will not automatically and immediately be omniscient. Only God has that power. So we have much to learn—but we will learn with the alacrity of minds free of sin's temptations and confusions, with willing and brilliant help freely available, in optimal learning situations and with ever-improving tools. Languages, skills, art forms, sciences, techniques, theories—think of what shalom-making will be like in such circumstances! It is breathtaking to imagine, especially when we know that whatever is actually the case in the world to come, it cannot be *worse* or *less* than the best we can imagine (as John found in the New Jerusalem) but only better.

All we do today, therefore, benefits not only today, and perhaps tomorrow, but also gives us practice in what we will do forever: creatively working the world in the company of our fellow humans and of the Son of Man, the Great Human, himself.

HUMAN VOCATION

All of Us, Some of Us, Each of Us

MAXIMIZING SHALOM: EVERYONE

All human beings are called by God to fulfill the creation commandments. We are to worship God, seek each other's best interests, and care for the rest of creation. There is no one who is exempt from these commandments, nor are there activities that are legitimate beyond these commandments. The Bible not only condemns acting wrongly or refusing to act rightly, it also condemns "empty" or "wasteful" words and activities. Beyond trivial issues, such as which flavor of toothpaste to purchase or whether one should lace up one's left or right shoe first, there are no "neutral" actions (Matt. 13:48; Eph. 4:29). One is either contributing toward shalom or one is not.

To assess whether one is, in fact, contributing to shalom requires a theological understanding adequate to the task. This understanding must be broad enough to encompass all that contributes to the flourishing of creation and the pleasure of God, and also fine enough to see how particular tasks contribute to the whole.

Such ethical clarity has become more difficult to obtain, moreover, because the world since the Fall in Genesis 3 became a significantly tougher place in which to make a living. Thorns and thistles—real and metaphorical—are everywhere, resisting and retarding our efforts. Every task, every job, every profession or trade, even every effort at leisure, seems to manifest a certain irreducible quotient of what we might sum up as *crap*: absurdity, waste, fragility, confusion, disappointment, frustration, exploitation, and the like. Almost everything we try to do is harder than it should be. We also must acknowledge that some work is not just annoying, or even vexing, but truly alienating. Turning screws on an assembly line all day or stitching endless piecework in a sweatshop is demeaning, unpleasant, and the very definition of "unfulfilling."[1] Human societies, furthermore, have developed evil patterns that privilege some and oppress others. The patterns change, and sometimes the elites do, too, but women, children, the disabled, and the different (ethnically, sexually, and otherwise) rarely enjoy privilege. Within such a world, human beings have to make our way as best we can, and that often means making the best of an unfairly bad situation. This sometimes amounts to sheer faithful endurance.

What more might it mean, however, to truly make the best of it, to maximize shalom in such a deeply compromised world? A Christian ethic that encourages everyone to remain in their "station," to accept the status quo as divinely ordered, to work away diligently in hopes of "pie in the sky by and by," is an ethic that ignores God's redemptive purposes within history and at the end of (this phase of) history. It can actually be a *slothful* ethic, by which I mean refusing the responsibility to seek as much shalom as possible—which might entail the attempt to alter entire social structures (and not just by those who have been given the authority to do so, but also by each of us, wherever we are in the hierarchy). This opportunity and obligation to make a positive difference reaches all the way down to one's own daily decisions: Either press for improvement or acquiesce in evil. Nicholas Wolterstorff writes,

> A Yes and a No is what must be spoken. Can we entirely alter what we do, so that here and now we practice the occupations of heaven? Of course not. Can we somewhat alter what we do, so that our occupations come closer to becoming our God-issued vocations? Usually, Yes.[2]

There is no defense for a work ethic that merely reinforces the economic and political order. In fact, our Christian understanding of creation and fall tells us that every economic and political order, however good, is also corrupt to some extent and therefore can be, and should be, improved. Aware of our place in God's plan of redemption and energized by a vision of a new world to come, Christians must be in the vanguard of efforts at improvement. We should keep a relentless pressure, both critical and creative, on the powers and structures of our world to be transformed as much as possible according to gospel values. Like the seeds and the leaven of Jesus' parables, which are diffused in order to influence everything around them, Christians must try steadily, and sometimes dramatically, to effect change—as Christians always have, whether in the development of constitutional government, the rise of science, the abolition of slavery, the empowerment of women, the recognition of universal human rights, and more.

It is true, to our shame, that there have been many Christians who have resisted one or another of these improvements. But the historical record is clear that Christian principles and Christian people have been crucial to the success of these campaigns for justice and compassion. Today and tomorrow, appropriately informed and skilled Christians must continue to bring insight to every social situation, even the largest systems of interaction—so large we often take them for granted as just "the world we live in," whether the economic market, or globalization, or geopolitics, or the environment—such that nothing is ignored and everything benefits from both critical and creative suggestion and investment.

One can do any legitimate job to the glory of God, even as we regret that the world has fallen so far that it generally produces one economy after another that exacts corrupt and corrupting work from human beings who are capable of so much more. The Apostle Paul encourages even *slaves* to do their work "unto the Lord," in the hope that the Lord will repay us far beyond our deserts with an eternal inheritance (Col. 3:23–24). "It is the Lord Christ whom you serve," Paul reminds us all—the Lord of the Church, yes, but also the Lord of creation, to the flourishing of which we are always called to contribute.

We must appreciate work, therefore, as a part of God's original blessing and calling of humanity, not as an evil introduced by the Fall that will vanish in the New Jerusalem. We are to undertake work gratefully and joyfully. It is a dignified thing to contribute to the goodness of the world. "God loveth adverbs," Puritan Joseph Hall has said, and Paul exhorts those Christian slaves, and all of us, to do our work—however mean, however mechanical—"heartily" (Col. 3:23).[3]

Indeed, there is work to be done by every person, save those incapacitated by defect, disease, or injury. Churches and Christian businesspeople need to be in the lead in finding ways of *letting* everyone work who possibly can work. Work is good for us to do. And as far as we can, we should try to provide, and engage in, creative and useful work that blesses the worker and the recipient of his or her labor. This is one crucial dimension of how a Christian view of the dignity of people and of work can make a difference in the workplace. Trying to employ people, and to employ them in good jobs, is not only a morally good thing to do but is also a quest we can expect God to bless: we can expect that God has arranged the world in order that businesses that try to do so will thrive.[4]

The last several decades of worry about offshoring/ outsourcing jobs to the less developed world has been only partly ameliorated by the fact that some North American businesses have since found, to their embarrassment and cost, that ruthlessly seeking what seemed to be the least expensive labor supply did not necessarily result in the best outcomes (quality, dependability, flexibility, communication, and so on).[5] Yet even as the cheap labor markets migrate from South America and East Asia to South Asia and eventually to Africa, a new challenge looms in the form of widespread mechanization.[6]

I don't have a Luddite bone in my body, and I am grateful for robots substituting for human beings in situations of both drudgery and danger. But even in the conservative spaces of the ivory tower, I have seen how eliminating administrative assistants to professors and "replacing" qualified and capable people with computers issued to faculty members has resulted in scarcely visible but significant inefficiencies. (We professors are stereotyped as clueless about correct and conducive policies and procedures for good reason.) I have also been aghast at the proselytizers for "distance education" and "instructional technology" who have degraded person-to-person education down to a truly "virtual" education that can equal the successes of traditional education only if the measurements focus on very basic informational or skill-based instruction.[7] Will we really be better off when there are finally no clerks to advise and assist us in hardware stores or clothing shops as we "self-serve" and, only if all goes well, we get actually what we need and save a few dollars? When inter-action with a knowledgeable human being will be restricted to expensive boutiques? I can only begin to imagine what happens in industries that uncritically adopt machines to replace people.[8]

Among those social improvements necessary in our time is space for rest and recreation—increasingly jeopardized, despite the rosy predictions of a generation ago about a leisured society, by globalizing economic pressure, tele-communication technologies that make us "available" at any time and any place, and a corporate ethos that rarely looks past the next financial quarter or two. The heat is on, and a reasonable work week—and a correspondingly reasonable work day and work year—has become, as it was in the early industrial period in the West, a crucial social issue. This issue affects not only the poor around the world who toil in factories and on farms but also financially prosperous but emotionally and socially ragged white-collar workers from Manhattan to Mumbai.

Beyond work lies the territory of other generic human activities that deserve Christian affirmation. We need a theological understanding of *art*, for example, as a worthy pursuit—from profound creations that offer us new ways of perceiving, feeling, thinking, and acting to the design of everyday items that increases our enjoyment of an appliance, a room, a front yard, or a person's appearance. Likewise, we need a theological understanding of *sport* as a worthy pursuit—in its formation of character, in its symbolism (fair play, honest effort, clear rules, penalties for infractions, unequivocal outcomes), in its contribution to physical and mental health, and so on. We need a theological understanding of *play* in which enjoyment is sufficient rationale, rather than play being justified in terms of improved productivity at work or in terms of shared activity to enhance familial, ecclesiastical, or corporate relations—however much these benefits also might be gained.

To be sure, art, sport, and play can be loved inordinately, as can anything else, as Augustine warns us throughout his *Confessions*. Like any other form of human culture, moreover, they can be corrupted and corrupting. My point is that it is also possible to regard them too lightly, especially for earnest Christians. We tend to emphasize only work and "religious" activities as worthy of praise, even establishing them as the framework within which everything else we do must be justified. (Art merely to decorate a church; sport merely to "get in better shape" to work more effectively; leisure merely to form relationships that offer opportunities to evangelize; etc.) God is interested in more than productivity and spirituality. God made the whole world, God is redeeming the whole world, and God expects us to cooperate in gardening and reclaiming the whole world.

Furthermore, part of cultivating the world is cultivating *ourselves* within it, in order to become the best possible version of ourselves. And that means becoming all that God has meant us to be, including the pursuit of art, sport, and play of all legitimate kinds.

MAXIMIZING SHALOM: PARTICULAR GROUPS

Within the generic human calling, various sorts of human societies have distinctive roles to play. Empires, states, nations, subcultures, municipalities, families, marriages, and friendships; professions, trades, guilds, corporations, shops, stock exchanges, banks, and insurers; transportation media, communication media, information media, schools, and museums; studios, galleries, performance halls, theaters, troupes, orchestras, bands, and ensembles; arenas, stadiums, teams, and leagues; nonprofits, charities, and cooperatives—all of these and many more are ways in which human beings have organized themselves to pursue some particular form of flourishing.

Some gloomy theologians have said that institutions were ordained by God merely to restrain evil. I think it is abundantly evident that they have produced positive goods, and of many sorts. One of the blessed ironies of God's providence is that sometimes even manifestly evil institutions benefit others, whether it is in the form of splendid art and architecture left behind as an empire withdraws, or in infrastructure that enables others to build better lives (such as roads, schools, hospitals, or a lingua franca) once the hegemony has receded, and so on.

In the Bible, different nations and tribes play different roles, as do different professions and trades within Israel, and even different families. Differentiation on a wide scale may be characteristic of modernity, but it has always been a part of God's ordering of the world. We do well to recognize and to receive gratefully what God has granted us in these various groupings. At the same time, we do well also to recognize and resist the typical selfishness of groups, the chauvinism and imperialism that so frequently mark them. The early Reinhold Niebuhr of *Moral Man and Immoral Society* asserts that societies are *always* collectively worse than the individuals that comprise them.[9] We need not go that far. But we should recognize that there is nothing necessarily benign about community. Community can make us better, yes, but it can also make us worse.

One of the great useless emphases of our time is the championing of *community* over *individualism*, as if the former is good and the latter bad—indeed, as if the former is a kind of cure for the latter. Surely the testimony of the last century or so, with its grim parade of "communities" of nationalists, imperialists, communists, fascists, Nazis, cultists, and terrorists, should tell us that community sometimes can be dreadful. Simply put, individuality and community are both basic to human life, and in our present era, after the Fall and before the Second Coming, they possess both benign and malign characteristics.

In this light, we can also lay to rest the perennial Christian argument over whether society will be best improved by the conversion of individuals or by the conversion of social structures. The correct answer is that *both* are necessary. The widespread conversion of individuals can have significant social consequences; an example can be seen in Latin America's experience of evangelicalism—which has resulted in a decrease in alcoholism, domestic abuse, and poverty.[10] But individual attitudes can also be shaped by new social expectations and forms, such as the delegitimizing of racism and sexism in North America. And spreading values at the individual level can provide grounds for alternative politicians and policies, and alternative companies and products, which thus results in large-scale structural change. Of course none of these approaches is capable of ushering in the Kingdom of God. Latin America and North America cannot yet pass for the New Jerusalem. Still, those societies are better in many respects than they used to be.

The fundamental ethical question for groups is whether and how they contribute to shalom. It is not enough to ask such groups whether they break any laws or commit any harm while maximizing return to their shareholders, the electorate, or whoever may be their primary constituencies. What must be asked is whether they are improving the world *and* whether they are improving it as well as they could.

What it means to improve the world will depend on the theological framework in which the Christian makes her judgment, and she needs a theology adequate to that task. According to such a theology, we might ask what exactly an insurance company does, and what *should* it do—with due regard not only for its shareholders and clients, but also for its suppliers, the companies in which it invests, and even its competitors. What does a rock band do, and what *should* it do—with due regard not only for its audiences but also for its songwriters, its backers, and other bands that it can help or hurt? What does a magazine or website do—with due regard not only for its readers but also for its advertisers, its publishers, its influence on particular conversations and subjects, and so on? Is the world better because of this group? Is this organization contributing *as much as it can* to shalom?

Such questions ought to both energize and direct a group, neither asking it to strive for an impossible ideal nor permitting it a complacency that can result in either stagnation or rapacity. We should ask both *Why are we doing this?* and *How can we do this better?* Christians who serve our creative God should want to ask these questions of every institution, starting with those that claim to be Christian.

Those are not the only ones; a whole set of questions must be asked: What is the purpose of this group? What is its characteristic way of increasing shalom, and what are the ways it is typically diverted from its work? Is this group still fulfilling that good purpose? Is there a new purpose it ought to serve instead? And if it is on track, is it making all the progress it could?

Groups, like individuals, can get confused and lose their focus. They can forget their ultimate objective, their true telos. They can get slothful and settle for mere routine. Alternatively, they can pridefully take on too much, whether too lofty a goal or too broad an agenda or too great a portfolio of responsibility. Then they spread themselves too thin and attempt many things badly rather than accomplish a few things well.

Still other organizations can struggle for survival, even as the need for their particular contribution has passed. There will always, in this age, be need for government, of course, and also for families, businesses, and other general forms of cooperation and authority. We recognize, however, that this whole system eventually will give way to the direct governance and provision of Christ in the New Jerusalem; but even now governors come and go, families blossom and fade, businesses contribute to, and then start to impede, the marketplace. Change and limitation are realities that affect groups as they do individuals. A proper ethic recognizes that what was true and good and beautiful yesterday may not be so today. What was a valuable contribution to the commonweal may not be one anymore. What was a fruitful organization is now in need of pruning or even liquidation and supersession. Christians properly venerate tradition and honor the work of the past, but we should not indulge in sentimentality and nostalgia. The Bible is full of reminders of the temporality of human life, and that includes groups as well as individuals. A realistic Christian ethic casts a clear, as well as compassionate, eye over all groups to ensure that they serve the great purpose of shalom, not merely their own interests. We dare not waste time and money propping up organizations whose worthiness has passed; rather we should give thanks for what has been and welcome what is to come.

A Christian ethic also recognizes that governments and businesses are not families or charities, and families and charities are not businesses, and so on. It is a mark of terrible ethical confusion in our time—not in the narrow sense of immorality, but of confusion about the *nature* of things, the *ethos* of each institution—that hospitals are being run as businesses, universities are being run as businesses, governments are being run as businesses, and even churches are being run as businesses. There is much for other organizations to learn from the practical wisdom of business, to be sure. The effort to succeed in a competitive market can promote efficiency, responsiveness, innovation, and more. But institutions that are essentially religious, or educational, or medical, or charitable must never simply *become* commercial enterprises. The bottom line of a hospital, school, government department, or church cannot ethically be a financial one—indeed the bottom line cannot ethically be exclusively financial for a business, either. *What good are you doing in the world?* must be the question at the end of each day.

A different sort of ethical confusion is evident when nonprofit organizations, charities, and even businesses are characterized as "families." This gives rise to the protest that you don't fire your family members or refuse to help a relative if he or she is in trouble. Yet, it is not merely all right for businesses to fire people, it is essential that they be willing to do so. The metaphor of "family" confuses supervisors who need to make hard decisions in as clear-eyed a fashion as they can, and it gratuitously wounds employees who now must add the pain of familial betrayal to the already painful experience of losing a job.

Likewise, it is not only all right but also essential for hospitals to put patient care above fiscal efficiency. It is not only all right for charities to decline to help certain kinds of people or to help them in some respects but not others but also essential that they make such distinctions. Otherwise they will run out of resources to do what they were called to do. Differentiation arising from ethical clarity is essential for the proper functioning of each kind of group.

What keeps this differentiation from devolving into sheer fragmentation, or even a kind of low-grade civil war among various sectors and groups encroaching on each other's turf (as when churches engage in electoral politics like political parties, or civic groups offer a sort of "community substitute" for churches), is the underlying purpose of the cultural mandate. Each sector of society and the groups and individuals within those sectors—whether education, healthcare, government, business, or the arts—maintain the central, shared concern to improve the earth, to garden the world, to increase shalom. They will therefore welcome and cooperate with others who have the same concern, while pressing on with their distinctive tasks.

In zones of overlapping concern and jurisdiction—such as the education of children—Christians should recognize and respect the legitimate interests of each institution. Of course parents as heads of families do have the primary responsibility to care for their children, but primary ("first, most basic") responsibility does not mean *sole* responsibility. The state also has intrinsic responsibility for the welfare of its citizens, especially those, such as children, who are especially vulnerable to others, including their parents. And the educational system has its own appropriate mandate to educate as well as it can. So when controversies arise, as they perpetually will, about who should teach what to whom, and whether pupils can legitimately dissent or even opt out, we must at least begin by recognizing the unavoidable complexity of the situation, rather than falling back on reductionist slogans: "Parents know best!" "Ask the experts!" or "This is the law!"[11]

Visions of shalom will vary, of course, and sometimes conflict. But it is essential to maintain that businesses, for example, can rightly be condemned as deficient if they clearly do not intend to contribute to the common good, but only to the good of their shareholders and executives. " 'Deficient' by whose standards?" comes the retort. And the Christian's reply is, "By *our* standards, which we believe are at least an approximation of the standards of the One who made the world, who sustains it, and who will bring it to judgment. Thus we believe that these are not arbitrary standards, not our mere preferences, but the very standards of reality."

To take a stand on such moral realism, the conviction that goodness is not a matter of mere preference but is as integral to the created order as space and energy, means to believe that businesses that abuse their customers, suppliers, and competitors will not ultimately succeed. That is the Christian conviction. Yes, they might well acquire wealth and power for a time. History and the Bible agree that some of the wicked do prosper *for a while*. But we should observe, first, that many do not. Wrongly oriented businesses are pushing against the grain of the original, good universe, and many bad businesses, as well as bad governments, bad schools, and other bad organizations, do fail. Abusing people within and without the organization tends to result in failure all round. Furthermore, those who lead groups that do not seek shalom, as well as those who serve in such groups, often pay a terrific toll in other parts of their lives, whether in romantic and family relationships, friendships, or physical and spiritual health. And however happily the powerful few may inhabit and then exit this life, after that is the inevitable judgment of history, let alone of whatever lies beyond. "My name is Ozymandias, King of kings [or the Third Reich, or the latest financial empire]: Look on my works, ye mighty, and despair!"—they cry, until their achievements sink, broken and impotent, into the sands of time.[12]

Christians call all organizations to function as their best selves, according to the clear purpose of serving shalom in their most characteristic fashion. And Christians therefore join their fellow human beings gladly at work in manufacturing, journalism, politics, art, advertising, education, medicine, and every other field as they help such organizations stay faithful to their highest and truest ethos—and thereby flourish.

MAXIMIZING SHALOM: EACH INDIVIDUAL

Each person is called by God to play a particular role in the gardening of the world. No one is useless, no one is free of responsibility, and each is called to the generic human task of contributing to shalom.

Even within oppressive social structures that tend to reduce individuals to machine parts—almost literally on assembly lines or metaphorically in large professional and financial firms—the individual human being matters. He or she is called by God to play a part that matters in the great garden of the world. Each of us does have a sphere of responsibility, and a considerable sphere it is: the total complex of our families, friendships, neighborhoods, workplaces, playgrounds, political involvements, and so on. We remember Paul's encouragement even to slaves that each of us has the solemn responsibility to choose whether to do our work "heartily," whether we advance God's concerns, and whether we serve the Lord Christ (Col. 3:23–24). The world is importantly better or worse depending on how each of us lives in it.

This calling is also a blessing. It sanctifies our work, makes it holy, as something God accepts from us with pleasure. One needs to remember that truth when changing the sixth diaper of the day, putting out yet one more fire at the office, struggling to pass one more confusingly phrased exam, or placating one more abusive customer. To persist in a truly awful job is an act of faith. Such persistence demonstrates that we not only trust God for our future but that we also believe God is not wasting us now. We have faith that God can bring good out of the most menial, and even oppressive, situations.

Furthermore, as C. S. Lewis eloquently reminds us, not only do we ourselves matter as individuals, but so do the individuals whom we influence each day:

> It may be possible for each to think too much of his own potential glory hereafter; it is hardly possible for him to think

too often or too deeply about that of his neighbour. . . . It is a serious thing to live in a society of possible gods and goddesses, to remember that the dullest and most uninteresting person you talk to may one day be a creature which, if you saw it now, you would be strongly tempted to worship, or else a horror and a corruption such as you now meet, if at all, only in a nightmare. All day long we are, in some degree, helping each other to one or other of these destinations.[13]

At the same time as we are encouraged by these affirmations, we recognize that we are limited in our abilities and even in our interests. Not only can we not do everything, but we don't even want to try. Is that bad?

In theory it might be splendid to be interested in everything. But let us consider the counterintuitive idea of rejoicing in our limitations. I have spent most of my career on the campuses of large universities. I am a reasonably curious fellow, but there are great reaches of scholarship on those campuses that frankly do not interest me much: accounting, chemical engineering, epic poetry, plant biochemistry, dentistry, most advanced mathematics, . . . All of these are fields that fascinate many people, and yet I can barely glimpse the magic therein. Those subjects are not dull; I am dull to them.

Yet this deficiency in me is also a blessing and equipment for my service in the world. For I already experience frustration when trying to pay all the attention I should like to pay to the things in which I am already quite interested. If every part of the full panoply of human inquiry was equally compelling to me, I would gain only vexation. So I am glad that there are whole areas of human investigation I can happily leave alone. The same principle holds for various leisure activities, various foods and beverages, and so on: God has endowed the world with a superabundance of goodness such that it is a positive mercy that we do not even *want* to enjoy it all.

We each therefore should seek to understand ourselves as thoroughly as possible in order to become the best version of ourselves that we can and make the best contribution we can. What am I good at? What am I not good at? What brings me joy and lets me bring it to others? What seems to result only in mediocrity or even simply a mess—despite, perhaps, my dreams of glory? Honestly: How can I best make a contribution to the world? This self-awareness is to be sought neither to indulge ourselves nor to neglect ourselves, but to participate fruitfully in the win-win-win of the Kingdom of God, in which everyone benefits by everyone contributing to shalom.

The ethic presented in this book provides absolutely no justification for picking the most lucrative, prestigious, and secure job available: "Since every legitimate job is valid, I think I'll opt for the cushiest." That is the Reformation doctrine of the worthiness of all vocations run to seed. The divine command always is to do what *maximizes* shalom.

PART II

OUR (TEMPORARY)

CHRISTIAN CALLING

Make Disciples

THE BASIC CALLING

OF THE CHURCH

HAD OUR FIRST PARENTS NOT sinned, and every one of us since them, all would be well. We human beings would live each day in loving relationship with God, each other, and the rest of creation. We would be developing into better and better versions of ourselves, flourishing in a never-ending upward spiral of skill, sophistication, virtue, and all the lovely fruit of the Spirit (Gal. 5:22).

Alas, aside from a few glimpses here and there, the Bible presents us with only two chapters at its beginning and two chapters at its end that depict a properly functioning world. The third chapter of Genesis drastically interrupts the Edenic paradise, and almost all the rest of Scripture depicts both the outworking of evil into creation and the reworking of creation's gardeners by God toward the salvation of the world. To work with God in this great mission of redemption, of getting back what was lost and setting it all right again, God calls us.

THE FALL: WHAT'S FUNDAMENTALLY WRONG

In the Fall, depicted in Genesis 3, humanity disobeys God. Not content to be created in the image of God, humans decide to "be like God" in some other sense. Not content to go about their lives in joyful communion with everything around them, they want to know more. They have so far experienced only goodness and can look forward to much more, so that the only remaining category of experience they would not have is the one thing God forbids them to seek and from which God has heretofore shielded them: acquaintance with evil.

By the fundamental sin of deciding for themselves rather than deciding according to the word of God, by proceeding to presume to know better what is best for themselves and disobeying God, and by experiencing the consequences of that sinful action, they do indeed now know good and evil. They are indeed "like gods" but only in this particularly terrible respect.

The consequences of sin show up immediately as both epistemological and ethical. In the woman's conversation with the serpent, in which God's express words are altered to make them both more severe ("Don't touch it") and less definite ("in case we might die"), we see a weird clouding of the mind that facilitates sin by the will. She literally doesn't get God's warning quite right, as if to leave open a deceitful alternative that the serpent is only too happy to provide. And then when God calls the human pair to account, Adam and Eve's finger-pointing away from themselves is not only morally wrong but cognitively wrong: it literally isn't the truth—the whole truth—of the matter.

This point about the irrationality, and not just the immorality, involved in sin shows up again in the very next story, in Genesis 4. Cain seems to be confused about how to honor God in sacrifice, but God corrects his misunderstanding and the implication is that Cain is free to try again. But instead of then proceeding to obey God in light of his new knowledge, Cain proceeds to kill Abel. This is a story so familiar to us that we must notice how irrational Cain's action is, quite apart from its immorality. For how can killing Abel possibly improve Cain's situation, which is that God is dissatisfied with him? "What was Cain thinking?" we might cry. The murder of Abel is an act of both wickedness (morality) and derangement (epistemology). So the Fall is a very bad thing, and the world is full of very bad things as a result.

We must be careful, of course, to remember that the Fall is only one part of the Christian story. Some Christians seem preoccupied with the evils of the world, as if the whole story is a Fall. They interpret and inhabit the world as if it is completely fallen, corrupted beyond repair, a valley of the shadow of death through which we must travel as quickly and safely as possible to reach the sunlit lands of the next life. So culture itself seems to them a dangerous waste of effort and resources. There is no point trying to rearrange flowers on tables in the dining room of a hotel on fire. It's all gonna burn anyhow—and rightly so. Forget politics and art and economics and all that stuff: Let's just get out of here and maybe help a few other people to escape also. Leave everything else alone—and behind.

Significantly, such an attitude sometimes shows up in a dim view of culture in its most extensive form, the form of the city. The city is the bad place opposite the good place, namely, the Garden of Eden. (Such Christians forget, of course, that

Eden was not a simply natural, wild place, but indeed a garden. As such, it needed tending, and human beings were created by God to tend it. So human culture is required there also!) The first city, such anti-urban Christians point out, was founded by Cain. Aha! That confirms that cities are evil, and thus all human culture downstream of the Fall is evil.[1]

The Bible does offer a fascinating dialectic between the evil city (Babel/Babylon) and the good city (Jerusalem/Zion). But before the Bible gets to all that (starting in Genesis 11), it suggests an interweaving of the good and the bad in the world directly after the Fall. From the story of Cain and Abel Genesis 4 goes on to show us at least two forms of cultural decline in the person of a thug named Lamech. Lamech marries two wives (so much for monogamy, the original norm of Genesis 2) and then boasts to them of his macho violence, his disproportionate killing of a man who had (merely) hurt him. Yet this horrid person fathers three symbolically interesting sons. One of them is the ancestor of nomads, those who dwell in tents and herd livestock; another is the first musician; and the third is the archetypal metalsmith. However suspicious one might be of cities, and however much one might disdain the loutish Lamech, in the gracious providence of God even this family produces cultural advancement through three creative and productive sons. (And, contrary to the tradition that our ultimate destiny lies far away from the urban in a bucolic paradise, the last city the Bible depicts is not Babylon the Great being hurled into hell, but the New Jerusalem descending from heaven to earth, in Revelation 21.)

Despite some promising developments, however, the world and its human gardeners clearly are doomed by the spreading stain of sin. The Bible sketches a relatively quick decline of humanity into a state so awful that God wipes us almost entirely off the face of the earth in the great flood, sparing only the righteous remnant of Noah and his family to restart the garden.

This drastic narrative—from creation to the Noahic "reboot"—takes up only a handful of chapters in Genesis (1-11). Then what we might call the time-lapse pace of the narrative slows down considerably to focus on the life of one man, Abraham, and on his descendants in turn. Indeed, his descendants—both physical and spiritual, Israelite/Jewish and Christian—take up the rest of the narrative of the Bible. And few of those characters in that very long narrative—including Noah and Abraham—avoid being exposed as sinners in need of God's help. Thus the vast majority of the Bible's story focuses on the third stage, salvation.

WHERE WE ARE IN GOD'S PLAN OF SALVATION

The "salvation" part of the story is ours. But it is too simple to say only that we live in "the era of salvation," since this era divides into at least three discrete sub-eras. Even further subdivisions can be important for understanding how this or that part of the Bible pertains to us, but let's focus upon the fundamental distinction between the Old Testament and the New, and recognize the earthly career of Jesus as the bridge between them.

If God intended the Old Testament to apply directly to all believers in all times, then we Christians should be applying it today in all its particulars—ceremonial, civil, liturgical, and so on. Yet few Christian groups advocate such a position today. (In our time, Christian Reconstructionism, also known as "Theonomy," comes closest to this radical view. People in this movement really do want American law, and the laws of other countries, to be based on the Torah—including capital punishment for homosexuals and disobedient children.) Most Christians instead recognize that that was then and this is now, and that was there and this is here. And when we give the matter further consideration, we find that most of us aren't Israelites.

Still, we see all around us Christians failing to make such distinctions. The American religious right, for example, advocates for the current state of Israel as if that state is directly fulfilling Old Testament prophecy and (a different claim) is entitled to the regard God requires for his chosen people. They maintain this view of Israel despite the manifest secularity of the vast majority of Israelis and of their state (which would disqualify them as "true Israel," according to the Biblical prophets).

"Health and wealth" preachers, for their part, claim divine promises of earthly prosperity that make some sense in an Old Testament context but do not so obviously fit in the very different economy of the New (Deut. 7:13; 8:7–13; 2 Chr. 7:14; cf. 2 Cor. 11:23–28). It simply isn't the case anymore that tangible blessing automatically comes to the righteous in this life. (It hasn't been automatic at least since the Book of Job.)

To notice the difference between the Old Testament and the New is not to disparage the Old, much less to dismiss it as irrelevant. In previous chapters I myself drew on the first few chapters of Genesis to make some points that are crucial in a Christian understanding of things, and I will continue to draw on the Old Testament as Holy Scripture in what follows.

We must be careful not to simply lop off the Old Testament as irrelevant to Christian ethics, even as we should recognize that we do not live in the Old Testament sub-era and ought not to simplistically apply its provisions to our place and time. Correct and fruitful reading of the Old Testament is a carefully acquired skill.

When we come to the next sub-era, then, the career of Jesus, many Christians happily set up ethical camp, so to speak. They long to follow Jesus just as the first disciples did. Whatever the charms of such nostalgia, however, we must not succumb to them. We are certainly not Jesus, nor are we the Twelve listening to him on a Galilean hillside—just as we are not Israel during the Exodus or Conquest or Kingdom.

Jesus is the center of God's great plan of redemption, through his incarnation, public ministry, crucifixion, resurrection, ascension, and second coming. The Church's earliest and most central confession was "Jesus is Lord." In the logic of the story and in the logic of salvation, therefore, the Gospels that narrate the life of Jesus are positioned at the beginning of the New Testament.

From these facts, however, some Christians have drawn some improper conclusions. In the history of Christian devotion, the tradition of *imitatio Christi*, the "imitation of Christ," looms large. Thomas à Kempis's spiritual classic of that name is only the most famous work in a long line of literature commending the life of Christ as the model for our own. Recently, this tradition has been radically simplified and popularized in the slogan, "What would Jesus do?"[2] This tradition of imitation comes straight from the Bible, of course. In his Upper Room Discourse, Jesus says that he is setting his disciples an example of loving service (John 13:15). His "new commandment" explicitly tells them to "love one another. . . . Just as

I have loved you" (John 13:34). Paul urges his churches to imitate Christ (Eph. 5:1–2; 1 Thess. 1:6). And the epistle to the Hebrews points to Jesus as our great example—the "Author and Finisher of our faith" (Heb. 12:2–3, King James Version).

So what's the problem with trying to imitate Jesus as closely as we can? It's a problem for this pretty basic reason: in many respects, Jesus is not our example.

For one thing, we are not Jesus. Jesus was who he was and did what he did in order to accomplish his distinctive mission. And that distinctive mission isn't ours. We are not called to fulfill the promises to Israel and to inaugurate the Kingdom of God. We are not called to be the Savior of the world and the Lord of resurrection life.

While we're at it, let's note that we are not all called to be Jewish, and male, and single. No one reading this book has been called to live two thousand years ago in the Levant under Roman oppression. And few of us are called to a trade, only to give it up for public religious teaching ministry in our thirties. Please notice that I'm not just cherry-picking odd little details about Jesus that are different from you or me, such as the color of his hair or his preference in music. The traits I have noted, and many others, were crucial to Jesus' *particular* identity and vocation, and none of us are called to emulate *them* as a matter of faithfulness.

Jesus calls us not to *do* his work but to *extend* his work. He promises, in fact, that his followers will perform "greater works than these" (John 14:12). We must take this seriously. Jesus' work was great, of course, but also limited. He played a particular role in the divine plan. That work was meant to inspire us outward and onward, not to confine us within particular limits that were proper for Jesus' calling but not for ours. Imbued with the Spirit of Jesus and acting as the

Body of Christ, we are to bear witness to Jesus Christ far beyond the extent of his own quite restricted preaching tours in Israel (with the occasional venturing beyond to a few Gentiles) and to make disciples of *all nations*. And the Church is engaged in that mission yet today, after two thousand years of labor.

So it is crucial to see that we are not supposed to live as if Jesus were present now in his earthly ministry, but *after: after* the crucifixion, the resurrection, and the ascension; *after* Pentecost and the giving of the Holy Spirit; and *after* the Gospels and the Book of Acts, which record the launching of the Church's distinctive era and mission. We live *after* the Old Testament and *after* the career of Jesus in a third sub-era of redemption, the age of the Church before the return of Christ in the consummation of history. "It is for your benefit that I go away," Jesus told his disciples (John 16:7), and we must take him at his word. We must not live as if he hadn't gone away and is present for us now as he was then, as if we are to follow him in that particular mode of ministry that had its place but is now over and done.

"What would Jesus do?" therefore is the wrong question for Christian faithfulness. If we keep asking it, we will keep making the perennial mistakes many Christians have made through the centuries, such as prioritizing church work over daily trades ("because Jesus gave up carpentry for preaching the gospel"); valorizing singleness, at least for clergy ("because Jesus didn't marry"); and denigrating all involvement in the arts, politics, or sports ("because we never read of Jesus painting a picture or participating in political discussions, much less kicking a ball"). Instead, the right question is something like this: "What would Jesus want me, or us, to do, here and now?"

Beyond this question of the imitation of Christ is another issue, one regarding theological and ethical method. And it's so important that we must pause for a while to consider it.

Many Christians, including some quite sophisticated theologians, seem to make the following mistake: because Christ himself has priority over all other figures in the history of salvation (which is true), then the Gospels that depict his life ought to have priority over all other books of the Bible, such as the prophets or the epistles. This argument sounds plausible, of course, but it is an important error and in at least four respects.

First, even though the Gospels do come first in the canon of the New Testament, they are probably not the earliest Biblical testimonies to Jesus. Paul's early letters, most scholars agree, predate most or all of the four Gospels. So if we seek the most primitive layer of "Jesus tradition," Paul's work would deserve priority.

But why seek that most primitive layer? So, second, we should not be privileging whatever we guess is the earliest material of the New Testament versus whatever is later, because all of it is inspired by God and therefore has the same status: Holy Scripture. Furthermore, any historian knows that sometimes later accounts are better than earlier ones precisely because those later accounts have drawn on several earlier accounts plus the perspective that only time can bring. So there is no good reason, whether theological or historical, for preferring "earlier" to "later," especially when all the books of the New Testament were composed in the same (apostolic) period. Such prioritizing would be as odd as preferring Mark's ostensibly earlier Gospel to John's later one.

Third, privileging the Gospels would make sense if Jesus had written them while his disciples wrote the other books. But the Gospels, of course, were authored not by Jesus but by other Christians as well: traditionally, Matthew, Mark, Luke, and John. So to privilege the Gospels is not to prefer Jesus to Paul or Peter, but simply to prefer Matthew to Paul, or Mark to Peter, or John to, well, John (1–3 John).[3] The elevation of the Gospels over the rest of the New Testament is particularly odd coming from educated Christians who should know better, and yet sound as if they have discovered a new red-letter edition of the Bible—except that their new version prints all the Gospels in red ink, while the rest of the Bible remains in black.[4]

Finally, the story of Jesus is, of course, the key to the Biblical story, as it is to all of human history. But to emphasize the Gospels over the rest of the New Testament is to forget that Jesus is Lord over all of history, Head of the Church that succeeds him in earthly ministry, and in fact Author of the whole New Testament via the inspiration of the Holy Spirit—as he is the God who inspired the whole Bible.

The better interpretative path, therefore, is to keep clearly in view what each of the books of the Bible has to offer us and to draw upon them according to their distinctive natures. We appreciate their genre strengths and limitations, and also the place of their subject matter in the Christian story.

We Christians therefore must not be forever trying to go back to the experience of the disciples trooping about with Christ in ancient Judea—nor, for that matter, nostalgically trying to recapture the experience of the disciples in the Book of Acts. The apparently unfinished nature of that book, in fact, has prompted many readers to conclude that God intends the rest of the Church to keep writing it, generation by generation, until the Lord of the Church returns, to fulfill the promise made at that book's beginning (Acts 1:11).

Richard Bauckham offers some crucial reflections in this vein that are well worth listening to at length:

> The difference between the testaments might be better expressed in terms of a difference of political context. Much of the Old Testament is addressed to a people of God which was a political entity and for much of its history had at least some degree of political autonomy. The Old Testament is therefore directly concerned with the ordering of Israel's political life, the conduct of political affairs, the formulation of policies, the responsibilities of rulers as well as subjects, and so on. The New Testament is addressed to a politically powerless minority in the Roman Empire. Its overtly political material therefore largely concerns the responsibilities of citizens and subjects who, though they might occasionally hope to impress the governing authorities by prophetic witness (Mt. 10:18), had no ordinary means of political influence.[5]

Our proper theological aim is to make the best sense of the whole Bible for all of the inspired instruction we can get on how to be God's people in the world here and now. Good theology also takes into account the ongoing work of the Holy Spirit in the life of the Church. As Oliver O'Donovan writes,

> There was no revealed political doctrine in the New Testament, prescribing how the state was to be guided. The early church had simply to proclaim God's Kingdom come in Christ. The political doctrine of Christendom was discovered and elicited from the practical experience of Christian political discipleship.[6]

We must be on guard, then, against the common Christian temptation to shrink the Bible to a few favorite books— whether Gospels, Epistles, Torah, prophecy, or what have you. And we should expect to find that the Holy Spirit did, in fact, lead the Church into more truth, as Jesus said the Spirit would—including truth about how to participate in new forms of society—once the canon was completed.

We have implicitly circled around a fundamental point of dispute in Christian ethics, so let us now take it on directly: What are Christians today to make of the deeds and words of Jesus in his earthly career?

At one theological extreme, Jesus' example and instruction are encapsulated in a dispensationalist scheme that relegates most of what he did and said to a bygone episode: Jesus came to offer the Kingdom to Israel, but Israel refused it, so God moved on to deal with the Church. The Sermon on the Mount is thus reduced to an intriguing artifact, legislation for a regime that never actually got started. The Sermon is therefore more or less instructive for us now in a manner similar to the way the Torah is more or less instructive for us now. I doubt that many readers of the present book are seriously considering this approach, which is not taught any more even at some former bastions of dispensationalism. So I will move on to consider the other extreme, which does have considerable traction in ethical discussions today.

This view affirms that Jesus meant literally what he said and intended us to do precisely what he did. Therefore, Jesus meant the Sermon on the Mount to be applied directly, as he meant everything else in the Gospels. Any alternatives to this literalism thus have to be viewed as disobedient compromises with the world; as failures to take up the cross with vigor and courage; as substandard discipleship and therefore ultimately sinful.

This forthright position has an enduring attraction for any serious Christian, of course. Its clarity and radicality combine in a heroic ideal of Christianity that rises impressively above most of our actual attempts to follow Christ. We must yet ask, however, is this clear and radical model actually coherent: with itself, with the Christian story, and with Christian history? I suggest that it is not, and it is important that it be exposed as such so that we may embrace instead an ethic that is more truly and fully Biblical. (It would also be pleasant to no longer suffer the accusations of despicable infidelity that are so frequently hurled at those who abandon this extreme version for something more realistic.)

As I say, this "clear and radical" version, as I am calling it, is incoherent. We need proceed no further than to examine the Sermon on the Mount itself. It is common for advocates of this position to tell us to do just what Jesus said in this sermon. But they do not really mean that.

Yes, they usually mean to turn the other cheek when struck and to return charity for violence. They mean to avoid hatred and lust, and to pursue reconciliation and good fellowship. Of course, that is all to the good, and I agree with them. Such keen Christians do not go on, however, to advocate the gouging out of eyes and the severing of limbs to improve one's likelihood of going to heaven (Matt. 5:29–30). Now, it's good that they don't, and I agree that we shouldn't. Yet these admonitions are right among the other passages that they are recommending to us with complete literalness. In the text, though, there are no obvious literary indications that in these particular verses we are dealing with hyperbole, not to be applied literally, while on either side of this passage there are verses that we obviously must obey literally.

Furthermore, some of those ethical injunctions may not be as clear as has frequently been asserted. Let us look particularly at the *locus classicus* on nonviolence/nonresistance:

> You have heard that it was said, "An eye for an eye and a tooth for a tooth." But I say to you, Do not resist an evildoer. But if anyone strikes you on the right cheek, turn the other also; and if anyone wants to sue you and take your coat, give your cloak as well; and if anyone forces you to go one mile, go also the second mile. (Matt. 5:38–41)

I do not pretend to understand all of what Jesus means here in this notoriously difficult text—difficult hermeneutically, and difficult practically. But I submit that he cannot mean us to understand the command "do not resist an evildoer" to be a blanket statement covering all instances of oppressive violence.

Let's not leap right away to the usual example of the marauder in the house at night. Let's instead take a different tack and work our way to the question of responding with force to violence.

Jesus does not mean, I think it fair to say, that parents should not resist evil in their children. How else could parents possibly fulfill their roles? It would be a bad parent who would refuse to prevent a child hurting another child or endangering itself. Nor does Jesus mean us to apply this ideal of nonresistance to church leaders, who are instead told explicitly by Christ's apostles in his inspired Word to exercise church discipline precisely in order to resist the evildoer (e.g., 1 Cor. 5). So this injunction doesn't apply to at least two kinds of societies, families and churches. And these societies happen to be the only societies in which first-century Christians would have had freedom to fully realize their ideals. I conclude, therefore, that if following such a rule in the "obvious" sense would render impossible the proper functioning of Christian families and churches, it certainly would destroy larger and more pluralistic social units, such as cities and countries. So, to put it mildly, I cannot recommend that we "simply" obey it. And I note that this "obvious" reading of the text has not been obvious to the Church from its earliest days, when some Christians continued to participate in the imperial armies, for example, while others taught that no Christian should do so.[7]

My sense is that many of the instructions of the Sermon on the Mount are indeed meant for us to take on straightforwardly and universally. But not all of them are. Jesus is a master of poetry and of parable, and we must be alert to his shifting genres. And if it is true that some of the Sermon is taught through hyperbolic imagery, as I think everyone must concede, then all Christians are in the same hermeneutical boat. Everyone is engaged in the same task of sorting out just what Jesus meant for us to believe and to do in this or that instance. No one can congratulate him- or herself for occupying the high and holy place in which they patently obey whatever Jesus said, unlike their disputants who must be pathetic and damnable compromisers.

I have argued, then, that this "clear and radical" approach is incoherent on its own terms, failing even to interpret its own favorite text in a plausible way. Second, this clear and radical position is incoherent with the Christian story. Christians are failing to see that while Jesus is announcing the Kingdom of God, he alone lives totally within it. His disciples don't—whether while he is around or afterward once he is gone. The Kingdom has not yet fully come, even though wonderful elements of it, and its fundamental ethos, are already here, to be enjoyed by the Church and to be shared with all others.[8] So since the Kingdom is "already, but not yet [fully]" come, we should not try to act as if it has already and fully come. Jesus' harder sayings point to this fact, as does the curious shape of his whole public career. Jesus demonstrates a morality, a spirituality, a dominion over nature, a control over death itself that is typical of the wondrous age to come, but these only flash out in brief signs in our era. Not everyone is healed, not all storms are stilled—not in Jesus' earthly career, and not since. We need an ethic that is consistent with this liminal period in which we live—between Jesus' first and second advents.

Third, I think we need to ponder that this ostensibly clear and radical position has never been instantiated in two thousand years of subsequent Christian history. Not once. No congregation, much less a denomination or national church, much, much less the whole extant Church, for even one day has succeeded in following this literalistic standard. This clear and radical hermeneutic might have been plausible to consider in the first century, because no one had yet fully attempted it. But how plausible is it twenty centuries later? Have all of God's people since then been manifestly disobedient to the call of God?

Well, yes, we have been. And perhaps we should just redouble our efforts. But one might suppose that if Christ did mean for us to live in this way, then the Holy Spirit of God would have empowered at least some Christians to do so. And I maintain that history shows that he has not. So I ask, what makes the ethicist today who advocates this radical ethic think that here and now things will be so different from every preceding episode of Church history?

This argument does not prove in any absolute sense that Jesus is not gravely displeased with his Church after he apparently was so clear about what he wanted from us. But as we weigh as carefully as we can what is most likely for Jesus to have meant, it seems to me very odd for him to have commanded what no Christians have managed to even closely approximate. I suggest that two thousand years of Church history tilts the burden of proof onto those who continue to aver that Jesus intended us to follow this "clear and radical" extremism.

Let me be clear that I have no intention of contradicting Jesus but of contradicting instead merely *some alternative and mistaken interpretations of* Jesus. I agree with many other Christian theologians and ethicists throughout Church history who believe that the main point of the Sermon on the Mount is both the call and the promise to be complete and mature. The perfection to which Jesus refers as he calls us to be "perfect, as your heavenly Father is perfect" (Matt. 5:48) is indeed that to which God is leading us. We are to be perfect, complete, and mature someday, and Christ calls us *toward* this destiny now.

Our ethical situation, therefore, is *downstream* of the career of Jesus. Indeed, it is downstream of Jesus' suffering and death, his resurrection, and his ascension. It is downstream of Pentecost and the coming of the Holy Spirit. And it is downstream of two thousand years of global Church history. What, then, is our calling now?

MAKING DISCIPLES: THE DISTINCTIVE CHRISTIAN VOCATION

"In Christ God was reconciling the world to himself" (2 Cor. 5:19), and we Christians are grateful for all that God has done, is doing, and will do in Jesus. But God is not saving the world entirely and solely through Jesus. Jesus himself tells us so.

When Christ took his leave of the disciples, he gave them one particular task, but there are two versions of it. Luke says that Jesus told us to bear witness of him (Luke 24:48; Acts 1:8). That is a bold command, given that witnessing to Jesus meant reporting truthfully what he said and did, identifying (with) him as telling the truth, and taking whatever consequences might issue from Jewish or Roman authorities who had already cooperated in Jesus' torture and death. Witnessing to Jesus would be hard, and many would do so only literally by way of the cross.

Matthew, however, has Jesus saying something different in the Great Commission: "Go therefore and make disciples of all nations, baptizing them in the name of the Father and of the Son and of the Holy Spirit, and teaching them to obey everything that I have commanded you" (Matt. 28:19–20). Obeying *this* commandment isn't hard. It's impossible.

It is difficult enough to change people's minds about non-trivial ideas. I do that for a living as a professor, and I can show you on exam paper after exam paper just how (un) successful I am at it. It is hard, and likely harder, to change someone's morality: to convince him or her that that favorite activity is actually harmful and wicked. But to make a *disciple* of someone is to change what and whom he or she *loves*.

Have you ever disapproved of the boyfriend or girlfriend in the life of someone you care about and then intervened, hoping to break them up? How did that go? No, converting people's *loves* is hardest of all. In fact, I have been trying to make a disciple of *myself* all my life, and that project has met with only checkered success.

The only way, therefore, for this command to avoid absurdity is for it to come the way it actually does come to us in Matthew's account: with reassurance that this impossible task is not ours to attempt alone. Here is the whole passage, and note what comes before and after the Great Commission itself:

> And Jesus came and said to them, "All authority in heaven and on earth has been given to me. Go therefore and make disciples of all nations, baptizing them in the name of the Father and of the Son and of the Holy Spirit, and teaching them to obey everything that I have commanded you. And remember, I am with you always, to the end of the age." (Matt. 28:18–20)

With God, the impossible becomes possible, and conversion— actual disciple-making—is the work uniquely of the Spirit of God (Matt. 19:26).

Jesus therefore calls Christians to this distinctive Christian mission. Let's note immediately, and we will reiterate this later, that the disciple-making commandment, what we will also call the *salvation commandment*, does not replace the permanent and generic call of God upon all human beings summed up in the creation commandments. Christians don't suddenly become something other than human upon conversion. And most of what most Christians do most of the time is generically human, not distinctively

Christian. A Christian doesn't go out to his Christian shed to retrieve his Christian lawn mower and fill it with Christian gasoline before cutting his Christian lawn in a Christian way.

Disciple-making, however, is the crucial task made necessary by the Fall. Jesus is humanity's route back to God. He at the same time shows us both how God is toward us and how to live toward God. He at the same time is our Savior who does for us what we cannot do for ourselves and our model for what there remains for us to do. He at the same time is the Lord and shows us how to be a servant of the Lord.

Helping people become Christians is fundamentally a matter of helping them to follow Jesus and become more like him. It is not a matter of recruiting them to join the world's biggest and best religion; or teaching them newer, truer ideas about things; or guiding them to refine their moral or aesthetic sensibilities—although it is, I suppose, all those things, too. Becoming a follower of Jesus, however, is fundamentally about finding one's way back to a right relationship with God, and that happens through connecting oneself with (and being connected to) Jesus.

As the Way, the Truth, and the Life, Jesus constitutes the center of our lives around whom everything else then spins correctly. Becoming a disciple of Jesus is the one and only way to become what we ought always to have been and aspire always to be: properly functioning human beings, living out our lives according to the creation commandments in the delight of God's blessing. So we Christians gladly join with the Holy Spirit of God in this work of calling people to Jesus, introducing them to him and helping them grow to full maturity, even as we ourselves are helped to do so by other Christians.

This task is one that only Christians can perform. We are the *ekklēsia*—literally, the ones "called-out" to do this extraordinary work. Why is it exclusive to Christians? It is not because Christians are intrinsically more spiritual or wise or holy than others. I acknowledge gratefully that by virtue of the Holy Spirit, who indwells and empowers us beyond our own qualities and abilities, we do become *more* spiritually aware, *more* wise (beginning with the fear of Yhwh; Prov. 1:7), and *more* holy (as "saints," those set apart for divine service and becoming more and more conformed to the image of Christ). But we have not been assigned this distinct and distinctive task because we merit such an honor. Instead, it is assigned to us simply in the nature of being Christian. Christians are the only people in the world whose religion is named for Christ. We are the only people in the world who put Jesus in the center, where he belongs. We are the only people in the world who proclaim, "Jesus is Lord." Therefore we are the only people in the world who can bear witness to Jesus, who can invite others to repent and believe this good news, and who can teach people how to become disciples of Jesus.

Everything else we are and do particularly as Christians connects with this mission. That is not to say that mission is the sole activity of the Church—contra much of the evangelical tradition and some of the Missional Church movement of our day.[9] To say so is to substitute what Christians *distinctively* are to do for *all* that Christians are to do. Again, the creation commandments have priority: We are humans first and last, and "Christians" only temporarily. There won't be any "Christians" in the world to come, in the sense of people bearing the label "Christian" to distinguish them from those who aren't rightly related to God through Christ: "No longer shall they teach one another, or say to each other, 'Know the Lord,' for they shall all know me, from the least of them to the greatest, says the Lord" (Jer. 31:34).

The Church engages in worship of God not because that is a peculiarly Christian thing to do but because that is the correct and healthful *human* response to God, to love God with all one's heart, soul, mind, and strength. Christians certainly ought not to engage in worship merely because it helps the Church perform its particular mission better, although it does. Similarly, the Church cares for its own in fellowship because that is what *people* do when they are rightly related in shalom and love each other as themselves—not merely because fellowship strengthens the Body of Christ for service to others, although it does.

Thus, it just isn't true, despite its frequent repetition in some circles, that "the Church is the one society that exists for the benefit of its non-members." That phrasing may be cute, but it is not correct. Nor, for that matter, is Kierkegaard's famous image of the Church as performers in worship with God as the audience. Worship is a dialogue between God and us in which God blesses us far more than we bless God, even as God gives us gifts with which to bless each other as well. The Church undertakes worship and fellowship in the win-win-win dynamic of the Kingdom of God: to love God, to love our neighbor, and to benefit ourselves simultaneously.

Here Dietrich Bonhoeffer's intriguing recommendation of the "secret discipline" of the Church might be worth another look. Bonhoeffer refers to the ancient Church practice of refusing admission to the Lord's Supper to all but baptized members.[10] Such a practice might seem contradictory, or even repellent, to our contemporary sensibilities of inclusion, hospitality, and anti-elitism. But the practice suggests that the Church thus maintains its integrity—literally, its integration with God in worship and with each other in fellowship—for the intrinsic importance of authentic worship and fellowship and also for the benefit of the world. The world will be much more richly blessed by a strong, good, lucid, passionate Church than by one that compromises its worship and fellowship according to the fads of popular culture or the lowest common denominator of those who happen to show up. Worship shorn of all terminology and ritual that is not immediately intelligible to the unchurched visitor, of all preaching that is not restricted to the vocabulary, categories, and concerns of the occasional attender, and of all spiritual conversation that probes beneath the manicured surfaces of conventional propriety cannot nourish a strong and well-formed Church. And it is only such a Church that can turn outward to offer the world a vigorous, definite, wise, and truly alternative society and mode of life.

The Church is the repository of the Christian symbol set, narrative, experience, and practice—the keeper of the ideas and actions that define us, motivate us, and guide us over against the scripts and agendas of other powers and interests. It is the community that aspires to bring forth the best possible array of these treasures according to the need of the moment, helping each other individually and helping ourselves corporately to believe, feel, and act as God wants us to do in the current situation. Only a regular return to connect again and again with this trove and this fellowship can keep us properly oriented and passionately inspired in our mission.

The Christian Church in the medieval West opposed an alternative structure, headed by a pope, to the normal hierarchies of power, headed by kings, thus subverting the claim of total allegiance typically made by monarchs and states.

The Anabaptists would later emphasize the voluntary nature of membership in a church against the automatic package of Christianity-and-citizenship assumed in both Catholic and Protestant realms in the early modern period. In fact, the Christian Church always offers an identity and community more basic than those that are normally taken to be primary and ultimate. David Martin puts the point starkly:

> Mohammed was a warrior and a family man whereas Jesus was neither. Again notice that Islam sanctifies a holy city and is about territory whereas primitive Christianity is not ... Christianity rejects the social logic embodied in genealogy, biological reproduction, and land, and attempts to set up spiritual and non-violent brotherhoods and sisterhoods outside that powerful nexus.[11]

Martin might be overdrawing the distinction somewhat. For early Christians did value blood ties: "whoever does not provide for relatives, and especially for family members, has denied the faith and is worse than an unbeliever" (1 Tim. 5:8). And the vision that inspired the early Christians was that of a New Jerusalem, a city come down from heaven to a new earth, which they would enjoy in resurrected bodies. But Martin is right to emphasize that the Christian community relativizes all other commitments, just as the Christian confession ("Jesus is Lord") relativizes all other loyalties. In the same way that individuals become healthiest and also most helpful to others when they maintain a dialectic of solitude and community, so the Church becomes most vital as it alternates between focus on its Lord and its own development, and focus upon the world in service.

Having said all that, we recognize that the Church is in fact missional in its *distinctive* task of witnessing to Jesus

Christ and making disciples. All that it does, including worship and fellowship, contributes to that task, even as we must be careful not to subsume all that it does under that task.

Before we proceed to discuss the Church's mission, however, we need to pause to dispute with those Christians who suggest that God's entire redemptive project focuses on the Church as both means and end—as if the world, both in the sense of the natural order and of global humanity, exists only as the "raw materials out of which God creates his church."[12] To identify the Church as the sole locus of God's redemptive concern is to badly misunderstand the scheme of salvation. Indeed, it is to invert it. God wants the whole world back, not just a selection of human beings. And God wants it back not to bask in the eternal adoration of the redeemed saints, per the Beatific Vision, but to enjoy the give-and-take of shalom with all God's creatures and among them as well. To repeat, therefore: The Church performs its distinctive redemptive calling within, and in the service of, the general call of God upon humanity to be stewards of the whole earth God loves. The Church is the locus of God's redemption of humanity, creation's governors, precisely so that the rest of creation, which must groan in the meanwhile, can be restored to proper health as well (Rom. 8:22).

Let's turn, then, to how God deploys the Church in its various modes.

THE CHRISTIAN VOCATION

All of Us, Some of Us, Each of Us

MAKING DISCIPLES: EVERYONE

In at least three respects, then, the Church is engaged in mission: as witness and example (per Luke's account) but also as agent (per Matthew's).

As *witness*, the Church experiences something remarkable and reports that experience to others. As Richard Bauckham says: "Witnesses are not expected, like lawyers, to persuade by the rhetorical power of their speeches, but simply to testify to the truth for which they are qualified to give evidence."[1] And the central experience of the Christian Church is *Christ*—not religious feeling or spirituality in general, not God or the divine in general, not faith or religion in general, but Jesus Christ. As Christians bear witness to Jesus Christ—in their reception of his revelation, their baptism in water and in his Holy Spirit, their enjoyment of his Church, and their work with him in the world—then the Church performs its distinctive task and adds immeasurably to shalom. We should note that even when the Church speaks more generally and less particularly about Christ, it may still add to shalom. But now it does so as just one among many agencies of social reform, charity, moral uplift, spiritual experience, and the like—and often not the most effective or inspiring of them.

Again, let us be clear that we undertake worship and fellowship not solely for the advancement of this mission. They are generically good things for all human beings to enjoy. But genuine worship of Christ, corporately and individually, and genuine fellowship with other Christians provide regular occasions for encounter with Christ, and in so doing give the Church something about which to testify to others. Indeed, surely a major problem in the effective witness of Christians in the West is the lack of powerful experience of Christ week to week, even year to year, providing such Christians with little fuel for our zeal and little experiential content for our message.

This honor of bearing witness to Christ would be glory enough, but Christ also calls the Church to be an *example*. Christians are to live in the light of the Kingdom of God, however imperfectly we perceive it and however inconstantly we practice its principles. We are called, that is, not merely to witness to something that happened over there and long ago, although what did happen is certainly crucial to our testimony: "God was in Christ reconciling the world to himself" (2 Cor. 5:19). Nor are we merely to witness to something that is happening here and now and among us, as if an exciting spiritual experience is all we have to offer. But what is happening within and among us can and should be visible to others who observe us. Albeit with the grace of the Holy Spirit, without whose ministry no truly spiritual thing can be apprehended (1 Cor. 2:13–15), Kingdom life can be seen and interpreted for what it is. We ought to be acting out at least an approximation of the Kingdom of God—in our individual lives, yes, and especially in our churches, families, and other Christian organizations. For the "eternal life" we are promised in the Gospel (e.g., John 3) is to be our present experience and our future hope: it is, to use a different translation of the same words, "the life of the age to come."[2]

So Christians care for the poor. We care for the financially poor, defying the power of Mammon by giving our money away with liberality and with faith that God will always provide what we truly need. And we care for the poor in spirit: the depressed, the lonely, the unloved, the misfits and "losers" that society scorns and hurries past. So Christians rejoice for and with each other, rather than offering grudging congratulations through teeth clenched in envy, because we know that in God's economy of abundance there will be plenty of success and honor to go around. So we put ourselves at each other's service, making the most of our talents, skills, and resources to the maximal benefit of all. So we celebrate the arts, play sports and games, cook good food, and otherwise declare that the world is yet a gift from God and that he is a generous Lord who enjoys our enjoyment. So we pray for the Day when suffering, sin, and absurdity are gone and all is light, goodness, and flourishing. And so we do whatever little bit we can to honor God, bless others, and fulfill ourselves. The Church is the new humanity, and as we live life as properly functioning human beings and not just as members of some peculiar, narrowly "religious" sect, we exemplify precisely the heart of our religion: faithfulness to the God of both creation and salvation, the God of abundant life (John 10:10).

Third, Christ calls us beyond the roles of witness and example to be actual *agents* of his mission. Among the most extraordinary commands of the Bible is this Great

Commission: "go . . . and make disciples." As we have seen, strictly speaking this mandate is nonsense. We cannot make even ourselves into good disciples, no matter how we instruct ourselves, remonstrate with ourselves, and pray for ourselves. The *imitatio Christi* model goes only so far. We must be born again by the Spirit. Christ must form himself in us. So how can Christ thus command us to *make* disciples of *others*?

This last, great command of Jesus' earthly ministry comes with the promise of his own authority and presence (Matt. 28:18–20) and also of the Holy Spirit (Acts 1:8). We are called to do what is actually divine work, the hardest work in the world: changing people's loves. And there is no way we could do this work unless the heart-transforming power of the Holy Spirit courses within us. But God *is* within us, and therefore "greater works than these" are commanded of us. We are to play an actual part in drawing men and women, boys and girls, to the Savior and help them respond to him as Lord.

Having surveyed these three great modes of our distinctive calling as Christians, we note several synergistic qualities of our work.

First, we see the win-win-win dialectic again. As Christians care for others, that ministry also contributes to our sanctification, which also adds to God's pleasure as God's good purposes advance. Likewise, as we become more holy, we also become more faithful and more effective in our mission, which also adds to God's pleasure. And we can count on God to be happy to grant us all that we need to keep becoming better people and more effective in God's service.

Second, we see that the creation commandments and the salvation commandment deeply connect. Our obedience to the former greatly aids in our obedience to the latter. We will be better witnesses to God's work in Christ and to the life of the Kingdom God brings as we experience that Kingdom life. We will be better examples of Kingdom life as we practice it in its fullness. And we will be more effective agents as our neighbors see the Kingdom life we live and are drawn, with the help of the Holy Spirit, to its impressive goodness.

Conversely, Christians who narrow their understanding and practice of mission to evangelism alone end up being less effective in that evangelism precisely because what they are witnessing to, exemplifying, and acting out is a much-reduced gospel, an important but thin slice of the abundant Kingdom life.[3] Proclamation of the Gospel is an essential part of both Christian mission and Christian life, but it is not the totality of either. When it becomes the only mode of Christian service to God, the message being proclaimed becomes less attractive because it is less vital and less evident in those proclaiming it. How do we expect people to be attracted to a society of people who live only to convert other people to their society? We will be better evangelists if we do not concentrate all of our energies on evangelism.

Too narrow an understanding of the Christian life shows up in many ways. Art, for example, is often dismissed or, even more frequently, ignored in Christian circles. Churches are constructed according to efficiency—maximum seating, lowest heating or cooling costs, best price—or evangelistic efficacy ("Will this building impress those we hope to convert?"). They reflect no regard for other values that have guided Christian architecture in the past: testifying to the grandeur of God, or fostering intimacy with God and each other, or any other spiritual-aesthetic principle. In such circles art is, at best, mere decoration or device. Any more than a modest interest in architecture, interior design, clothing, or cosmetics is under suspicion as sheer worldliness. For does not the Bible itself warn against such things? Paul writes,

> I desire, then, that in every place the men should pray, lifting up holy hands without anger or argument; also that the women should dress themselves modestly and decently in suitable clothing, not with their hair braided, or with gold, pearls, or expensive clothes, but with good works, as is proper for women who profess reverence for God. (1 Tim. 2:8–10)

I suggest that Paul is warning against extravagance here, however, not against beauty. He wants the focus in worship to be on God, not on oneself and particularly not on one's bodily adornment. The God upon whom we are to focus is a God who loves beauty—the inner beauty of the spiritual, yes, but also the external beauty of the physical. For this is the God who lavishes beauty even upon the flowers of the field (Matt. 6:28–30) and who actually expects an effort on our part to provide beauty even in worship. This God, as the rabbi Paul knew well, required considerable outlay of materials and skill in the construction of the Tabernacle and the garments of the priests (Exod. 25–27, 35–39). God required perfumed incense in worship, and the sacrifices on Israel's altars themselves were to offer a pleasant aroma to God (Exod. 29:18, 25; 30:34–37; Lev. 1–2). God later blessed Solomon's temple in all its magnificence (1 Kings 6–8). God's prophets chided Israel for mediocre offerings that would offend even an earthly governor (Mal. 1:8). And we have seen already that God intends to construct the New Jerusalem in breathtaking splendor.

The appearance of Christian churches, Christian homes, and Christian bodies communicates our values. *We are known by our art.* If we keep our churches, homes, and bodies bereft of art (or, alas, bereft of good art), we are saying something about what we hold to be Kingdom values—and what we are saying is heretical, namely, that God doesn't care about beauty.[4]

But just a minute. Isn't the world in an emergency situation? So how do we justify painting pictures while the *Titanic* is sinking? Shouldn't we frantically be doing all we can to get people into the lifeboats?

This powerful metaphor is common, but wrong, and we need to discard it once and for all. The world is in trouble, true, but in a kind of trouble not very much like a rapidly sinking ship. Instead, the world is like what the New Testament actually describes it as being like: a garden, a city, a war, a planet—which are all long-term and complex systems.

Furthermore, we serve a God of abundant power and resources, and God has furnished this planet, and us, with abundance also. We are not in a situation of scarcity, but in a situation of badly distributed and badly used abundance. It is simply not right to tell the artist to leave off his work, sell his art supplies, and get busy with evangelism or the relief of the poor. Those Christians whom God has called both to support and to engage in evangelism and poor relief—they are the ones who are responsible for those tasks, and they are the ones to be blamed if the tasks languish.

It would be senseless to try to make (bad) missionaries out of (good) artists. The world would suffer the loss of the good artistic work that they would have done. The salt and light they would have brought to the artistic community would be lost. And many people who would be attracted by artistic work and testimony to investigate the Christian Church would instead be repelled upon encountering an aesthetic desert, no matter how eloquent our preaching and excellent our morals. Thus, again, our evangelism ironically would be hampered precisely by an excessive focus on evangelism. The salvation commandment must be properly related to the creation commandments, or all will be compromised.[5]

MAKING DISCIPLES: PARTICULAR GROUPS

All Christians, and all Christian groups, share a responsibility to proclaim Christ as Lord, to live as disciples, and to welcome others to become disciples as well. Throughout history, moreover, various Christian groups have been formed to accomplish particular tasks: missionary societies, medical organizations, relief and development agencies, educational institutions, fellowships of various kinds of professionals, and so on. Particular congregations and denominations have been given both gifts and opportunities from God to do distinctive work, most obviously in the sense of ministering within particular localities (the church in Jerusalem versus the church in Philippi) and thus to particular kinds of people (Jews in Jerusalem and Gentiles in Philippi).

Modern societies are characterized by the increasing and widespread differentiation of social sectors and thus of social organizations. And the modern Church has become differentiated as well. Particularly since the mid-twentieth century, special-purpose groups have proliferated both within congregations (support groups for divorced people, youth groups of various levels, men's and women's fellowships, and the like) and beyond—indeed, *especially* beyond, in what are sometimes, and mistakenly, called "parachurch organizations," such as InterVarsity Christian Fellowship, World Vision, Wheaton College, Women's Aglow, Pioneer Girls, Neighborhood Bible Studies, the Fellowship of Christian Athletes, and many, many more.[6]

These groups are called "parachurch" mistakenly, I suggest, because they do not, in fact, work *beside* the *Church*, but are themselves truly the Church of Jesus Christ deployed in particular ways to accomplish particular purposes. True, they are not congregations and in that (important) sense are not churches. But they are not, as the term "parachurch" seems to imply, stopgap devices to make up for some kind of deficiency in the work of congregations. Most of them do work that no congregation or denomination can do, or could ever do as well, precisely because they are so focused— and often also because they are ecumenical to at least some degree.

Evangelical organizations on university campuses have blessed generations of students by offering them age- and context-appropriate religious education in an evangelically ecumenical environment that has introduced their members to other traditions and to the evangelical consensus that binds them together. This experience is unlikely to be gained in any other way. A Baptist or Pentecostal or Presbyterian campus group may well offer particular benefits to its members but not these crucial benefits. Moreover, groups such as the Navigators and Cru can achieve a critical mass of members, drawing from across denominational lines, to accomplish certain things on campus that an array of independent denominational groups never would. Such is not always the case, of course, but my point is that there are important and intrinsic limitations to denominational divisions, no matter how lively the denominations may be, that can be overcome by such ecumenical special purpose groups—or what I call *paracongregational* ministries.

Certainly there are attendant dangers to such organizations. They can spring up on the basis of some initial charisma of leadership and urgency of need only later to flail about, bereft of the wisdom and stability that a more established organization could bring to their work. They can easily go astray under leaders whose entrepreneurship is not matched by managerial ability or spiritual maturity. And they can wastefully diffuse among several similar organizations resources that would be better spent on one just one.

On the other hand, these organizations can emerge more quickly if they are independent of established ways and means, and with innovative ideas and forms unlikely to emerge from established groups. And they (sometimes) can fade away more easily, and properly, when the moment of their usefulness is past, rather than being propped up indefinitely by large congregations or denominations that refuse to prune them back.[7]

Particular denominational traditions have particular qualities to offer to the world and to other traditions. There is a great opportunity that has largely been missed to date in any ecumenical movement—whether that which usually bears the name, dating from the Edinburgh Missionary Conference of 1910 and now institutionalized in the World Council of Churches, or in the various evangelical ecumenical organizations exemplified by the World Evangelical Alliance. That opportunity is to learn from each other and particularly from each other's *differences*.

John Howard Yoder has trenchantly criticized a particular version of diversity:

We see here at work the ordinary ethos of liberal Western ecumenism. One assumes that it is proper for each denominational community to have "their thing," perhaps thought of as their "gift" in analogy to the language of 1 Corinthians 12, or as their "talent." One assumes that each denomination's particularity is somehow "true," in that others should listen to it respectfully rather than calling it heretical as they used to. At the same time, one assumes that the kind of "truths" which the others hold is not over-powering, since that "respectful listening" does not obli-gate one to agree with them, or even to weigh seriously the reasons they give for their views.... Thus the price of this good-mannered ecumenical openness to hear one another at our points of distinctiveness is a pluralism that may replace the truth question with a kind of uncritical celebration of diversity.[8]

Yoder is quite right. A shallow relativism leads to a shallow engagement with the other, ending with, as Paul Griffiths writes about interreligious dialogue more generally, "a dis-course that is pallid, platitudinous, and degutted. Its prod-ucts are intellectual pacifiers for the immature: pleasant to suck on but not very nourishing."[9]

My recommendation instead is that we do not stop ask-ing evaluative questions. We ought unapologetically, if also respectfully, to interrogate various other traditions in order to learn something that can truly improve our own. Perhaps the Presbyterians really do know more than we do about due process in church government. Perhaps the Orthodox really do know some things we do not about iconography. Perhaps the Mennonites really can teach us the meaning of "enough." Perhaps the Pentecostals can help liberate us from dull and disembodied worship. Baptists who have learned to improve their procedures from Presbyterians, their art from the Orthodox, their finances from the Mennonites, and their worship from the Pentecostals do not thereby become worse Baptists, but better ones. And so it should go around the ecumenical circle.

I suspect that God has not bestowed on any denomination the single fully pure and comprehensive tradition precisely in order to humble us and to draw us together in mutual regard, mutual edification, and mutual service. Ecumenical encounter that does not result in change all around is worse than useless: it confirms in each participant a smug self-containment that reinforces each tradition's inbred weaknesses.

Our differences can serve God's purposes in yet another way. Mindful of Yoder's warning about superficial mutual affirmation stemming from a woolly relativism, I offer the following proposal with some trepidation. I yet offer it as both important on its own terms and as suggestive of broader applications.

The Christian traditions that oppose any use of force (usually simply equated with *violence*) characteristically claim that Jesus shows us an alternative way to deal with the world's violence. Jesus does not fight fire with fire, they say, but rather submits to immolation, so to speak, only to emerge triumphant from the ashes on the other side of death. We, too, must not resist evil, but instead must be willing to sacrifice ourselves as we trust the God who has overcome death and all other enemies in Christ's cross and promises resurrection for all who will follow this path.

This appears to be a plausible reading of at least much of the New Testament. Yet I have found it increasingly difficult to square this ethical view with the whole Bible as the Word of God. The Old Testament presents a God who resorts frequently to violence to accomplish divine purposes. Moreover, God calls the people of God to do the same—not always, but often. And what about the New Testament? Jesus' cleansing of the Temple seems to be an act of violence. God instructs the Church to obey and pray for those who wield the sword in the interest of justice (Rom. 13:1–7; 1 Pet. 2:13–14). And what is one to make of the apocalyptic Jesus riding in triumph over his enemies on a field of blood, in the service of the God who pours woe after woe upon the earth? Jesus is both the Lamb of God and the Lion of Judah. He is the Prince of Peace, who makes peace both "by the blood of his cross" and also by the strength of his right hand, the sword that proceeds from his mouth, and so on. I can no longer see such martial images being explained properly along pacifist lines.

I warn again against any resort to "WWJD?" Just because Jesus in his earthly ministry did not resort to violence (except for that Temple cleansing, and the cursing of the fig tree ...), it does not mean that we are to eschew all force ourselves—particularly when we do see this same Jesus forcibly subduing his enemies in the Apocalypse. Since we live neither in the era of Jesus' earthly ministry nor in the era of the Last Judgment, I suggest it is at least an open question how Christians are to engage the challenges of this world, whether on the individual level of a thief or murderer entering one's home, or a thieving and murderous horde entering one's village or nation.

I have come to agree with the view of the majority of Christians in the majority of Church history: Christians are to join with others, and with God, in using force to resist evil and promote good via economic restrictions, police forces, judicial systems, and armies. This violence is an ugly, regrettable, and temporary expedient that will be done away in the world to come precisely by the imperial power of the returning Christ who loves peace and quickly brings shalom to our war-torn world. In some situations, however, violence is the least bad option, and Christians should not leave to others the hard, bloody, and dirty forms of peacemaking.

How, then, can Christians possibly bear witness to such a complicated understanding of violence, justice, and shalom? I cannot claim to resolve fully these deep matters—and that is my present point. Perhaps only the mind of God can fully encompass them. No one theological scheme, nor any single Christian tradition or group, can say and show all that there is to say and show about our peace-loving God—who sometimes resorts to violence to restore peace to a violent world. I suggest, then, that in at least some instances God calls a majority of Christians to join with others in the forceful restraint of evil and promotion of good, and that God simultaneously calls a minority of Christians (and others) to a vigorous peace witness. Only the combination of these callings can testify to the regrettable evil inherent in the use of such force; to the need to resort to violence, but only when all other means of resolution have failed; to the requirement that any violence be contained to the greatest extent possible; to the recognition that this life and our place in it is not the highest good; and to the deeply anomalous place that force has in God's economy. This complex testimony does not delegitimize violence entirely, but it delegitimizes it absolutely, so to speak, as a terrible necessity that in the Kingdom of God will have no lasting place.

Let us retreat from this awful subject to one that perhaps will make my larger point more agreeably. It makes sense to say that some forms of corporate worship are better than others. Those forms of worship that neglect preaching, for example, or marginalize the Eucharist, or skimp on prayer; those that discourage participation by the laity; those that do not call participants to their best efforts, but allow or even cultivate mere slack observance—all of these kinds of worship are simply deficient. But there is no order of service one can construct that encompasses the positive qualities of a Roman Catholic mass plus a charismatic revival plus a Quaker meeting. An amalgam that incorporates elements of each is no magic solution, either, but is simply a fourth alternative with its own deficiencies relative to the others.

I suggest in this light that no single worship form can help all people everywhere meet and celebrate God equally well, nor can any single worship form express the richness of God and the variety of God's blessings on the widely variegated people who bear God's name. Therefore we can affirm multiple worship forms as genuine and good rather than feeling obligated to rank them, let alone denounce them. To be sure, as we have seen with respect to denominations generally, each worship tradition might well benefit from learning from the strengths of other styles. It would thus become a better version of itself.

Such a dialectic requires a willingness to recognize what is better and what is worse in other traditions to improve one's own ministry—and perhaps even to remonstrate with the others for their benefit. Such a dialectic, more fundamentally, acknowledges that to articulate the whole counsel of God wildly exceeds the capacity of any one theological, liturgical, devotional, or ecclesiastical tradition. This attitude of humility avoids both chauvinism and relativism and ought to result in both the strengthening of each particular group and a greater fellowship of mutual edification among groups. Without such an attitude, ecumenism will remain as it is now, which is formally the same whether one looks at liberal or conservative varieties: lowest-common-denominator theological and liturgical affirmations of little import and a certain amount of cooperation in basic, albeit often important, Christian ministry, whether social action, evangelism, or whatever.

Yoder offers some creative observations about the positive role of minority traditions:

> Minority groups can also exercise pioneering creativity in places where no one is threatened. They can do jobs nobody else is interested in doing, and thereby gradually draw attention to some realm of social need for which it would have been impossible to find an imposed solution.... The presence on the stage of a very different position, even if not a possible model to be imposed as official policy by a majority, or even to be negotiated by a sizable minority in a coalition situation, still does change the total spectrum of positions, and thereby moves the balance point of the system.[10]

We do not all have to think the same way, worship the same way, testify the same way, and serve the same way. We may even be called to take up apparently contradictory positions in order to, together, encompass the complex richness of God's truth and care in a situation. By all means let us scrutinize alternatives carefully and beware those that will compromise the cause. But let us also keep minds more open to the idea that even in exactly the same situation, different Christian groups will be faithful in saying and doing quite different things. And let us be especially careful not to crush minority testimonies just because they are minorities and *ipso facto* they must be wrong. They may yet have a vital role to play.

A final point about vocational diversity can be made about the particular call of Christ on particular groups. Let's focus on congregations, but the same principles apply to Christian educational institutions, Christian youth organizations, Christian social services, and so on.

It ought to be obvious that every congregation worthy of the name demonstrates certain traits and performs certain practices—acknowledging that Christians may disagree about whether other items also belong on a list of minimal requirements. Surely a congregation that never prayed, read Scripture, or cared for the poor would fail anyone's definition of a genuine Christian church. Yet beyond these generic qualities and actions, each congregation is also called by Christ to particular work. This should be obvious from its geographical location and cultural makeup. Yet many churches fail to take such fundamental realities thoroughly into account.

Many congregational leaders have never analyzed their own geographical and cultural particulars, nor have they analyzed their congregations in these respects. The pastors know very little about the ethnic makeup, the spending patterns, the leisure preferences, the educational backgrounds, the religious heritages, the networks of kinship and affinity, and the other basic social realities of those whom they are attempting to serve and serve with. Census and other survey data that help advertisers, banks, and politicians influence communities are ignored by church leaders, who lead instead on the basis of their collective impressions—perhaps accurate, but impossible to verify, falsify, or improve objectively. Worse, pastors can place too much trust in their own experiences as sufficient data upon which to construct a picture of the communities they serve, rather than recognizing the extreme narrowness of *anyone's* experience and the need for other sources of information to supplement one's own small fund of anecdotes.

Without this awareness, many congregations therefore have never asked a fundamental question: "What particular things can and should we try to do, both for ourselves as a church and for those God has called us to serve?" They certainly have never asked the corollary question, "What shall we deliberately *not* do, or at least not do very much of, in order to faithfully execute God's particular plan for our ministry?" Churches all too often attempt to do a little bit of everything, and end up with mediocrity and ineffectiveness on every front.

I am not advocating an extremely narrow focus, as if a church ought to target, say, only fun-loving teens and ruthlessly pare away everything that isn't amusing. (I am not making up this example.) The result would be a club or a special-purpose group, not a congregation, and a shallow one at that. Nor am I giving comfort to churches who insist, explicitly or not, that every member be of a particular race, or class, or political outlook. A degree of heterogeneity is assumed in New Testament churches so that each congregation experiences and exemplifies the expansive, welcoming love of God that breaks down walls of social division.

A church that is located in a working-class area, however, is not obviously obliged to set up an advanced program in adult religious education in the way that a university church is so obliged—although it should have a good adult education program appropriate to its membership. A church that is located among recent immigrants would normally focus on meeting the peculiar needs of those people rather than attempting to maintain some sort of generic and artificial balance of "all things to all people." Each congregation ought to free itself from any guilt feelings because it does not minister to every conceivable group. Instead, Congregation A might well refer prospective members to Congregation B precisely because Congregation B is good at serving such people, and Congregation B can reciprocate.

It is easy to imagine abuses of such a principle. Congregation A can send all the people it deems troublesome or discomfiting to good-hearted Congregation B. Congregation B, in turn, can congratulate itself on its spiritual superiority to Congregation A. I trust that no one will mistake my point. I am suggesting that congregations—and all other Christian organizations—work hard to see themselves as this distinct group of people that Jesus Christ has called to this place at this time, and then trace out the healthy implications of their distinctiveness for ministry, even as they bless others who are different and called to different work.

MAKING DISCIPLES: INDIVIDUALS

Since we are convinced that God loves the whole world and is calling it back, and since we are convinced that God has called Christians to go out everywhere to work with God in this mission of salvation, then we can expect that God seeks to deploy Christians as witnesses, examples, and agents everywhere. This point, I trust, is now obvious, if it wasn't before. But it carries significant implications.

One implication is that God has called each of us as particular individuals, in our distinctive particularity, to be co-workers. Yet some Christians today seem to be distinctly uncomfortable with talk about individuals. Many are understandably reacting against what they see as excessive individualism in the modern world and in response have embraced *community*. But there is a temptation to substitute an excessive or even exclusive emphasis on what is, in fact, one *pole* of an *ellipse* for excessive emphasis on the other.

Human beings are both created as individuals and enveloped by communities. It is not good for us to be alone, and yet we always remain persons with individual dignity. In the Old Testament, we see the importance of many individual lives (Adam, Eve, Cain, Abel, Noah, Abram, Sarah, Rebekah, Joseph, Rahab, Ruth, Hannah, Samuel, David, Hosea, Jeremiah, Daniel, Esther, and Nehemiah, to name a variegated lot) even as God also deals with the people of Israel as a group. The Old Testament oscillates between emphasis on the corporate and on the individual. Ezekiel and Jeremiah in particular call God's people to account even as they highlight the individual responsibility of each person (Ezek. 18; Jer. 31:29–30).

The New Testament depicts the people of God as a family or nation, an *ethnos*, and yet also as a voluntary society. It is a particular family or nation. One is invited to join by God, and one freely joins by faith and continues to enjoy it by faithfulness. The New Testament thus again fulfills the Old. True Israel is constituted by individuals who act like true Israel. Likewise, the Church is made up of those who trust God, declare that Jesus is Lord, and behave accordingly.

God wants the whole world back. So God wants people of God to be in every walk of life, in every social stratum, in every ethnic group, in every location precisely to maximize God's influence and draw the world most effectively to God's heart. Thus God strategically deploys individuals, not just groups.

There is a circular logic here that is nonetheless important. I am situated where I am, and I am the person I am, precisely to do what only a Christian such as I am can do; namely, to witness to, to exemplify, and to effect conversion in my particular social matrix. I alone have this set of relatives, friends, co-workers, enemies, neighbors, and so on, and I alone am this sort of person. Therefore I alone can exert the particular benign influence on each of these people that I alone can exert. This can sound nonsensical, of course, but I don't think it is. Instead, it is vital to the realization that God has not made mistakes in making each of us who we are and placing us where God has in order to get done what God wants to get done.

I illustrate this point by referring to one of the great accomplishments of contemporary cinema, the James Bond series. These movies have starred actors such as Sean Connery, Roger Moore, Timothy Dalton, Pierce Brosnan, and Daniel Craig—and, indeed, George Lazenby. Now, among the less plausible features of this entirely implausible series are the striking good looks of these men. When Sean Connery or Pierce Brosnan enters a room, everyone notices. Thus it is ridiculous to suppose that James Bond, looking like that, could be a truly *secret* agent for longer than about two seconds.

I, on the other hand, routinely enter, dawdle in, and exit rooms without anyone paying the slightest attention. I could be an excellent secret agent. "The name is Stackhouse: John Stackhouse."

To put this lightly (and I promise to resume a serious theological tone in a moment), we ought to give thanks to God that we are not more gorgeous than we are—or more intelligent, or more creative, or more rich—because if we were much more gifted, we could not function the same way in *our particular* roles. People might write off our testimony to the Lord's blessing in our lives with the ready retort, "Well, that's easy for you to say." Or they might never feel they could identify with us, living as we do in a bubble of blessing, and so they could never confide in us. Or they might try to push their way into the Kingdom of God for the wrong reasons, to enjoy the trappings rather than the substance of the gospel of renewal, and that would be bad, too.

To say this is not to disregard the fact that God does make some people extraordinarily beautiful, intelligent, talented, and so on—but God does so to fit them for their particular callings, not because they are particular favorites. One day, thank God, we all will be more splendid than we are today. But for now we are "under cover," playing the roles we have been given to achieve key mission objectives that could not be achieved were we to drop our disguises and appear in the glory that God has prepared for us (2 Cor. 3:18; 4:17; 1 John 3:2). Thus we should accept ourselves and our situation because we trust that God has wisely and kindly assigned us to be a certain sort of person doing a certain sort of work. After all, it's only for the next few decades, and then we get to go home and truly be ourselves!

I think this picture of being called by God to participate in a series of assignments during a lifetime mission is far more helpful than the common metaphor of our being issued roles in a play. The image of drama has a venerable herit-age in Christian thought, and it has its uses. But drama *isn't real*—and our lives are. We are not playacting. The challenges are real, the threats are real, the deprivations and sufferings are real—and so are the outcomes real. You, too, may find it much more encouraging to keep remembering that you are not being called to act in a play, but actually to accomplish a particular set of tasks as a particular sort of person in your particular situation to advance God's purposes as only you can.

On a more speculative note, I have long wondered why God did not more quickly and thoroughly sanctify certain people: straightening out their tangled theology, or ethics, or lifestyle, or whatever. Of course some people resist God's work in their lives. We all do, to some extent. But what about the apparently quite sincere, serious, and spiritual people for whom I could personally vouch? Why has God let them persist in odd beliefs, attitudes, or behaviors?

Take one acquaintance, a Bible scholar of international reputation who maintains views of the Scriptures that I find disconcertingly liberal, while his piety is warmly evangelical. Take another acquaintance, a woman who swears frequently, drinks heavily, and smokes a pack a day . . . and is a brilliant and effective evangelist. I have come to surmise that perhaps God is not hurrying along their sanctification in these notable respects—partly because they don't matter as much as the "weightier matters of the law" (Matt. 23:23), but also because the scholar would never have been appointed to his position of influence in a major university had his views been more conservative, while the evangelist never would have gained and retained the audiences she has among the religiously alienated if she were more straitlaced. These brothers and sisters function as "bridge people," whose combination of the genuinely good and the apparently not-so-good equips them for their distinctive task of connecting Christianity with those far from it.

Come to think of it, aren't we all "bridge people" in one way or another? God paradoxically and pragmatically can use all sorts of things about us to achieve divine purposes: what we think are our attractive traits, yes, but also perhaps some traits we would gladly do without—and eventually shall.

From these reflections on limitations and deficiencies, we turn to the positive issues of spiritual gifts and membership in the Body of Christ. Really, these two go together. Each of us is gifted by the Holy Spirit to participate in the Body of Christ, whether in edifying each other or in furthering our work of mission in the world:

> Now there are varieties of gifts, but the same Spirit; and there are varieties of services, but the same Lord; and there are varieties of activities, but it is the same God who activates all of them in everyone. To each is given the manifestation of the Spirit for the common good. To one is given through the Spirit the utterance of wisdom, and to another the utterance of knowledge according to the same Spirit, to another faith by the same Spirit, to another gifts of healing by the one Spirit, to another the working of miracles, to another prophecy, to another the discernment of spirits, to another various kinds of tongues, to another the interpretation of tongues. All these are activated by one and the same Spirit, who allots to each one individually just as the Spirit chooses. (1 Cor. 12:4–11)

However much our spiritual gifts draw upon the natural talents we possess—those talents themselves being gifts of God—spiritual gifts are special in that they are focused on the Church's own life and its particular mission in the world. Most spiritual gifts are special also in that they evidence supernatural power, demonstrating a Spirit at work beyond normal human ability and motivation—whether in healing and prophecy, or in giving and compassion (Rom. 12:8).

In some cases our spiritual gifts will not be directly related to our workweek skills. The high-powered executive might delight to serve others by preparing and pouring coffee after worship on Sunday, while the stay-at-home parent might brilliantly direct a Sunday school or soup kitchen. Everyone is gifted; everyone is called. Good church leaders will help people identify those gifts and callings, and put them to work where they are best suited.

(Putting people's spiritual gifts to work does not necessarily entail putting them to work within the context of the local congregation, however. Some people may be better suited to serving in paracongregational ministries, or perhaps their spiritual gifts—such as evangelism or hospitality—will be best used outside explicitly Christian organizations entirely.)

There are no useless Christians, because there are no useless members of the Body of Christ. The living Spirit flows through each of us and gives us good work to do. Paul continues:

> For just as the body is one and has many members, and all the members of the body, though many, are one body, so it is with Christ. For in the one Spirit we were all baptized into one body—Jews or Greeks, slaves or free—and we were all made to drink of one Spirit. Indeed, the body does not consist of one member but of many. If the foot would say, "Because I am not a hand, I do not belong to the body," that would not make it any less a part of the body. And if the ear would say, "Because I am not an eye, I do not belong to the body," that would not make it any less a part of the body. If the whole body were an eye, where would the hearing be? If the whole body were hearing, where would the sense of smell be? But as it is, God arranged the members in the body, each one of them, as he chose. If all were a single member, where would the body be? (1 Cor. 12:12–19)

A crucial axiom here is that each of us is a *member*, not a *microcosm*. We have particular gifts of ability and opportunity, and corresponding limitations. We are not shining little spheres, nor perfectly complete human bodies. Instead we each have a distinctive shape: a hand, an ear, an eye. We must not strive to be "well-rounded" in the sense of performing every kind of ministry with equal success. Nor must we try to be self-contained, needing no one else. Of course it is good to be as useful as possible. Of course it is good to avoid sloth that improperly burdens others. Yet we are called and equipped by Christ to be members who perform only a restricted range of service and who require the help of other members, not only to accomplish the larger goals of the Body but also to grow ourselves into health and maturity.

The Bible tells us to "bear one another's burdens" (Gal. 6:2). This does not imply a pathological scenario, as if the Church were a sad bunch of cripples desperately leaning on each other for support—although in some important senses it is surely that. But it tells us that the ideal is not a Stoic or Nietzschean individual independence. The Biblical ideal, we recall, is shalom: a healthful interdependence of strong, growing creatures who both recognize and rejoice in their need for, and service to, each other, God, and the rest of creation.

We surely must avoid any improper individualism. Furthermore, while we should delight in our own particular ministry, we must honor the ministries of others that differ from our own. Just because we are enthusiastic about what we are doing—or perhaps because we are not enjoying it!— we must not begrudge others their particular service and chide them for not joining us in ours.

Equally, we must not feel guilty because we do not take on their ministry, however impressive it is. Instead, we must commend them to God and stick to the particular work God has given each of us to do. During a faculty meeting at a Christian college, a professor announced that he was resigning to pursue a calling among the poor of that city. It was a moving address, and afterward little knots of conversation formed in faculty offices. In one such conversation, a distinguished senior professor was so overcome by admiration for his younger colleague's call that he openly doubted the worth of his own career, spent entirely in the academy. Yet, as a friend pointed out to him, this senior colleague had blessed the Body of Christ with decades of fruitful Biblical scholarship, while the departing younger professor had not. Serving the poor is good. So is teaching the Scripture (cf. Acts 6:2–5). Few people can do both. We should be content to be mere members of a Body that collectively does many things.

Paul's classic passage about spiritual gifts continues, and we should observe at least one more point he makes:

As it is, there are many members, yet one body. The eye cannot say to the hand, "I have no need of you," nor again the head to the feet, "I have no need of you." On the contrary, the members of the body that seem to be weaker are indispensable, and those members of the body that we think less honorable we clothe with greater honor, and our less respectable members are treated with greater respect; whereas our more respectable members do not need this. But God has so arranged the body, giving the greater honor to the inferior member, that there may be no dissension within the body, but the members may have the same care for one another. If one member suffers, all suffer together with it; if one member

is honored, all rejoice together with it. Now you are the body
of Christ and individually members of it. (1 Cor. 12:20–27)

This part of the teaching on spiritual gifts tends not to be
preached on as thoroughly as the rest, and I wonder if it is
because the teaching becomes progressively more radical
as we near the end of chapter 12 and head into chapter 13,
the famous passage on love. In most of our churches, we do
precisely the opposite of what the Holy Spirit commands us
to do via Paul in this text. We lavish honor on those who
are already conspicuous in the larger world, and we take for
granted those who do the hidden, even repellent, but necessary, work of the Church. I say this as a preacher and a musician myself, and thus someone who tends to be up front and
in the spotlight. Don't people gifted in these latter ways routinely get lots of attention and honor? So what about those
involved in less respectable work?

I think Paul might be indulging in a little irony here, calling "less respectable" those ministries that the proud, worldly
Corinthians would have been inclined to ignore or depre-
cate. Yet consider these "less respectable" ministries: caring
for babies in the church nursery; teaching the junior high
kids; preparing and taking meals to shut-ins; shoveling the
snow off the church sidewalk early on a freezing Sunday
morning; and poring over the church accounts to make sure
they are in order. These are truly vital services, but where
are the audiences for these faithful, effective, and important
workers? Where is the applause, or at least the fervent amens,
for these members of the Body—the sort of encouragement
that speakers and singers enjoy so routinely? A mark of the
Church functioning properly surely must be the practice of
inverting the normal hierarchy of honor and making sure

that every member receives the recognition that he or she deserves according to the values of the Kingdom of God.

For Paul's teaching on spiritual gifts proceeds to unfold into his paean to Christian love in I Corinthians 13, the "greatest" of all gifts and ministries, and one that any member and all members can and must undertake as the supreme mark of the Christian Church. Yet, again, we love each other, we love God, and we love the rest of creation both as individuals and as congregations. Thus we see both a duality and a dialectic brilliantly depicted in the inspired imagery of each Christian as a valued member of a complex body.

TAKING TIME SERIOUSLY: WHAT IS OUR CALLING HERE AND NOW?

The temporal dimension of vocational discernment is crucial. What is it that Christ calls us to do *all* of the time? What does he call us to do *some* of the time? And what does he call us to do *now*?

Human beings are always supposed to love God, love our neighbors, and care for the rest of creation. Christians are always supposed to be bearing witness and making disciples in a posture of perpetual worship and in a community of conspicuous love (John 13:34–35).

Within this constancy are patterns of life in which some actions are appropriate and others are not. Such rhythms come in a wide range: work, leisure, and rest; creating, criticizing, and revising; friendship, courtship, marriage; beginning, middle, and end:

> For everything there is a season, and a time for every matter
> under heaven: a time to be born, and a time to die; a time to
> plant, and a time to pluck up what is planted; a time to kill,
> and a time to heal; a time to break down, and a time to build
> up; a time to weep, and a time to laugh; a time to mourn,
> and a time to dance; a time to throw away stones, and a time
> to gather stones together; a time to embrace, and a time to
> refrain from embracing; a time to seek, and a time to lose; a
> time to keep, and a time to throw away; a time to tear, and
> a time to sew; a time to keep silence, and a time to speak; a
> time to love, and a time to hate; a time for war, and a time for
> peace. (Eccles. 3:1–8)

In this list, the Preacher includes both one-time events (birth
and death) and continual rounds (planting and harvesting).
This time-boundedness is the nature of our lives and, while
the Preacher seems pretty dour about it all, the Christian sees
it as providential (Matt. 5:45; 1 Cor. 3:5–6).

There are indeed special episodes in life in which
something must be done that will not be asked of us again.
Childhood is such an episode. Marriage is such an episode
for many. The parenting of small children and the parenting
of teenagers can be usefully seen as distinct episodes. Student
days, starting a business or professional practice, retirement,
caring for elderly parents or handicapped relatives—all of
these pose special challenges, opportunities, and limitations
within certain periods of time.

A young journalist once interviewed an older woman in
a Canadian city. The up-and-coming broadcaster listened for
an hour and became steadily more amazed at the septuage-
narian, whom she at first had been inclined to pity as just
"old" and therefore "uninteresting." But it turned out that
her interview subject had married, loved, and buried two

husbands, had raised four children, and was now enjoying twelve grandchildren. She also had earned three university degrees, and upon the completion of her Ph.D. began an academic career that resulted in two landmark studies of aboriginal peoples. She had served churches, civic boards, and charities. And now she was learning her sixth language.

"How did you possibly accomplish all that?" exclaimed the interviewer, her professional poise now abandoned under the impress of the other woman's life story.

"I have had the great blessing," she replied, "of getting to do everything I wanted to do in life. I just never tried to do it all at once." For, as it turned out, she had not begun her second degree until her family had been raised, and did not complete her doctorate until she was nearing sixty. She got her university post, turned out those two books, and retired ten years after beginning. To everything in her life, there was a season.

God does not promise all of us such a life. But we would do well to accept God's pace. We should look around particularly for what we can enjoy doing only at this particular time of life and in these particular circumstances, not letting its special opportunities slip away as we complain about its special limitations.

I remember my later teens and twenties as years in which I impatiently resented the fact that I knew—I *knew!*— how to fix this congregation, or that student group, or this school, or that organization, and yet no one cared about my opinion. I thought my merely being right (I was more confident then) would be enough and that everyone involved would be quick to hear, quick to agree, and quick to praise me for my admirable insight. I was sociologically clueless, not recognizing my complete lack of social status and how crucial that was in order to be heard by people with the power to make changes.

I tell my students now to rejoice in their lack of social status. One of the great things about being young is that *no one cares what you think*. That can be vexing, yes, but it can also be liberating. One can explore ideas and convictions, try on identities, investigate causes, and disturb very few. Nowadays, alas, whole rooms of people *demand* to know what I think, and many of them even pay me for my opinion. That might sound agreeable, but it is also deeply daunting. Now it matters what I think, and whether I change my mind, and my freedom is in many respects curtailed. Sometimes we can and should rejoice in the limitations of a particular time and place, even as we look forward to greater freedom to serve in different respects in different situations.

More generally, Jesus himself offers us a striking picture of timeliness, of living at a divinely ordered tempo. He did not hurry into the public part of his ministry. Then when he did begin it, as Mark Buchanan observes, he

> did it in an attitude of nearly unbroken serenity, almost lei-sureliness. He never seemed to be watching the clock. He could get tired, but He had no qualms about falling asleep just about anywhere . . . or having luxurious dinners out. He could be wonderfully responsive to the demands of others—a gruff centurion, a panicked father, a desperate widow—but never got caught up in their anxiety. Just as often, He could without a twinge of guilt walk away from demands and expectations. When the disciples interrupted His prayers because "everyone is looking for you," He responded by say-ing, "Let's go somewhere else" (Mk. 1:37–38). Or when news reached Him in Capernaum that His friend Lazarus was

dying in Bethany, he stalled. . . . Even after He "set His face like flint" to go to His death in Jerusalem, He meandered.[11]

Jesus lived this way, with such preternatural poise, because he had a clear vocation and a constant relationship with his Father in the Spirit. He died without the normal marks of success—marriage, family, wealth, popularity—and yet could say, "It is finished," and commend his spirit assuredly into the hands of his Father. This astonishing clarity and companionship is offered to the rest of us in the way of discipleship. François Fénelon gave this advice to himself:

> [Cheered] by the presence of God, I will do at each moment, without anxiety, according to the strength which he shall give me, the work that his Providence assigns. I will leave the rest without concern; it is not my affair. . . . I ought to consider the duty to which I am called each day, as the work God has given me to do, and to apply myself to it in a manner worthy of his glory, that is to say with exactness and in peace.[12]

Time is therefore no enemy, but a resource we can expend and a medium we can negotiate with confidence because we do so according to the express will of God. *There is always time to do the will of God.*

This principle explains God's command of regular rest and recreation—daily sleep, yes, and weekly Sabbath, plus regular festivals of delight, such as those prescribed in the ancient Hebrew law. Embracing such rest without resentment but instead with relish demonstrates faith: faith that God will provide for me and for my dependents without my constant striving; faith that God can run things quite capably without me for a day, or a two-week vacation, or when

I'm finally dead; and faith that God's depiction of shalom as involving healthy relationships of family and friends, which can be cultivated only by regular time together, is superior to our culture's depiction of shalom as constantly more efficient and conspicuous production and consumption. God gives us time to be whole people, in a network of thriving relationships. And even though, as we shall see, our circumstances in a given place and moment may press us hard to devote time to everything we should, the principle of regular rest and recreation remains a given, to be honored as fully as we can to our benefit, and to be ignored at our peril.

There won't always be time to do everything I might want to do, or aspire to do, but there will always be time to do what Jesus calls me to do.

CONCLUSION: MISSION AND VOCATION

Over the past century or so, there have emerged three, or perhaps four, typical conceptions of Christian mission. Evangelicalism and certain strands of Roman Catholicism have emphasized personal evangelism: saving souls. Their exemplar might be evangelist D. L. Moody, whom we met earlier as he claimed, "I look on the world as a wrecked vessel. God has given me a lifeboat and said to me, 'Moody, save all you can.'"[13] Liberal Christianity, both Protestant and Catholic, has taken up another form of gospel service and tried to save society by restructuring it. Nowadays, the religious right in various countries, and especially in the United States, has brought the spiritual and the social back together, but in a decidedly limited agenda of saving souls (and not whole persons) and saving society in narrow terms of sexual morality without attending to other social dimensions at all, whether capitalism's excesses, globalization's dark sides, or nationalism, consumerism, and other blights on the social landscape—let alone literal blights on the literal landscape of ecological degradation. Finally, of course, there is the view of "mission" all too evident in all too many pews and pulpits—namely, that God's mission is to provide for our constant and ever-increasing happiness.

The sovereign Lord aims much higher and broader than any of these blinkered concerns. God aims to rescue, revolutionize, and renew all of creation, and bring it to maturity in global shalom. Jesus came preaching, yes, but he came preaching *the Kingdom of God* (Mark 1:14), and everything he did and said demonstrated huge, even planet-wide, Kingdom values. His miracles were signs, pointing to the truth about God and what God intends for the whole world. Jesus also attended weddings and dinner parties, blessed little children and old people, prayed alone and taught others to pray, rebuked errant disciples and vicious enemies, cherished friends and honored his mother—and all of these actions also demonstrated God's way for us in the world.

Those Kingdom values help us refine the Reformation doctrine of vocation that moved Christianity out of the two-tiered system of super-Christians (monks, friars, priests, nuns) and ordinary Christians (everybody else) to validate all Christian living. Kingdom values help us go beyond this general validation of all legitimate pursuits to compel us to choose the *best* among extant choices.

A range of options in a given case can seem legitimate in Reformational terms; we are not supposed to simply pick our favorite, but ask: What will do the *most* for the *Kingdom*?

What job will make the most of my gifts, make the most impact, and make for the most shalom? What leisure activity will bring the *most* creativity, recreation, joy, playfulness, or rest—whatever is *most* important at that time? What relationships, among the many I do have or might have, should be cultivated, and in what directions—and what relationships should perhaps be pruned back or dropped altogether?

We hardly want to promote a religious mania that consciously asks for God's explicit will every moment we make a decision. God has provided us with experience, tradition, Scripture, scholarship and art; with community wisdom; and with freedom he expects us to exercise. We shouldn't have to pray for God to tell us to avoid certain options and select others. We already know what is right, and we should instead pray simply for the moral strength to do what we know we ought to do. As W. H. Auden puts it, "We can only / do what it seems to us we were made for, look at / this world with a happy eye, / but from a sober perspective."[14]

Most of us don't have to fret about the dangers of compulsive praying. Instead, we tend toward a pattern of practical atheism, of acting as if we don't believe God exists. So we might do well to cultivate the regular asking of the question, "What is the best way to honor God and advance the Kingdom in what I am doing and what I plan to do next?" The next time you are choosing a movie, the next time you are choosing a date, the next time you are choosing a book, the next time you are choosing a job, this question ought to be asked. For if it is not asked, and asked frequently, then other values will be determining our choices.

It all matters. God cares about it all. So if someone ever were to ask, therefore, "What are *you* doing for the Kingdom?" we might well reply with *any* of the following:

- I'm mowing the lawn.
- I'm washing the dishes.
- I'm making a puzzle with my three-year-old.
- I'm paying the bills.
- I'm composing a poem.
- I'm talking with my mother on the phone.
- I'm teaching a neighbor child how to throw a ball.
- I'm writing the mayor.
- I'm preaching.

Everything. Everywhere. Everyone. Every moment. That is the scope of God's call on our lives, and that is the dignity our lives enjoy.

PART III

RESPONDING TO THE CALL

OF JESUS

PRINCIPLES FOR THE NORMAL

HOW, THEN, SHOULD ALL THIS work out in the real world? How should we understand that real world in the light of Christian teaching, and then participate in it most faithfully?[1]

A MIXED FIELD, MIXED MOTIVES, AND MIXED RESULTS

Jesus once described the Kingdom of God in this unexpected way:

> The kingdom of heaven may be compared to someone who sowed good seed in his field; but while everybody was asleep, an enemy came and sowed weeds among the wheat, and then went away. So when the plants came up and bore grain, then the weeds appeared as well.
>
> And the slaves of the householder came and said to him, "Master, did you not sow good seed in your field? Where, then, did these weeds come from?"
>
> He answered, "An enemy has done this."
>
> The slaves said to him, "Then do you want us to go and gather them?"
>
> But he replied, "No; for in gathering the weeds you would uproot the wheat along with them. Let both of them

grow together until the harvest; and at harvest time I will tell the reapers, Collect the weeds first and bind them in bundles to be burned, but gather the wheat into my barn." (Matt. 13:24–30)

This parable comes between two more familiar parables in Matthew's Gospel, the parable of the sower casting seed upon four different kinds of soils and the parable of the tiny mustard seed growing into a large plant. Those parables seem relatively straightforward compared with this one, and perhaps get more attention as a result. But this one opens up a vital perspective for us on the world as Jesus recognizes it to be. Jesus explains:

The one who sows the good seed is the Son of Man; the field is the world, and the good seed are the children of the kingdom; the weeds are the children of the evil one, and the enemy who sowed them is the devil; the harvest is the end of the age, and the reapers are angels. Just as the weeds are collected and burned up with fire, so will it be at the end of the age. The Son of Man will send his angels, and they will collect out of his kingdom all causes of sin and all evildoers, and they will throw them into the furnace of fire, where there will be weeping and gnashing of teeth. Then the righteous will shine like the sun in the kingdom of their Father. Let anyone with ears listen! (Matt. 13:37–43)

"The field is the world," Jesus teaches, and that field is mixed indeed, populated by the children of God and the children of the devil—two different and opposed constituencies. Yet those two populations are so intertwined that uprooting the latter might also damage or destroy the former. The economy of the world as it is somehow requires that these two sets of inhabitants, these antagonistic neighbors, be allowed to become fully themselves, maturing until the time of harvest, when all will be uprooted, judged, and rewarded with blessing or curse. As Augustine warned, now is not the time for apocalyptic confrontation with the enemies of Christ—particularly since some might yet become Christ's friends before the end of the age.[2]

With the world itself already corrupted by the effects of the Fall, and with the enemy inspiring human agents to divert the earth's resources to their useless endeavors, mar the earth by their ugliness, and impede those who are being inspired by God to pursue the well-being of the earth—in short, to act like "weeds"—what should we expect of life today?

We should expect sin, rather than being surprised by it, time and again, as the news media breathlessly report on yet another scandal. We should simply *expect* some politicians to engage in graft, and some officials to accept bribes.[3] We should *expect* some executives to sell out their companies, shareholders, and customers for personal gain. We should *expect* drunk driving, drug pushing, ruthless cartels, sexual assault, stock manipulation, terrorism, and a hundred other evils. Expecting sin does not mean accepting it, much less ignoring it. Expecting sin entails something practical: planning for it. It means refusing to live as if we were in Eden or the New Jerusalem, and instead intentionally structuring our lives, individually and corporately, with the expectation of wickedness.

Beyond outright sin, we should expect waste. It should not shock us that governments, armies, and corporations waste money. It should not shock us that schools, hospitals, and charities waste money. It should not shock us that all manner of institutions waste people's time and talents, and the earth's resources. For the Bible tells us that human work has become much harder than it should be, that "thorns and thistles" are everywhere (Gen. 3:17-18), that the field of the world is full of literal and metaphorical weeds. Indeed, beyond the dark realities of sin and waste, we should expect stupidity and absurdity as well.

Within this landscape of evil, furthermore, there is obscurity, such that weeds can look like wheat and vice versa. The way forward is not immediately evident, and results are hard or even impossible to predict. The field presents us not only with deep and widespread evil but thick ambiguity as well. Many Christians, alas, have not taken the reality of this ambiguity seriously enough to actually expect it and to plan for it. Whether the Christians are liberal or conservative doesn't matter. Each sort has tended to see the world in plain polarities of good and evil (even as they differ as to what deserves which label). But wolves in sheep's clothing, projects that start well and then fail, and roads to hell being paved with good intentions are everywhere. Ambiguity is a factor with which we must realistically reckon.

To be sure, not all is unclear. Most of this book so far has dealt in categories and commands that I have tried to depict as clear. Now, however, we confront the application of these clarities to the murky terrain we must traverse on the way to the city where the shadows will disperse and "the righteous will shine like the sun in the kingdom of their Father" (Matt. 13:43).

As we peer into this fog, we must also peer inward to recognize the haze of our own ambivalence. Not only is the world out there mixed, but we ourselves also harbor mixed motives and traits both good and evil. We perceive that we do in fact hate our enemies; we do in fact crave luxury, power, and fame; we do in fact turn away from the light and prefer the darkness—at least at times and, paradoxically, at least a little all the time. As Aleksandr Solzhenitsyn warned us, the line distinguishing good and evil does not run between countries or peoples or classes, but within our own hearts.

We must reckon, then, not only with what is bad out there but also with what is bad in here: in our individual selves and in even our most sacred institutions, whether families, churches, or other Christian organizations. Reckoning with those realities means structuring and conducting our lives to recognize and restrain the evil both within us and without us as best we can—and to respond properly when those restraints fail, as they so often do. We should not wait until our motives have resolved into perfect purity before we attempt to do God's work; few of us could be considered entirely sanctified as yet. Furthermore, instead of being shocked by impure motives in others, we should simply *presume* impure motives in others. Because we do not demand from them an unrealistic purity, we can decide with clear eyes whether to support them, cooperate with them, and praise them for their successes.

Realistically, we ought to expect politicians and parties to engage in crass practices, repellent compromises, and strange alliances. We will always wish it were otherwise, and we will demand legality at least and high principle at best, but we will not wring our hands and despair of politics until a thoroughly good political option appears. For we would then have to wait for Jesus' return and remain useless politically in the meanwhile (perhaps contributing the limited blessing of chiding everyone else for failing to be as good as we think he or she ought to be).[4] We will expect our leaders—in government, commerce, the professions, and also the Church—to be tempted, often successfully, by power, money, and fame.

We will expect school boards to be assailed by wildly con-
flicting agendas, families to be riven by divergent interests,
courts to be perverted by various forms of social engineering, universities to parrot the views of the powerful, and corporations to seek financial success over community service.

All of these negative expectations arise not out of despair,
which enervates and immobilizes, but out of clear-eyed
empirical analysis and our own theology, which together
both illuminate and motivate. Christian theology, which
contains a robust doctrine of sin, includes also robust doc-
trines of providence and redemption. God set up institutions
to bless us, despite their corruption, and God continues to
work through them. God also rules history and aids those
who press for greater shalom in those institutions. God is not
discouraged by the evil evident in ourselves and our world.
God is sad about it, angry at it, and grieved by it, but not
discouraged. God works away at it, knowing that this labor
is certain to produce fruit. And God has called us to do the
same, as human beings and as Christians.

God's expectations thus include both fruit and weeds. As
disciples of the Master who told this parable, we must develop
similar expectations. Realism requires that we expect good
results: Jesus is Lord. But until his Kingdom fully arrives
in glory, we do not expect perfect results, and we are not
shocked or greatly discouraged by bad results. The combination of evil, ambiguity, and our own moral mixedness should
guard us against the utopian temptation and conform our
expectations better to what Jesus told us to expect: both per-
secutions and progressions, sins and successes, accidents and
accomplishments, resistance and renewal.

The Old Testament exemplifies this realism. The Torah
does not mandate total righteousness or anything close to

it—as law never properly does. Law sets out, instead, minimal standards of goodness, fairness, and prudence. The Torah (the word also means "instruction") nonetheless lifted Israel above its ancient Near Eastern neighbors. No other legislation that we know of is so generous to the needy and vulnerable, so concerned for the welfare of each individual and family against the concentration of wealth among a few, and so rich with joyful celebration of its deity. But this legislation also allows for slavery, differences in the treatment of women and men that most of us moderns find unacceptable, and so on. The Law deals with the actual people in that actual context and, as instruction, calls them to walk forward and upward. It doesn't require them impossibly to leap straight up into perfection.

Guided by this realism, we will not typically hold out for all-or-nothing solutions—in government, in benevolent societies, in workplaces, or in homes. True, sometimes one has to draw a line and say a definitive yes or no. Some decisions—such as whether to confess the faith, whether to preach the gospel, whether to support fellow Christians in need, and whether to care for the poor—are simply binary. Yet even in these categories there is a need for prudence. *How* should we confess the faith and preach the gospel *in this context*? What means should we use to support fellow Christians in need or to care for the poor? Should we advertise what we do as loudly as possible? Perhaps, but also perhaps not: Jesus and the apostles sometimes "went public" and sometimes stayed private. Must we be as confrontational as possible? Perhaps we must (Jesus and the apostles sometimes were directly confrontational to their enemies: Matt. 23; Acts 4–5), but also perhaps not (as Jesus and the apostles sometimes were not: Matt. 26–27; Acts 24–26). A good cause does not justify just any choice of action—although those inclined toward what they like to think of as "the prophetic" tend to feel this way and sometimes leave wreckage in their wake. Instead, Christians ought to weigh our choices carefully, according to the intelligence, intuition, and inspiration we are given, in order to do the most good possible—to *maximize* shalom. And that will mean to *think politically* in a fundamental sense, for politics is "the art of the possible."

Many Christians refuse to acknowledge that "half a loaf is better than none," to wisely "pick your battles," to prudently "live to fight another day." They see any compromise as derogatory toward the holiness of God and faithless toward the power of the Spirit. Only total victory will do. And such Christians are right—they are right about the *ultimate* outcome in the Second Coming of Christ. They are *not* right about the *penultimate* stage in which we currently serve God. In this era, we live in a mixed field that is still growing, not at the harvest when everything will be sorted out once and for all.[5]

In the midst of this mixed field what does the normal Christian life look like? Can we hope for more? And what happens when the normal disappears into the darkness of the borderline situation?

THE NORMAL . . . AND BEYOND

In a culture saturated with information—in which a wide range of new media compete for our attention—issues often come to the surface in the form of crises. A crisis is not necessarily a bad thing, but it is an urgent thing, a moment in which a choice must be made (from the Greek *krisis*, "decision"). At such moments, a single action or individual, sometimes a small group, can sometimes tip the balance. So we alert the troops, marshal the resources, and plunge into the fray. But before we do all that, we should also pause and pull back to gain an adequately large view. If we don't, if we remain in perpetual close-up, then we will be stuck in perpetual crisis mode, reacting to whatever suddenly appears on our screens, jumping to conclusions, and taking emergency measures. If we are going to participate intelligently and effectively in cultural struggles, we need to keep several broad principles in mind.

First, we have to realize that crises emerge out of processes, not out of nowhere. Processes usually take a while. We don't just suddenly develop a credit problem when the bank mails us a warning notice. Corporate boards rarely just suddenly fire an executive. Learning problems in a classroom don't just suddenly appear on examination day. And street protests are rarely triggered by a single event, no matter how dramatic. So those who wish to influence crises must appreciate the metaphors of inertia and momentum in regard to processes. Steering a society is like altering the course of an ocean liner. Ocean liners have tremendous inertia; they are hard to get going and, once they are going, they require the application of sustained and substantial force, and thus great patience, to steer. If an iceberg comes into view, the ocean liner had better start changing course a long distance away. What is true of steering societies is usually true of changing smaller communities (such as businesses or charities or churches) as well. They, too, have considerable inertia and tend to run the way they are running now, to be corrected only with considerable force and patience. And what is true of those smaller organizations is, frankly, true even of most of us individuals. Self-help books tell us—at least the wise ones do—that breaking habits is hard, and establishing new habits, whether in diet, exercise, parenting, or praying, is long, slow work.

Once we have recognized process, it becomes evident that those who control the process generally control the crisis. For the process generally sets the terms of the crisis—how the situation appears (compared with how it looked a while ago), what facts are being considered as important (and what are now out of view as irrelevant), and what options are available (and what no longer are). The process generally sets up the crisis so that it is most likely to break a certain way. If a drunken pilot has had the ocean liner heading steadily for the rocks, even if a more skilled captain jumps in at the last minute, the ship will still crash. Control of the process usually entails control of the crisis, no matter who enters the picture once the crisis emerges. Any good politician knows that. Any Christians who want to affect the real world need to know it, too.

A second principle is that cultural processes are difficult to control, and even fully comprehend, because history is not made up of straight lines—nor is it made up of circles. Yet many people visualize one image or the other, thinking they can accurately predict historical outcomes either by extrapolating linearly from current trends or by expecting that things will come around to the way they used to be. Sometimes history does proceed for a while in reasonably continuous ways, whether fairly flat lines (as in the typical life of peasants throughout most of the Middle Ages) or fairly steep ones (the economic rise of the Western working class after World War II, particularly in America). And there are indeed cyclical patterns in history, whether the overextension and collapse of empires, the rise and fall of tyrants, or the business cycles on the management of which so much of our current economic stability depends. Yet these lines are not ever merely straight, nor are they ever merely circular. The Middle Ages did see technological and political changes that disrupted and sometimes improved the lives of peasants. Not everyone in the Western working classes enjoyed upward mobility—certainly not those whose livelihoods were replaced by mechanization, economies of scale, and outsourcing or offshoring. Empires and tyrants do not, *pace* Spengler and Toynbee, rise and fall the same way, and business cycles are still prone to great unpredictability, as the dot-com bubble and NASDAQ meltdown at the turn of the millennium, and the global recession starting in 2008 have reminded us all too vividly.

History is made up of *multiple* lines with *multiple* curves, and thus history has very limited predictability. This is both a hopeful reality and a cautionary one. It is hopeful because when some levels of history seem to be moving in a bad direction, often others are moving in a good one. Many Christians today are convinced that modern society is morally far worse than it was, say, a hundred years ago. And if one consults certain indicators—such as the incidence of divorce and abortion, the decline of church attendance, the vulgarity of popular culture—such a conclusion may be justified (although American church attendance is actually higher than it was a century ago, versus the general pattern of decline in the British Commonwealth). Yet consider how things are today versus a hundred years ago: If you had to be poor, would you rather live now or then? What if you belonged to a racial or ethnic or religious minority? What if you were coping with a disability? Suppose you were female?

Or a child? I suggest that the less you look and sound like me—a middle-class, middle-aged, white man—the better it is for you today. So we must be wary of the jeremiads that damn everything in sight and be grateful for what God yet is doing—for God is the source of all good, including all good social trends (James 1:17).

To live as if tomorrow will be just like today, next year just like this year, and the latter decades of my life like the earlier decades, is to ignore reality. We must eschew simplistic claims about "what has happened" and "what must be done." (That caution alone would shut the mouths of many a pundit, including Christian preachers, broadcasters, and, yes, professors.) We must beware even of sophisticated analyses; they can offer us only more or less educated guesses—no matter how many charts and graphs our favorite futurist might bedazzle us with. Who saw World War I coming? Who predicted the founding of the State of Israel? Who foresaw the Vietnam War, Watergate, the Iranian Revolution, the fall of the Berlin Wall, the end of apartheid, Bosnia, Rwanda, 9/11, the various Arab Springs, or the Donald Trump presidency? Beyond a few science-fiction fantasists, who anticipated transistors, microchips, the Internet, fiber optics, the iPod, or Skype? Who predicted the rise to world significance of Riyadh, Shanghai, or Bangalore? Who prophesied the global tide of Pentecostal and charismatic varieties of Christianity?

What is normal, what is predictable, is both a degree of continuity—else we would be utterly unable to conduct our lives—and a degree of discontinuity, for which we can only try to prepare and then encounter with resilience. Whether change is good or bad, it is a fundamental part of life now, and increasingly so in both scope and degree. Realistic Christian living in the world requires that we stop thinking in straight, simple, and single lines, or round, simple, and single circles. It also requires that we do what we can to direct the lines of history toward good outcomes, in full recognition that our efforts may be thwarted or even have unintended and undesired effects. We must do our best, under God, for ourselves and for the world. We strive for shalom, and all the time: in the processes, as well as the crises, of life.

Does such an attitude somehow imply a lack of faith in God's power? Does it settle for a kind of procedural worldliness and low horizon of possibility in which God no longer does great things, and neither do we? Let us turn to the question of the normal and the wonderfully not-normal. After that, we'll have to confront the fact that many of us live in badly sub-normal situations.

THE NORMAL AND THE MIRACULOUS

Jesus promised his disciples that they would do "greater works than these" after his ascension and their reception of the Holy Spirit at Pentecost (John 14:12). I see no reason to doubt that he included miracles among those works, particularly as the Book of Acts depicts the disciples healing the sick, flinging away venomous snakes, raising the dead, and predicting the future. A miracle, basically defined, is an event that does not arise out of the normal course of things—what we usually call "nature" in this discourse. Thus a miracle by definition is "supernatural." A miracle occurs because of an addition to the system, a boost that enables wonderful things to happen that ordinarily do not and cannot happen given the normal functioning of the world.[6]

The greatest and most important of these events in our experience is the Holy Spirit's conversion of human beings from spiritual death to spiritual rebirth and eternal life. But subsidiary miracles are expected and reported in the New Testament as well, as we have noted. I am not convinced by cessationist arguments that authentic miracles were supposed to mark only the apostolic period; rather, I believe that the Church should expect a miracle *when a miracle is required*.

As we have had reason to observe, God normally works in normal ways through normal means—that is why they are normal. We must be clear about that reality. Otherwise, we may hunger for miracles as if they were normal, although there is no indication in Scripture that they are. The apostles seem busy with just the sort of activities we would expect such people to undertake: preaching the gospel, setting up churches, counseling individuals, training leaders, writing instructions, enjoying fellowship, engaging in worship, and the like. The miracles serve to underline what they underlined in the work of Jesus himself: the gospel of the Kingdom of God come in Christ and the consequent mission of making disciples. Wherever miracles are necessary to emphasize this truth today, we should pray for them and, indeed, expect them.

For most of the history of the Church, however, God has worked through the normal means of non-spectacular work. I do not say "non-supernatural" for the work of the Holy Spirit in convicting people of sin and convincing them of the Lordship of Christ is the Spirit's regular work. There is otherwise never enough energy in the system to produce the New Birth. But the Spirit tends to channel this energy through conversation, preaching, reading, charity, reflection and repentance, and other normal means.

One must speak carefully here. To emphasize these normal means can sound like one or both of two kinds of mistake. The first mistake would be to treat as normative what has been merely the history of the Western Church, as if our experience has been "just right" and therefore should stand as the measure of all other Christian experience. The modern Western Church manifestly has been compromised by false beliefs, lack of faith, and worldliness, so we must not say to our brothers and sisters in Africa or South America or Asia, "Settle down, stop all of this excitement, put on the proper robes, and get back to the (Western) liturgy." Our siblings in the Two-Thirds World might well be enjoying experiences of God's power that would come to inspire and inform us if we would be open to them.

The second mistake would be to sound as if we ought not to seek such miracles in our own day and time, as if such events were *abnormal* in the pejorative sense. Again, I do not doubt that the modern Western Church badly needs a lot of things, one of them being more confidence that God is working powerfully among us and wants to do more than we have been willing to do in God's service. Spectacular miracles, both as signs of God's power truly being operative in other modes (such as evangelism and social reform) and as significant accomplishments of God's purposes in themselves (such as God's desire that the sick be made healthy) can and should always be prayed for. Miracles might do us a world of good in certain circumstances.

Having said that, however, in genuine hope and what is, I trust, a measure of genuine humility on behalf of my particular Christian community, it remains evident in both the pages of the New Testament and the history of the global Church that spectacular miracles are indeed rare and are not to be the normal fare on which the Church's faith is nurtured. Nor are they to be the normal mode in which the Church's work is accomplished. The teaching of the gospels and the epistles focuses on holiness of character, integrity of life, purity of witness, and persistence in service. I reiterate that these are themselves miraculous in the sense that they require the Holy Spirit's power. They cannot be effected by human power alone. Yet the New Testament does not focus on exorcism, healing, resurrection, prophecy, or other obviously supernatural events. Nor does the history of the Church. Nor should we.

We need to steer between two evangelical catch-phrases: "Expect a miracle," and "Pray as if it all depended upon God; work as if it all depended on you."[7] Whatever "it" is, we must *not* work as if it all depended on us, for that is a sure route to exhaustion, self-pity, and bitterness. Rather, we must do our part heartily—in the power of the Holy Spirit—and also expect God to do God's part, whether through other Christians, other people, events elsewhere in creation, or direct intervention. Trusting God to work does not entail expecting a miracle in the sense of divine activity beyond God's normal modes of operation (through the power God has already vested in creation and through the Spirit who indwells the Church) because God evidently chooses to use miracles rarely.

This principle applies on a broad landscape—indeed, to all Christian life. Yes, we can and should pray for healing, whether from a cold or from a cancer. God might use the normal means of healing (via the body's own devices or via medicine), or God might directly intervene, or God might do neither. But we are expected both to pray and to do our part: to look after the sick person as best we can, recognizing our dependence on God for *any* sort of healing. Yes, we can and should pray for the success of an evangelistic campaign by our church. God might use the normal means of persuasion (friendship, family relations, preaching, charity) and then directly intervene (for only God can convert a person)—or God might not. But we are expected to pray for divine help and also to do our part: to care for our neighbors as best we can, including proclaiming the gospel to them as best we can, while recognizing our dependence on God for *any* evangelistic success.

Likewise, we can and should pray for just and compassionate legislation from our governments, for wholesome entertainment from our media, for wise and informative education from our schools. Here, too, however, we need to remember that God normally works through normal means. The Holy Spirit normally flows over the extant contours of the cultural landscape, pouring in where openings have been made, moving around obstacles, smoothing rough places, and usually surging most powerfully in channels that have been cut. All of this means that we must work with God to fashion that landscape as best we can and not to expect many flash floods of Holy Spirit power to sweep down and carry everything before them. That sort of miracle can happen, and perhaps it would happen more often if we would pray that it would. But, again, the Biblical and historical evidence would lead us to think that the normal mode of the Spirit's work in social matters is to work with what is there, ameliorating what is bad, strengthening what is good, and sometimes helping press recalcitrant features into new and better shapes.

David Martin is especially perspicuous on such things. As a sociologist, and a faithful Christian, he urges us to be realistic about the nature of social challenges:

> If, for example, sociological analysis shows that the conflict of Catholics and Protestants in Ulster is a particular instance in a class of conflicts, so that given [the occurrence of a certain group of factors] . . . C and P are bound to clash, then ecumenical breastbeating becomes a rather otiose activity. . . . The ordinary liberal and (intermittently) Christian assumption that the solution is basically a matter of goodwill is undermined. The situation may at certain previous junctures have been willed, but it is now determined and goodwill cannot be relied upon to mend it.
>
> . . . Of course, if everyone were to will the good simultaneously then the structural constraints might be ameliorated or even abolished, since everyone would simultaneously desire not only peace and harmony but also justice. But one knows on good sociological grounds, let alone on good theological grounds, that an immediate and universal desire for peace and justice is not humanly or statistically likely.[8]

Indeed, we might say, such an event would be a miracle.

If we take the previous points together, then, we would see that God has equipped us to negotiate the world, and to negotiate *with* the world, so that good things happen and bad things don't. We can ask God for sensitivity, skill, and wisdom, we can attend to processes, we can apply our resources to them, and we can try to steer any crisis to a good resolution. We are not to stand on the sidelines, moaning over situations in which we have refused to invest ourselves and invoking God's miraculous power to achieve what our disobedience has not. To practice this sort of piety—a perpetual oscillation between indolence and crisis-mode begging of God to perform what are in fact political, psychological, and sociological miracles—is not to glorify God at all. It is instead to dishonor the means God has put at our disposal and to disregard the commandments God has clearly given for human life in general and Christian service in particular. Living without miracles is conceited—"Father, I don't need you anymore, and I can handle it myself"—but living in reliance on constant miracles is juvenile: "Daddy, it's too hard! I don't want to try. *You* do it."

Sometimes, however, normal life gives way to extraordinary and even excruciating circumstances. What do we do then, in the borderline situations?

FACING THE BORDERLINE

FUNDAMENTAL ISSUES

The following example of an ethical dilemma is so often used that its horror can recede into a sort of dark cartoon: the SS pounding at the door of the Dutch house at midnight, the frantic hiding of Jews in attics or basements, and the officer demanding, "Are there Jews here?"

The home invader who threatens one's family, the terrorist who under torture might reveal information that would prevent a disaster, the use of nuclear weapons to end an otherwise even costlier war, and of course the "trolley problem"—everyone has their favorite instance of a borderline situation in which normal ethics might have to be compromised in the interest of the greater good.

It is a maxim of jurisprudence that extreme cases make bad laws. I think, however, that the extremity of these hypothetical situations is beside the point. The choices available to the conscientious, responsible, realistic Christian are just two, no matter how high or how low the stakes. The first is this: Always refuse to do something that is forbidden by Scripture (or perhaps, by extension, by Christian tradition), no matter what your intention or the expected consequence. The faithful Christian commits the matter to God, who will make sure that things turn out properly according to God's sometimes mysterious plans, and who never requires the believer to do what is evil in order that good may come. The second choice is to do whatever will be truest to the revelation of the will of God, taken as a whole, recognizing that in a topsy-turvy world sometimes one must do here and now what one would never do in Eden or the New Jerusalem. That is, the Christian determined to further God's purposes in the world will sometimes do something that is objectively impure but that nonetheless is the best of the available options and will produce the most shalom in the situation.

These two options sometimes are mapped onto the classic ethical categories of "deontological" (one ought to act according to one's *duty*, no matter the outcome) and "consequentialist" (one ought to act to produce the best possible outcome). I contend that the second view ought to trump the first one if the two collide. That is, normally one ought to follow the clear moral guidelines set out in Scripture, tradition, and so on. In normal life, we don't have to guess, or convene an ethical symposium, about whether to blaspheme, or tell a lie, or murder someone. This point is a simple one and easy to skip over, but it is crucial. God's Word and the Christian ethical tradition are full of straightforward wisdom as to what is and isn't the right thing to do, and it can be self-serving and disingenuously disobedient to obfuscate what God has taken pains to make clear. Thus the burden of proof is always on the Christian who suggests that, in this particular case, some non-traditional action ought to be considered as the will of God.

I want to argue here, however, that one's *fundamental duty* is not to follow the rules but to listen to the voice of

Jesus to know how *to produce the best possible consequences.*
Seeking to maximize shalom is what it means to do the will
of God, and sometimes that will mean departing from one's
conventional duties.

"Duty" proponents typically chide "consequence" proponents on two counts: First, that consequentialism opens
up a dark door to a casuistical calculus that arrogantly presumes to judge what really is best in a situation, despite the
manifest instructions of Scripture; and, second, that consequentialism exposes Christians to the dangers of rationalized
self-interest in their decision-making. Those who hold to the
consequential view chide upholders of the duty principle on
two counts also: First, that their view is incoherent, for there
is no way to both love your neighbor and follow the "don't
lie" rule by telling the Nazis where that neighbor is hidden,
or even by remaining silent, which is not lying but would
signal the same thing; and, second, that the "do your duty"
approach amounts to a childish expectation that God will
deliver them from all ethical difficulty and never require that
they trouble their consciences. I propose to acknowledge
these mutual charges and then leave them behind, since both
sides have their retorts (this exchange has a long history) and
neither side persuades the other. Instead, the approach I offer
combines regard for both duty and consequence, seeing our
God-given duty as our *normal* way of proceeding with confidence that God has so arranged the world that if we do our
duty the best consequences will ensue. It is only in *abnormal*
situations that maximal shalom is to be gained by departing
from the norm.

So now I want to combine some principles already established in this discussion with some further theological material that ought to be stipulated by anyone in this conversation

to trace out more fully how we are to hear Jesus' voice in extraordinary circumstances.

The first consideration is to recall where we are in the Christian story. We are not Jesus, and we are not in the time of Jesus. We are downstream of Pentecost and the Book of Acts. We are also well short of the New Jerusalem. Most of the readers of this book are in countries in which Christians enjoy citizenship in democracies, in more or less open economic systems, and in more or less free arenas of ideological exchange and contest—none of which were the conditions of Jesus or the apostles. We also do not expect the Lord to return, and the present system to end, within our lifetimes, as the early Christians apparently did—although we hope and pray that this will happen.

With these greater freedoms and the necessity of living for the long haul the question of responsibility arises. If we can vote, should we? If we can run for office, serve in the police department, or join the military, should we? If we can work in corporations, investment houses, movie studios, or news organizations, should we? If we can teach in public universities, sit on public school boards, or write books for public consumption, should we? These are questions that do not find ready answers in the New Testament for the simple reason that they do not arise in the experience of the New Testament Church. Such opportunities to participate in public life were not available to Christians in that culture. Some of our modern institutions didn't exist back then, of course, but in regard to the opportunities that did exist at the time, either the doors were closed against them or they had no choice in the matter (such as being pressed into military service)—or the early Christians expected all such questions to be irrelevant in the light of the Lord's imminent return.

It seems to me that those Christians who continue to advocate a New Testament era ethic that depends on the strong expectation of the imminent coming of the Lord are indulging in a weird kind of "second naïveté" (Ricoeur). To encourage Christians generally to keep away from government—indeed, to encourage Christians to keep themselves disentangled from any institutions that engage in coercion—because the old order is passing away and Christ is soon to return is to willfully ignore the passage of two thousand years. Since the time of the early medieval Church, Christians have had many opportunities to shape government—and other social institutions and relations—for the better. Let me make clear that I believe Christ really could return at any moment, and I pray that it will be soon. But it may well *not* be soon, so to act as if one knows it will be is presumptuous and irresponsible. And to advocate that we all strictly follow a New Testament ethics governed by a strong expectation of the Lord's imminent return when one is two thousand years down the road and knows that Christ may not return for another two thousand is strangely atavistic.

Such an attitude gets Church history exactly backward. Many Christians of this outlook sneer at Christendom as a fall from grace, as if the Church sold its soul under Constantine and has gotten it back only here and there, in small sects and marginal prophets, ever since. Oliver O'Donovan remarks that

> it is not, as is often suggested, that Christian political order is a *project* of the church's mission, either as an end in itself or as a means to the further missionary end. The church's one project is to witness to the Kingdom of God. Christendom

is a *response* to mission, . . . a sign that God has blessed it. It
is constituted not by the church's seizing alien power, but by
alien power's becoming attentive to the church.[1]

The emergence of Christendom, that is, should be construed
not as a grotesque deviation from authentic Christian mission
but as a natural result—with all of its attending challenges—
of missionary *success*.[2] Over the three centuries preceding Constantine, the Church had spread not only broadly
throughout the nations of the Roman Empire but also up
and down the social scale. In fact, there is evidence that at
the time of the Great Persecution at the turn of the fourth
century, the two emperors chiefly responsible, Diocletian
and Galerius, were married to women who were disposed
favorably to Christianity and perhaps were even Christians
themselves.[3] Thus for the succeeding emperor to embrace
Christianity (however slowly and piecemeal Constantine did
embrace it) might have seemed like a dramatic reversal of
paganism, but it was really just the last social domino to fall
to Christian influence, the remaining social stratum to be
penetrated by the gospel.

The Christian responsibility in and for the world looks
quite different in such circumstances—circumstances not
of despicable capitulation but of evangelistic effectiveness.
To be sure, the emergence of Christendom did pose a new
set of threats to the Church as well as opportunities for
it—particularly the threat of relaxing the Church's missionary zeal, softening its demands of sanctity, and contenting
itself with the status quo as if it were the Kingdom of God.
Wherever such attitudes ruled, and wherever they persist
today, they need to be confronted and the gospel standards
proclaimed afresh. Such confrontation and proclamation,

however, ought to be conducted with appreciation for the good that has attended Christendom and, indeed, for the missionary success that bore it in the first place.[4] To say that we are now in a situation different from what Jesus and the apostles faced (as we are also in a situation different from that of Constantine and his court) is not to set aside Jesus and the apostles. It is rather to ask whether anything in the Christian ethos ought to change when the opportunities to obey the commandments of God have changed so radically.[5] To these commandments again we now turn.

The second consideration is to recall the creation commandments and the salvation commandment, and their relation to each other. Some Christians have opted to obey the Great Commission and to leave the rest of creation to the care of non-Christians and God. Others engage in creation care but draw the line at any sort of violence. Because serving in the justice system requires both compromise and coercion, such Christians avoid both by avoiding the system itself, trusting God to run it as best God can through non-Christians.

I reply that God has not set aside, nor even circumscribed, the creation commandments for Christians. So any ethic that implies otherwise is immediately suspect. If we think the only way to honor God is to withdraw from doing our best to promote shalom, then despite our efforts to stay pure, we have not avoided contradiction—and sin—after all.

Yet, comes the rejoinder, the Church does its best for shalom by refusing to join with the worldly powers in the coercive work of government, the justice system, the military, and so on. By maintaining an alternative community, the Church bears witness to greater ideals than individual or national self-interest, greater than expediency and efficiency, and greater than the zero-sum logic of secularism that always requires the sacrifice of some for the benefit of more.

I have always respected this radical viewpoint—impressively detailed by John Howard Yoder and defended beyond Anabaptist circles by Stanley Hauerwas, Ronald Sider, Jim Wallis, and many others. I also respect the modest posture of "faithful presence" advocated by James Davison Hunter, a chastened American culture warrior.[6] And, as I will affirm again, I'm not persuaded that such Christians shouldn't continue to maintain their witness, powerful as it is precisely in its almost typological purity. At the same time, I will honor Brother Yoder by refusing to retreat into the relativism he so hated and say bluntly that I think it is wrong for *all* Christians to hold to this sort of view. Indeed, I think it is best that *most* Christians take another, more participatory, and thus more morally dangerous and ambiguous stance. I say so on the basis of two further considerations.

The third consideration is to return to the Christian story to witness God involved in violence, deception, and other contraventions of "normal" morality. The Old Testament depicts God as killing individuals, nations, and once even the whole inhabited earth in the Flood. God deceives God's enemies, causing some to panic before an imaginary threat God supervises (Judg. 6–8). God uses nations against other nations (Habakkuk), and other creatures against humans (as in the storm and the great fish of the Book of Jonah). God even allows Satan to work mischief on divine favorites, whether Job or the Apostle Paul (2 Cor. 12:7–10). And in the New Testament, Jesus warns of the Day of the Lord during which God will judge all, punish the wicked, and eradicate all of God's opponents from the earth in a global spectacle that results not only in the joy of the blessed but also in the "weeping and gnashing of teeth" of the damned (Matt. 13).

Furthermore, God's people achieve divine purposes by killing others, whether in assassination, as in the story of Ehud (Judg. 3), or in attacks on whole peoples, as in the conquest of Canaan (Deut. 20:17).[7] God brings salvation through liars, such as the Hebrew midwives (Exod. 2:15–20) and the prostitute Rahab (Josh. 2–6). God puts prophets through agonies both physical (Ezekiel) and marital (Hosea). God calls other prophets to take up arms and kill God's enemies— even prophets as admirable as Samuel and Elijah. And in the New Testament, God sends the Son of God to the Cross and God's witnesses (literally *martyrs*) to their deaths.

I recognize that God seems not to call the apostles to any ethically ambiguous action. But in the brief sketches we have of them in the New Testament, we must recognize also they are never depicted as facing an ethical dilemma; we have no instructive analogies to the Nazis pounding on the door asking for hidden Jews. We never see them in such a situation. Nor are they ever in a position of social and political authority in which they have the opportunity to wield power on behalf of others or of the gospel. So the strongest argument from the apostolic practice against what I am saying is, at the end, only silence. I acknowledge that the apostles do not say and do the sorts of things I am discussing here. But I affirm that they are never shown to be in positions to make such decisions, and thus are never depicted as *refusing to do them*, either. So it is parlous to say with confidence what they *would* do if the circumstances were (almost unimaginably) different.

I have tried hard in the foregoing tally of violent episodes to avoid exaggerated or inflammatory language.

I think God did just those things I have listed, and so did God's people under his command. So the ethical imperative against Christians being involved in anything coercive or anything else that would normally be seen as evil (such as consigning an innocent carpenter-cum-rabbi to crucifixion) cannot be made on the basis of some putative holiness of God that excludes such things. The holiness of God as actually depicted in the Bible somehow includes all of these actions. Perhaps, then, the case against any sort of coercion wielded by Christians can be made on the basis of a fourth consideration.

This fourth consideration is the distinction between God's work and ours, between what is proper only to God and what we are to do in resemblance to, and in cooperation with, God. Since we were created in the image of God to engage in godly work in the world—namely, caring for the rest of creation—and since we are always to love God and our neighbors as ourselves, then we must continue to obey those commandments. Finding refuge from them in the salvation commandment will not do, as we have seen in other contexts. Indeed, we can say that if Christians refuse to work for justice in coercive ways because they affirm that coercion is always wrong, what do they make of a God who finally will coerce the whole universe back into line?[8] To be sure, there are Christians today who believe, as some Christians have believed in the past, in a non-coercive God who merely woos or lures or suggests. But this is not orthodox, Biblical teaching, whether it is couched in terms of process thought, New Age syncretism, or liberal sentimentality. No, the only recourse is to distinguish between God's work and ours in such a way that helps us avoid ethical dilemmas.

Perhaps there are grounds for such a distinction. I have insisted on the uniqueness of Jesus' role in salvation. He alone is Savior and Lord. So what might be good for Jesus to do (such as judge the world) is not proper for us to do. Along this line, Paul quotes the Old Testament to instruct the Church not to retaliate when mistreated: "'Vengeance is mine, I will repay,' says the Lord" (Rom. 12:19; Heb. 10:30). Human beings cannot be entrusted with the prosecution of vengeance, which requires both more data and more intellectual and moral refinement than we can bring to the task.

I myself oppose capital punishment on similar grounds. Our justice systems—including international courts and war crimes tribunals—are so porous, so fallible, so amenable to improper influence, that we cannot risk putting innocent people to death, as we manifestly have done. I recognize that there are cases that seem utterly obvious (Hitler, Stalin, Mao, Pol Pot). But I cannot think of a way to draw a clear line between them and, say, their lieutenants, and then *their* lieutenants, and so on in an almost infinite regress. Since we believe in a God who will repay each according to his or her deeds, and since our society can afford to protect itself from dangerous people through incarceration, we simply do not need to practice capital punishment; we can let God assign in the next life whatever is truly due a person. We hopeful and compassionate Christians can work for prison systems that provide the best possible context for repentance and amendment of life for all convicts, even these who have transgressed the most. At least we can campaign, as Christians historically have done, for humane conditions for our fellow human beings, including the worst murderers—not because they clearly deserve it, but because God loves them and wants us to do the same.

Yet society does need to be protected, and it seems obvious it must be protected by violence—legal, authorized, monitored, and minimal violence, but violence nonetheless. Some people distinguish between "coercion," which might be modified by the adjectives in the previous sentence, and "violence," which would not be. I recognize this distinction, but I do not want to be seen as disguising the true nature of my proposal. Whether it's called coercion or legitimate and proportionate violence, somebody has to exercise it in the divinely instituted role of government. Why would God's own people not play a part in such a system?[9]

God's own people did play parts, and sometimes key parts, in precisely such systems of worldly government. Some of the most familiar Bible heroes devoted their talents to helping pagan, even oppressive, empires. Joseph was made prime minister of Egypt. Moses was an adopted grandson of Pharaoh and doubtless later a courtier. Daniel was a leading administrator of *two* empires, the Babylonian and then the Medo-Persian. And Mordecai, Esther, and Nehemiah were leading figures in the latter empire as well. Jeremiah was given a prophecy to explain such paradoxical callings, callings that reflect the embeddedness of all of us in the world:

> Thus says the LORD of hosts, the God of Israel, to all the exiles whom I have sent into exile from Jerusalem to Babylon: Build houses and live in them; plant gardens and eat what they produce. Take wives and have sons and daughters; take wives for your sons, and give your daughters in marriage, that they may bear sons and daughters; multiply there, and do not decrease. But seek the welfare of the city where I have sent you into exile, and pray to the LORD on its behalf, for in its welfare you will find your welfare. (Jer. 29:4–7)

That passage is often quoted far too glibly. Remember that "the city" in question is *Babylon.* God calls us, with a deep strangeness, to make our way, and to make shalom, as well as we can *even in Babylon.*

I have suggested that a Christian community that tries to engage in evangelism while leaving off participation in other activities that instantiate Kingdom values (such as art, commerce, and political renewal) will thereby compromise its very evangelism. I suggest now that a Christian community that tries to witness to the world by shunning participation in other activities that instantiate Kingdom values (such as order, justice, security, and freedom) will also thereby compromise its very witness. This fact is deeply ironic because such "peace and justice" communities typically see the matter in exactly the opposite way. They fear that involvement in these activities will compromise their Christian testimony. But I suggest that the contrary is true. I agree with them that God is the God of the land of milk and honey, the God of the peaceable kingdom, the God of the New Jerusalem. But along the way, and precisely in order to get there from here, God is not ashamed to be the God of the Conquest, the God of the destruction of Jerusalem, and the God of Armageddon. It is not enough to say that God is willing to be crucified rather than retaliate, and so we should never promote violence upon others for righteousness's sake. God has a long record of visiting violence upon God's enemies in this life, as well as in the life to come, and God called many of God's people to visit violence on God's enemies as well. All of this is part of the testimony of the Church, and however unpleasant or even terrifying it is—for it is a terrifying thing to fall into the hands of the living God (Heb. 10:31)—it is true.

FACING THE DILEMMA

What, then, of the so-called borderline situations, situations in which every option seems bad in some way?

> "You shall love the Lord your God with all your heart, and with all your soul, and with all your mind." This is the greatest and first commandment. And a second is like it: "You shall love your neighbor as yourself." On these two commandments hang all the law and the prophets. (Matt. 22:37–40)

The Bible is a rich resource to help us understand in detail what it means to love God and to love our neighbors as ourselves. Our ethics must not rest on either a shallow love ethic or a ruthless justice ethic—or even a well-intentioned shalom ethic—with all of their vulnerability to oversimplification and rationalization according to our interests and sensibilities. We must not try to maximize shalom according to our own judgment in defiance of explicit teachings of God's Word, nor will it suffice to conduct our lives in accordance merely with a few key verses or principles we have adduced from Scripture. The Bible tells us not only generally to seek shalom but also gives us considerable specificity as to the definition of shalom—and of love, justice, and other key elements of shalom. We are not free to simply snatch these words from the Bible, write them on a banner, and then fly it over whatever we would like to do.

We are to heed the *whole* Bible, bearing in mind the wisdom of the Christian tradition, the deliverances of scholarship, the provocations of art, and the wisdom we gain from reflecting carefully upon experience. We are to consult our fellows in the Church and others as well, seeking to profit from their various perspectives. And throughout this deliberation we are to trust the Holy Spirit of God to guide us to the action that makes the most sense of all of these resources in the interest of maximizing shalom. We should not wait until all the pieces of the puzzle nicely fall into place and the way forward opens up before us utterly clear and bright. We walk by faith, not by sight. But we also must not precipitously charge forward on the basis of our favorite simplistic principle and a superficial reading of the situation. Instead, we must do our part, our *cognitive* part, as responsibly as we can, and trust God to supervise that process such that it will bring Christ's command to us in the here and now.

If we do engage in such thorough study and deliberation, we will see that we live in a world into which God has thrust us to join in the difficult missions of both cultivation and salvation, and the way God does it sometimes involves dirt and blood. As Reinhold Niebuhr cautions us,

> A simple Christian moralism is senseless and confusing. It is senseless when, as in the [First] World War, it seeks uncritically to identify the cause of Christ with the cause of democracy without a religious reservation. It is just as senseless when it seeks to purge itself of this error by an uncritical refusal to make any distinctions between relative values in history. The fact is that we might as well dispense with the Christian faith entirely if it is our conviction that we can act in history only if we are guiltless. This means that we must either prove our guiltlessness in order to be able to act; or refuse to act because we cannot achieve guiltlessness. Self-righteousness or inaction are the alternatives.[10]

Let us consider the case of Dietrich Bonhoeffer and the plot to assassinate Hitler in which he was definitely, though marginally, involved. What do we make of this situation and the choices Bonhoeffer made? Let us note a fact that is often overlooked: the plot *did* fail, and Bonhoeffer was executed because of his involvement in that plot—scant days before the Allied forces liberated his prison. Had he remained out of the plot, he likely would have survived the war and brought us another thirty or more years of theological fruitfulness. So the consequences of Bonhoeffer's actions do not obviously justify them.

Yet it also remains obviously true that Hitler did fall because lots of other Christians, along with their compatriots, were flying planes, driving tanks, sailing ships, and shooting guns in opposition to the Third Reich. Maybe Hitler would have eventually fallen as a result of the German people coming to their senses, repenting, and resisting him, or by some other means besides war. Maybe. But we do not know that (though some may try to infer it from certain pacifistic convictions). What we do know is that armed resistance *was* effective and liberated many from a demonic regime. The decision to bomb Hiroshima and Nagasaki made a similar, awful sense to those charged with that decision. The apparent choice was either to opt for a bloodbath as Japan roused its citizen militia to fight to the death for the emperor (although who can say when God might have prompted the Japanese people to stop fighting?) or to opt for what was hoped to be a horrific warning by way of the extinction of one city, and then another—and, the record shows, that option *did* end the fighting and the horrible death tolls on *both* sides.

Some Christians have affirmed that no price is too great to pay to maintain ethical purity, and if God allows carnage as a result of our refusal to participate in coercion, then that is, to put it bluntly, God's responsibility. It is not effectiveness that is their concern, they say, but faithfulness. I will deal with the question of effectiveness versus faithfulness below. Right now I want to acknowledge that this view does have a powerful logic, and the question thus remains: *Is it God's will that Christians eschew the use of force?* The use of force has proven effective at least sometimes in restraining evil and promoting good, however many times we can easily show that it has done the opposite. And restraining evil and promoting good are the call of God to *all* humanity in the creation commandments. To eschew the use of force and then leave it entirely up to God and non-Christians requires a very strong confidence in one's interpretation of the Bible—and not in the comfort of a classroom or library or pulpit, but in the Situation Room, in the battlefield, and in the living room at midnight as one stares into the eyes of a marauder.

To refuse all ethical compromise means that one must think not only that Bonhoeffer was wrong to bless and assist an assassination attempt, but so were the citizens of Le Chambon-sur-Lignon, and Raoul Wallenberg, and Oskar Schindler, and the many others who used repeated and systematic deception to rescue Jews from the Nazis. One must think that they should have trusted God to rescue the Jews without their having to lie—in the face of God's apparent refusal to miraculously rescue Jews all around them. Or does anyone want to defend the idea that God *wanted* all the Jews rounded up by the Nazis, and so Bonhoeffer, Wallenberg, and the others were actually resisting the will of God? There seem to be no pure choices in this real-world borderline situation, and it would be good to know what the opponents of Christian realism think ought to have been done in these cases.[11]

Bonhoeffer's chief legacy regarding this question is his ethical reflection that led to his actions, but his *actions* of deceiving the Gestapo and aiding the intended tyrannicide are important to consider as well. Both his thought and his example have prompted many people to consider the possibility that God may well call us to the borderline, to do something that is in fact consistent with the thrust of Scripture and yet at the same time is something that normally would not be done and one day will never have to be done again. I have come to the dark conclusion that Bonhoeffer was right to participate in the plot against Hitler.

One must not see here a carte blanche for whatever seems advantageous, let alone personally or corporately convenient. Maximizing shalom must never be perverted into "maximizing profits" or "maximizing my personal welfare" or "maximizing our political position." We must recall that one ought to practice straightforward goodness as the norm, expecting both recognition and praise from some and incomprehension and resistance from others. Christians must not underestimate the importance and the power of what David Ford calls "prophetic gentleness or patience."[12] Usually the ethical challenge is not figuring out what to do, but summoning up the courage and goodness actually to do it. Bonhoeffer did what he did, however, because he could not see that any other action/inaction would result in something better in this darkly extraordinary situation.

Opening up the possibility of such an action does not grant license to disobey God's clear instruction whenever we think we might be able to achieve a little more shalom another way.[13] One must elect to do the thing that is normally wrong only after pleading with God for another, easier, clearer way to act, and then proceed only after imposing every anticipatable limitation on the evil to ensue. The ethically paradoxical choice must be the last resort. And if one is to engage in such ethical improvisation, it must be what all good improvisation is: First mastering the normal (and complex) rules and patterns, and only then transcending them (not merely breaking them) to effect something better than would have been produced by routinely following them.

Sometimes, some of us must improvise. In certain extreme situations we cannot settle for living "correctly" according to some neat ethical calculus we have devised and congratulate ourselves for our integrity while chalking up the result to "God's will"—which amounts to blaming God for whatever happens next. We are responsible to care for the earth and to love our neighbor as best we can. If we think we can do that better in an unusual way that leaves us vulnerable to second-guessing and maybe even to error, we should do it. For what is the alternative? It is to shrink back from this possibility and settle for the safety of the rulebook, the comfort of the clear but circumscribed conscience.[14]

Most of the time we know what to do and must simply do it. Sometimes, however, the politician has to hold his nose and make a deal. The chaplain has to encourage his fellow soldiers in a war he deeply regrets. The professor has to teach fairly a theory or philosophy she finds repellent. The police officer has to subdue a criminal with force, even sometimes deadly force. We are on a slippery slope indeed—and one shrouded in darkness, with the ground not only slippery but also shifting under our feet. So we must hold on to God's hand, and each other's, and try to make the best of it.

References to the daily work of politicians, chaplains, professors, and police officers draw us away from Bonhoeffer's extreme situation to what is, alas, the *actually normal* situation of so many people today: living in corrupt social systems that implicate them in wrongdoing of one kind or another.

I remember listening to a group of young Christian professionals at a dinner in Hong Kong. They were recalling with affection the recent visit of a North American theologian who, with great earnestness, challenged them to take a "full Sabbath" every week. They all seemed to like and respect the man very much, and they had made time in their busy schedules to hear him out. But each one of them, around the table, responded to this teaching with the smile of incredulity. The idea that they could take an entire 24-hour period every week for worship and leisure was simply preposterous.

They explained to me, a newcomer to Hong Kong, that in the 1980s and 1990s, as Hong Kong was being handed over from the British to the Chinese, one could get ahead in one's work and make considerably more money by working an extralong day and coming in on Saturdays. So many people ended up doing that, however, it then became the new norm. Now it was almost impossible to avoid working what Europeans and North Americans would call a very long workday and return to work at least Saturday morning, if not the whole day. The cardiologist at the table suggested that he likely had the shortest workweek of anyone there, and no one disagreed. Sundays, for these pious Christians, meant attending church both morning and evening, with the afternoons devoted to visiting with parents—usually, in fact, shuttling between two sets of parents in the case of married couples. So where was this restful Sabbath to be found?

More malignantly have come to me the testimonies of students who have lived and worked in the Philippines, South Asia, the "Stans" of the former Soviet Union, Eastern Europe, or across the great continent of Africa. They all speak of bribery as simply the cost of doing business. And these have been serious Christian people who incurred great expense to go to Canada for theological education.

> "If you want your goods off the docks and into your warehouses, you'd better be prepared to pay."
>
> "If you want those dozens of business forms processed by the government clerks, you'd better be prepared to pay."
>
> "If you want to avoid thugs damaging your property at night, you'd better be prepared to pay."

To maximize shalom in their situations, they have concluded, they must collude in what is manifestly an evil situation. They cannot do the good they can do in their city and country, cannot serve their neighbors, cannot make shalom according to their talents and opportunities, unless they pay certain prices, some of them literal.

None of this reasoning, to be sure, implies that everyone everywhere ought to capitulate to such regimes. Part of our human duty is to seek ways to avoid perpetuating such wicked and wasteful ways, and my students long for changes in the economies, politics, and ethics of their respective countries so that these measures can be avoided. And should they have opportunity to work for such changes, of course, then they must, including banding together both with other Christians and with people of other outlooks to denounce and resist harmful practices.

Closer to home for most readers of this book, we pay taxes to support institutions and initiatives in which we do not believe. Indeed, governments spend our money on things that outrage us. Similarly, we purchase goods and services from companies that might be exploiting workers, or squeezing suppliers, or crushing competitors, or abusing animals, or dominating markets in cartels. Considerable good has come from the efforts of consumer activists who have pressed for fair trade, just treatment of workers and animals, free market competition, and the like—but we are a long way from a Happy Valley of production and consumption. Is Amish-style withdrawal the only proper response? And if Christians purchase our own purity at this price, then what of the rest of the world we no longer influence because we are no longer there, exercising alternative values as best we can, calling the world to higher values, pressing our neighbors to greater integrity and compassion, and creating better opportunities for work and recreation? What would happen to Hong Kong if all the serious Christians left it so they could faithfully practice a weekly Sabbath? Then, among other losses, the cultural pressure to reduce the work week and encourage a less mechanical view of cultural flourishing would be significantly lessened. Would God's purposes really be advanced more effectively if all the serious Christians abandoned Manila, or Mumbai, or Mogadishu, or Montreal?

One final note. The Apostle Paul warns Christians not to engage in "unequal partnerships" (literally, "unequal yoking") with unbelievers (2 Cor. 6:14-18). This passage has been used to justify various degrees of Christian separatism throughout Church history. But the Paul who expected Christians to have regular interactions with non-Christians (1 Cor. 10:25-33) and even expected Christian converts to remain married to nonbelievers (1 Cor. 7:10-15) can hardly be understood here to be advocating wholesale withdrawal from those outside the faith. Instead, Paul wisely warns Christians against voluntarily entering into partnerships such that our freedom to follow Christ will be compromised, relationships in which there will come stark choices to be made between "light and darkness," between Christ and the devil.

As I have been saying, Christians can join with our fellow human beings in the common enterprise of making shalom. And sometimes, as we have seen, we will find ourselves in situations in which we must make hard, even paradoxical, choices in order to obey Jesus and maximize shalom. Paul is not speaking here against the principles we have been outlining. Instead, he tells the Corinthians—who seem constantly tempted to try to eat their ethical cake and have it, too, as somehow combining acquiescence to a decadent culture with discipleship to Jesus—that a true disciple of Jesus must not willingly put him- or herself in a relationship in which one will predictably be forced into actual sin, into actually pursuing an agenda other than God's.

In our world of globalized interdependence, no one's hands can remain completely clean. Do we then despair? I suggest instead that we pay our taxes just as our Lord both recommended and did (Matt. 22:21; 17:24-27), that we follow normal Christian morality as far as we possibly can, and that we do our best to maximize shalom whenever and wherever the situation constrains us from doing the normally right thing. Otherwise we can only flee to the desert, carry a bad conscience (which does no one any good), or end up capitulating hopelessly to the blandishments of the world. Far better to accept the realities of the mixed field we inhabit for now, and do all we can to improve as best we can each situation we encounter.

FAITH, HOPE, AND LIBERTY

FAITH IN GOD'S PROVIDENCE

The Christian life is one of faith: trusting in God for salvation—of oneself, one's neighbors, and the world. A vital aspect of that faith is trusting the work of God *in* oneself, *in* one's neighbors, and *in* the world. Another is trusting the work of God *through* oneself, *through* one's neighbors, and *through* the world.

The concerned Christian can forget to trust God in these ways and take on herself the burden of converting her husband to Christ, keeping her teenagers away from sex, or persuading her father to give up drinking. She can try on her own to convince the school board to pick different books for the library, or the city council to rezone her neighborhood to remove unsavory businesses. She can forget that only God can convert people in regard to this fundamental choice or that lifelong habit. She also can forget that God uses a variety of means to achieve his purposes, and what she does is only part of his plan. Such forgetting usually has the bitterly ironic result of actually interfering with God's work. She becomes, alas, a stereotype: a pest to her husband, a nag to her children, a harpy to her father. The school board and the city council ignore her as that odd, strident woman who shows up at meetings with no supporters and seems to speak only for herself. She overplays her hand, arrogates to herself the work that God wants others to do, fails to even consider building alliances, and so remains frustrated, ineffective, bitter, and alone.

Christian groups as well can "work as if it all depended on them." They can be suspicious of other Christian groups in the same arena, perhaps because they are from a different denominational tradition or embrace a different political philosophy. So Christian groups that have so much in common fail to cooperate and lose the chance to achieve together what they cannot achieve alone. Other Christian groups may be willing to band together with other Christians, at least of certain "acceptable" sorts, but refuse to make common cause with non-Christians. They fail to see that, at least for *this* issue and on *this* occasion, Muslims or Marxists might share the same goals and support the same plan.

Increasingly in our day we have seen Christians set aside such attitudes and form various alliances in the effort to accomplish various goods. And many Christians have learned the hard way about the quid pro quo of politics: the strings that may be attached to promises and favors, the compromises that move things forward despite the dismay of the purists, and the trade-offs that are usually expected to maintain access to power. Sectors of American fundamentalism in particular have veered from one extreme to another, from pious withdrawal to political enmeshment, in just the last generation or so.

We need a new Christian realism that trusts God to work through the various means God has shown that God is pleased to use: brave, persevering individuals, yes, but also families, churches, organizations of other kinds, alliances of various sorts, rulers, and even whole nations. And the Bible shows us that God is willing even to use those who do not believe and honor God. At the same time, we should attempt to discern what God is doing in the world and to cooperate with that mission—with our theology of sin ready to hand, looking hard for what motives may be in play, what traps are set, what consequences may ensue, and what prices must be paid.

Some Christians will recoil from such suggestions, instead retreating to Christian communities of what they hope will be purity of heart and cleanness of hand. Such communities may well play a useful role, reminding us of the ultimate holiness of the Kingdom of God and revealing for what it is the convenient temptation to believe that all that we do is somehow both shrewd and good. Still, in the nature of the case such communities will exercise only slight effects on cultural life. I do not mean to dismiss the efficacy of their witness or of their prayers. But in the world as God has seemed to ordain it, and from the pages of scriptural history in which God is shown to act politically, it appears that the adage is true: Political decisions are made by those who show up. The monastic movement, important as it was in nurturing Christian piety and promoting evangelism, shaped broader contours of European culture only as monasteries became significant landlords, educators, artistic centers, and advisors to the powerful.

The question for each Christian is whether I will discern and cooperate with what God is doing in this or that situation, in faith that God is indeed busy already in such work and will help me join in it fruitfully alongside others.

IRONY, PARADOX, INTEGRITY, AND EFFECTIVENESS

The Apostle Paul warns us against congratulating ourselves on the outcomes of our labors: "I planted, Apollos watered, but God gave the growth. So neither the one who plants nor the one who waters is anything, but only God who gives the growth" (1 Cor. 3:6–7). Given the mixed field in which we live and work, we should expect the outcome of our labors often to be obscure. Pastor Mark Buchanan puts it trenchantly: "To pray well is to cultivate holy patience and perseverance. It is to practice holy waiting, which means often to keep on praying in spite of the poor results."[1] Who can say what the central, let alone the total, impact of our work might be in any given instance, let alone over a whole lifetime? Frank Capra's film *It's a Wonderful Life* has reminded several generations now how interwoven our lives are with those of others and that a small action here can affect great matters down the line.

Furthermore, we recognize that our actions can have consequences quite other than we intend. Ironies abound in the fallen ecology in which we make our way. Welfare programs can encourage sloth, while workfare programs can crush the innocent. In seeking to protect their children from danger, "helicopter" parents may render them too soft and naive to be able to cope with life in the world. Teachers try to bolster their students' self-esteem through constant praise, and in the process they obscure the connection between industriousness and achievement so that the students' inflated self-esteem pops against the sharp demands of reality. Technology makes it easier for employers to demand more output but no less labor. Low-fat snack foods encourage binging and, because they are loaded with sugar, greater obesity. And desperately extreme evangelistic confrontations ("Prepare to meet thy God!") can so irritate people that further communication is impossible.

As replete with ironies as is our world, we must not throw up our hands and retreat into quietism. We have faith in the God of paradoxes who, on the jumbled landscape of our broken world, draws straight with crooked lines. We trust that the God who specializes in bringing good out of evil will make something beautiful out of our efforts to love God and our neighbors in creation. Indeed, God often brings good out of our failures, and even our sins.[2] For in the aftermath, we sometimes learn humility, and faith, and other vital lessons we would learn no other way. Moreover, other people can sometimes receive our gifts better from meek hands and chastened voices. At the heart of our religion, after all, stands the Cross, the supreme paradox of human history: shame/glory, suffering/joy, wrath/love, horror/gratitude, death/life, end/beginning. The Cross shows us that we won't always win. And it shows us that we always, finally, *do* win—through the Cross, and through our crosses.

As we take up our crosses to follow Christ, therefore, we are encouraged by the Apostle Paul's affirmation:

> For by grace you have been saved through faith, and this is not your own doing; it is the gift of God—not the result of works, so that no one may boast. For we are what he has made us, created in Christ Jesus for good works, which God prepared beforehand to be our way of life. (Eph. 2:8–10)

"Our way of life" is to be performing whatever good works seem to be given to us by God to do. We need not be paralyzed by our inability to discern with certainty what to do or to foresee all the consequences of our actions. We trust that God will show us what we need to be shown in order for us to respond as God wants us to respond. God promises to guide us, so we trust that promise and carry on with good works.

Those good works are good in two ways. The first is the way of integrity: doing what the Spirit prompts us to do out of obedience to the Lordship of Christ and out of faith that God is good and what God commands therefore is good. Faithfulness means doing our duty.

Many individual Christians, and also churches and Christian organizations, congratulate themselves on their faithfulness over against any consideration of *effectiveness.* "Our job is not to be effective—that's God's business—but to be faithful." How convenient it is for such Christians to fly the flag of faithfulness as their numbers dwindle, their evangelism remains fruitless, and their social ministry stands unwelcomed by others: "We're small, and uninfluential, and disparaged by others, but that's just because we are so true to the gospel." I grew up hearing this from conservative Christians, and nowadays one hears such rationalization also from those on the religious left as they reassure themselves about what they are pleased to call their prophetic fidelity.

Such Christians lack a full definition of Christian faithfulness. Hear again this familiar parable:

> For [the Kingdom of heaven] is as if a man, going on a journey, summoned his slaves and entrusted his property to them; to one he gave five talents, to another two, to another one, to each according to his ability. Then he went away.
> The one who had received the five talents went off at once and traded with them, and made five more talents. In the same way, the one who had the two talents made two more

talents. But the one who had received the one talent went off and dug a hole in the ground and hid his master's money.

After a long time the master of those slaves came and settled accounts with them. Then the one who had received the five talents came forward, bringing five more talents, saying, "Master, you handed over to me five talents; see, I have made five more talents."

His master said to him, "Well done, good and faithful slave; you have been faithful in a few things, I will put you in charge of many things; enter into the joy of your master."

And the one with the two talents also came forward, saying, "Master, you handed over to me two talents; see, I have made two more talents."

His master said to him, "Well done, good and faithful slave; you have been faithful in a few things, I will put you in charge of many things; enter into the joy of your master."

Then the one who had received the one talent also came forward, saying, "Master, I knew that you were a harsh man, reaping where you did not sow, and gathering where you did not scatter seed; so I was afraid, and I went and hid your talent in the ground. Here you have what is yours."

But his master replied, "You wicked and lazy slave! You knew, did you, that I reap where I did not sow, and gather where I did not scatter? Then you ought to have invested my money with the bankers, and on my return I would have received what was my own with interest. So take the talent from him, and give it to the one with the ten talents. For to all those who have, more will be given, and they will have an abundance; but from those who have nothing, even what they have will be taken away. As for this worthless slave, throw him into the outer darkness, where there will be weeping and gnashing of teeth." (Matt. 25:14–30)[3]

The definition of faithfulness here is *results*. It is *effectiveness*— not mere integrity, and not just effort, either, as some would prefer to view the story. The first two slaves double their master's investment in them. That's what the master cares about. He does not care how they did it or how hard they worked at it.

The third slave does not make any money at all, but rather retains his master's original investment in him and hands it over upon the master's return. This slave is the very picture of integrity—without effectiveness. He carefully guards what the master gives him, as many Christians guard their faith, their purity, their witness. And when the master returns, they have not compromised one iota. The original investment is returned in full. It's all there, intact and complete. But the master is furious. He gifted the slave with the talent not to have it preserved but to have it multiplied. And he punishes the slave as a total failure, as "worthless" and thus fit only for removal as so much trash.

The fundamental commandments of God all entail performance, accomplishment, effectiveness: cultivate the earth, love God and your neighbor, and make disciples of all nations. Notice particularly this last one. If one confines oneself to Luke's accounts of Jesus' last words to his disciples, one can be forgiven for understanding the mandate to be simply to "bear witness," whether anyone listens or not (Luke 24 and Acts 1). But Matthew's account makes it quite clear: the command is to "make disciples," not merely to drop the gospel at the world's feet like a brick and then turn away, satisfied with another job well done.[4] We must engage the world and stay with the world until the world—or, at least, lots of the world—has joined Jesus' band.[5]

True faithfulness combines integrity and effectiveness. Indeed, these two elements work together. Keeping integrity in full view will guard us against adopting inappropriate methods of attracting and retaining the world's attention, against minimizing the scandal of the Cross, against growing churches—or businesses—by any means possible. Keeping effectiveness in equally full view will guard us against self-righteousness, insularity, and sloth. A church must have integrity to be effective in the genuine work of disciple-making, and a business oriented to proper goals must have integrity to be effective in serving the world. Likewise, a church concerned for true effectiveness is a church alive to the transformative and fruitful power of the gospel and its possibilities, just as a business concerned for true effectiveness generally enjoys a fresh and expansive sense of its identity and its creative possibilities.

Finally, a concern for faithfulness will mean assessing situations as carefully as possible and then expending our resources wisely for maximum effect. We aim at making the best of each situation. Since our resources are always finite, we will not attempt to solve every problem at once, react to every threat with full force, or jump at every opportunity—just as God does not try to teach us everything at once, make us perfect immediately, and solve the world's problems at a stroke.

We will need to exercise a holy prudence, even a kind of sanctified ruthlessness, about what—in a world bristling with problems and crying with needs—we should do. We need to keep our minds on the big picture, ready to freely interrupt the parade of small particulars in our carefully optimized schedules to care for the wounded stranger by the side of the road. We must be true to our vocations and be wise in their fulfillment. We will remember that we are not called to root up all the weeds, but to get about the work we are given to do. Serious Christians thus will strive to abide in

Christ (John 15) so that we can know what his will is in this moment and trust him to somehow take care of all that he is *not* calling us to do.

We must be willing sometimes to overlook minor issues to focus on major ones and to sacrifice lesser goods to gain greater ones—a principle that is very hard to accept for certain binary-minded Christians, those who think that compromise always involves tolerating a certain amount of evil (which it usually does) and therefore must always be avoided (which is the way to get very little accomplished in the real world). Again, we must recall that God has been tolerating a considerable amount of evil throughout the world and throughout history, and God has not tried to fix everything at once. God, instead, is tirelessly and relentlessly embarked on making things better. We should therefore be more godly and less fastidious. And we can do so with peace and joy, retiring each night to sleep in a world of unfinished business, because we hope in the God who one day will make all things new.

HOPE

The Christian hope comes from believing, and living in, the Christian story as disciples of Jesus. We are in that story, and we are "in Christ," as Paul enjoys repeating. Thus we look ahead to the New Jerusalem with eager sureness. We know the Lord of history, and he has told us how the story will turn out. Our hope is sure—as certain as anything can be for us, since God's faithfulness is as certain as anything can be for us. We thus undertake our work in the world without despair and without desperation (both of which entail, literally, being *without* hope), but instead with confidence—literally, with faith (*con fide*)—in the One who is entirely faith worthy. Glenn Tinder chides us:

> Christians who are very anxious about the fate of God's truth must have forgotten the doctrine of the Holy Spirit, which implies that God does not send his truth into history like a ship that is launched and then forgotten. He is the source at once of the truth human beings face and of the inspiration that enables them to recognize it as the truth and, in a measure, to understand it.... Need Christians, then, fear that God's voice will be drowned out by human error?[6]

We live our lives now—what Bonhoeffer calls the "penultimate"—with the ultimate, our hope, ever in view. And here is another dialectic with practical implications. Because the ultimate is what finally and forever counts, we ought to sacrifice whatever is penultimate to gain the ultimate. Yet we ought not to be reckless with or indifferent to the penultimate. Instead, we ought to value it highly. The ultimate is the consummation of, and not merely the successor to, the penultimate. The ultimate validates the penultimate as worthy of our respect and care. In short, we take the present world very seriously—and not too seriously.

It is time, however, to confront an apparent contradiction from Scripture that threatens to upend this scheme:

> But by the same word the present heavens and earth have been reserved for fire, being kept until the day of judgment and destruction of the godless.... But the day of the Lord will come like a thief, and then the heavens will pass away with a loud noise, and the elements will be dissolved with fire, and the earth and everything that is done on it will be

disclosed. Since all these things are to be dissolved in this way, what sort of persons ought you to be in leading lives of holiness and godliness, waiting for and hastening the coming of the day of God, because of which the heavens will be set ablaze and dissolved, and the elements will melt with fire? But, in accordance with his promise, we wait for new heavens and a new earth, where righteousness is at home. (2 Pet. 3:7, 10–13)

To many Christian ears, this passage has sounded like annihilation. The lesson drawn is that we should focus all of our energies and resources upon evangelism. Since it's all going to burn anyhow, why bother with art, sport, business, or anything other than full-time evangelism?

The first thing to note is that the author of the epistle doesn't draw the same conclusion from his own eschatology. The implication for him instead is that we should lead "lives of holiness and godliness, waiting for and hastening the coming of the day of God." Christians are to continue to live lives clearly dedicated to the priorities and principles given to us by God. Without any indication otherwise, we should assume that this means that Christians should continue to obey the creation and salvation commandments, and their elaborations in the rest of Scripture—and not jettison most of those mandates in the interest of last-minute, all-hands-on-deck evangelism.

Second, the imagery of fire here is parallel to the image of water, which immediately precedes this passage: "the world of that time [Noah's day] was deluged with water and perished" (2 Pet. 3:6). The "world of that time" was judged by God, purged by the Flood, and renewed by way of Noah, his family, and the animals on the ark. There was great discontinuity with the world as it had been, but also great continuity.

God did not create a completely new world ex nihilo, but instead cleansed the (continuing) world of what was evil, preserved what was good, and brought it into a new era. I suggest that the same pattern is in view in this passage in 2 Peter, except via fire instead of water. (It is an open question whether this passage depicts literal fire with which God will purge and rearrange things, or whether this fiery language is symbolic of purgation and renewal by other means.) The fundamental idea is not total destruction but judgment; what is good will be preserved to enjoy a better context in a new order—"where righteousness is at home."

Third, even if annihilation *is* in view, I nevertheless reiterate my paradoxical assertion that our evangelism is better if we do not restrict ourselves to it. Even if it *is* all going to burn, moreover, we ourselves will undergo a better process of sanctification to fit us for the life to come if we do not restrict ourselves to a single activity, evangelism, that will be entirely unnecessary in the world to come.

Finally, we must appreciate that this passage must be integrated with the many other apocalyptic passages in the Bible, the vast majority of which do not speak in such apparently totalistic language. Yes, fire and destruction are usually in view in those passages, too, but those images are consistent with the themes of God removing what is bad and purifying what remains for the glorious and total shalom to come. To reiterate, however, I suggest that even this extraordinary passage in 2 Peter is better understood as not speaking in terms of total destruction and a brand-new restart.

The Christian hope is of renewal—but renewal as in purgation, healing, and vitality to enable the maturation of the seeds already planted, the ripening of the life already begun, the confirmation of the patterns already established, the flowering of the Kingdom that has already come and will yet come in fullness.

The Christian hope teaches us to wait on God: to listen for the voice of guidance we expect and to receive the equipment we know he will provide. Precisely because we hope *in God*, we can act with confidence. But precisely because we *hope* in God, we do not perpetually rush forward into the next thing with our ready-made programs and provisions, but rather cultivate the humility that awaits *God's* direction and supply.[7]

LIBERTY: OURS

In our discussion so far we have touched on zones of freedom in Christ. We are free, first, from sin and death. No longer must we obey sin and fear death. We are free to choose the good in the hope of eternal life.

Out of his experience of wrestling with sin, fearing death, and longing for a good God, Martin Luther rejoiced to affirm that the Christian is free from worrying about his destiny, is therefore free from egocentricity, and so is free truly to love God and his neighbor. God has secured for the Christian blessings beyond measure, and certainly beyond our deserts. So the Christian is now freed from self-concern to be truly altruistic.[8] We can extend this insight to affirm that the Christian is thus free to tend the earth without self-ishness. And, according to the salvation commandment, the Christian cares for his fellow Christians and seeks to make disciples among his neighbors out of love, rather than concern for his own gain.

We can go beyond Luther's point by recalling the win-win-win concept. If I know my destiny is secure in Christ,

I might be capable now of genuine altruism to my family and friends, but why would I care for others whom I dislike or even who oppose me? I do so not only out of grateful regard for God's preferences—for Christ has commanded me to love such people—but also because Jesus promises to reward my obedience (Matt. 6:3–6,17–21). So I do not have to try heroically to summon a purely selfless *agapē* that, frankly, will never arise. I can instead cheerfully love God in the multiple (not mixed) motives of benefiting *everyone* involved. Such is the reinforcing circle of genuine shalom.

Liberty is mine, to enjoy both the delights of the world and the opportunities for service to God and neighbor. The Christian is not to live merely by obeying a set of rules, not merely by conforming to a new law (whether the Sermon on the Mount or even the whole New Testament). A Christian should certainly not be antinomian, either, living blithely and self-indulgently free from all guidelines or commands, for the commands of God remain upon her. But these commands are part of what we might consider her human "operating system." They are not a set of arbitrary injunctions that will bend her life out of shape and cramp her potential, but structures of the good life that will cause her to flourish and to contribute to the flourishing of others. They describe the way things actually are, or should be, and she observes them to her everlasting benefit:

> The law of the LORD is perfect, reviving the soul; the decrees of the LORD are sure, making wise the simple; the precepts of the LORD are right, rejoicing the heart; the commandment of the LORD is clear, enlightening the eyes; the fear of the LORD is pure, enduring forever; the ordinances of the LORD are true and righteous altogether. More to be desired are they than gold, even much fine gold; sweeter also than honey,

and drippings of the honeycomb. Moreover by them is your servant warned; in keeping them there is great reward. (Ps. 19:7–11)

Furthermore, the particular commands of God upon her life as an individual, her particular vocation, are merely the clarifications of her true essence, purpose, and destiny. Within those statements of the identity and meaning of her life, God then expects her to exercise the freedom both to consult with God as necessary (via prayer, Bible study, attention to preaching, conversation with other Christians, and so on) and to make good decisions based on the resources God has provided to help her to decide and act. God does not want us to be volitional invalids who need God to decide everything, to walk around in a mystical cloud in which we consciously experience God's guidance every moment on every particular. That isn't healthy faith; that is religious mania. Yes, we should enjoy "practicing the presence of God," "pray without ceasing," cultivate an attitude of responsiveness to God. As we do so, however, we are free to play chess, to drive our kids to school, to research a report, and to order new stock for the store without compulsively engaging in some sort of divine instant messaging because these actions are the sorts of things that are entailed by what God has shown us to be our vocation. God wants us to be spiritual adults who have taken the time necessary to discern God's will and who then get on with doing it—in confident freedom.

The Christian remains a human being who retains the terrible license to disregard the call of Christ, the voice of the Holy Spirit, the teaching of the Church, and the divine law in her heart. She can still indulge in sin. The burden of freedom is ours, whether to take up our cross, fulfill our vocation, and live as free adults, or to live as slothful, shirking juveniles who refuse the responsibility entailed by such glorious and dangerous liberty.

With these principles of freedom in view, we turn to the important fact that the New Testament emphasis is not on freedom for the Christian to live freely per se, but on freedom for the Christian to live freely *for the other*. Most of the discussion about Christian liberty in the New Testament occurs in Paul's writings, and his main theme is the paradoxical freedom to refuse to use one's freedom in order to bless other Christians:

> For you were called to freedom, brothers and sisters; only do not use your freedom as an opportunity for self-indulgence, but through love become slaves to one another. For the whole law is summed up in a single commandment, "You shall love your neighbor as yourself." (Gal. 5:13–14)

> But when you thus sin against members of your family, and wound their conscience when it is weak, you sin against Christ. Therefore, if food is a cause of their falling, I will never eat meat, so that I may not cause one of them to fall. (1 Cor. 8:12–13)

> "All things are lawful," but not all things are beneficial. "All things are lawful," but not all things build up. Do not seek your own advantage, but that of the other. (1 Cor. 10:23–24; cf. 1 Pet. 2:16)

Let's be clear that the actions in question are not sinful. If they were sins, they would simply be forbidden. Paul's point instead is that these actions are legitimate in themselves but become illegitimate if enjoying them will somehow impede the spread of the gospel and the edification of the Christian community. Good things are to be freely foregone in the interest of *better* things. Here is the benign inversion of the "lesser of two evils" principle to that of preferring the "greater of two goods." One sacrifices something one is legitimately free to undertake and enjoy so others will benefit. And once again we see God's emphasis on *effectiveness* and *results*.

Paul's example of eating meat that has been offered to idols needs translation to make sense in our own context, of course. We might think today of Christians who feel free to drink alcohol, watch movies with controversial content, or party in dance clubs. Such Christians will consider the example they set for younger or weaker believers who may lack their perspective and self-control and follow their lead into a situation in which they will founder. Less typically, perhaps, we might think of Christians who will take clever tax deductions, drive hard bargains, and assume high risks in investments or loans. Again, such Christians will be careful of the encouragement they may appear to be giving to less sophisticated Christians who might then feel free to cheat, exploit, and gamble.

Liberty is a precious and dangerous thing, and the Apostle urges us to recognize that while freedom is a splendid part of new life in Christ, penultimately it is an instrument that we freely take up or lay down, so to speak, as need requires.

LIBERTY: OTHERS'

The issue then arises of other people's liberty. The principle of granting and respecting freedom is fundamental to the Christian religion. In the first chapter of the Bible, God creates humanity and immediately commands us. Despite its implication of authority, however, the very idea of "commanding" implies the freedom to obey or disobey on the part of the one commanded. One doesn't command a fork, a flower, or a flood.

Our freedom is far from absolute. The commandments of God guide us to the best paths, to the highest vocations, to the realization of our fundamental purpose and ultimate destiny. Disobeying God's commands is to enjoy the freedom only to harm and finally to destroy oneself. The passenger on a ship crossing the Pacific is free to jump overboard, yes, and free to swim in the ocean for a while, but ultimately free only to drown. It is not in his nature to enjoy indefinitely such a degree of independence. His freedom is curtailed by his several limitations.

Among the respects in which our freedom is properly curtailed is the legitimate freedom of others. One must not act as if one is the only passenger aboard, eating all the food, monopolizing the swimming pool, and so on. One hurts others by abusing one's freedom, and one also hurts oneself, losing health by gluttony, friendships by selfishness, and so on. It is to our own advantage, as well as to the advantage of others—whom we are commanded by God to love as ourselves—to observe proper limits to our freedom. And what is true of individuals in relation to others is usually true, and in very similar respects, to families, tribes, corporations, churches, and states. Unbridled freedom never results, in fact, in the maximization of shalom even for oneself.

As God has granted each of us freedom, so we must grant freedom to each other. This is a difficult principle for many Christians to understand and practice, as it is for anyone who is highly confident of the universal applicability of his or her own ethic. It is a natural impulse to insist on beliefs and behaviors that appear simply *right,* whether according to a particular Christian tradition (e.g., Roman Catholic, Orthodox, Puritan, or evangelical), a particular variety of Islamic *sharia* (from Wahhabi to Isma'ili), a particular variety of communism (Leninist, Maoist, or what have you), or a particular version of democracy and capitalism (whether Burke's or Smith's or Keynes's or Rawls's). Those who are convinced of the rightness—the righteousness—of their cause tend toward hegemony as a deeply attractive, even automatic, political mode, whether in a family, a church, an organization, or a state.

Yet confidence in one's religion and hope for the future could lead in quite a different direction: toward patient, hopeful tolerance of others based on the belief that God is in ultimate control and eventually will bring God's good purposes to pass even through the granting of broad freedom to God's creatures.[9] The Bible reminds us that God grants us the basic liberty to refuse to honor God, to refuse to care for each other, and (thus) to refuse even what is in our own best interests. God knows that love and community cannot grow out of coercion—a truism that in our day perhaps deserves emphasis: *Love and community cannot grow out of coercion.*

God does not always free us from the consequences of misusing our liberty, although God graciously offers to forgive us our sins, to ameliorate and help us deal with what we might call the temporal consequences of our sins, and to bring us to eternal life in the world to come. God also lets us refuse that redemptive package, and thus be left to face the full, final, and fearsome consequences of our freedom.

Created in God's image to do godly work in the world, we are to grant each other a measure of freedom as well. Yes, we have to insist on a certain degree of conformity and engage in a certain measure of enforcement of that conformity to enjoy the benefits of society. Families must agree on mealtimes if they want to enjoy the blessing of table conversation; churches must agree on meeting hours, regular practices, and proper discipline if they want to enjoy worship, fellowship, and mission together; businesses must agree on hierarchies, teams, hours of operation, and the like to optimize their work together; and so on. In Western societies in which individualistic liberty increasingly seems to be the supreme value, we have to make these points about cooperation and curtailment more frequently and insistently.

Still, we ought to grant as much freedom as we can to individuals and to groups to pursue their vocations—or, indeed, to refuse or to fail at that pursuit. We must be on guard against adopting an overbearing attitude toward others, a condescension that too easily tips over into control. We must also eschew a different kind of condescension that pretends that all is well and therefore requires no effort from me. "Oh, they're just different, doing their own thing. That's fine, and I'll just focus on my own thing"—even if I see someone engaged in destructive behavior. Instead, we ought to maintain a respectful compassion for our neighbors, giving them their space, but also knocking on the door of that space if they seem to need help. We must remember that good parents, good teachers, good spouses, and good friends offer both accepting love and transforming love: I love you as you are, and I thus respect your difference and freedom; I am also dedicated to helping you to overcome your problems and to flourish—in whatever way I can, in whatever way I believe will be truly helpful, and in whatever way you will accept.[10]

We must be wary of the much less benign motivations of some who seek greater state control over individuals and institutions such as families, churches, and nongovernmental organizations. And we especially need to seek liberty for everyone to exercise his or her God-given freedom to choose about ultimate things, and particularly about God himself. Glenn Tinder is especially helpful on this theme:

> On Christian principles, affirming liberty expresses trust in God and mistrust of human beings, particularly human beings as organized in society and the state. Human beings do not know how to create faith or eradicate sin. Christians believe that God does. Individuals are left free in order for them to be fully accessible to God. It cannot be denied that many Christians have despised or attacked liberty from a concern for faith and virtue. But did they not, in that way, manifest a confidence in state officials that might more appropriately, at least for Christians, have been placed in God?[11]

These are the main grounds for the Christian support of liberal democracy. It is not only the least bad of the available alternatives, but it manifests positive and crucial Christian values such as justice, the dignity of all people, due process, transparency, honesty, liberty, responsibility, love of one's neighbor, and the humility to recognize the fallibility of both individuals and systems, including the state itself. Of course, liberal democracy is a far cry from the shalom of God's direct and perfect rule in the New Jerusalem. Liberal democracy is corrupt in every real-world instance. It cannot even guarantee the perfect outworking of its own values, which often collide in particular cases. Christians therefore must speak out against the presumption or pretension, let alone the typical self-congratulation, of any political system or regime, including democratic ones. Yet Christians also should recognize the roots of liberal democracy in the soil of our own religion, and we should commend and defend it as the only form of government we know of that even attempts to include all of these values.

Recognizing and granting liberty to others stands in tension with granting them liberty to harm themselves or others. Within a liberal democratic state, John Howard Yoder writes, Christians must face some political and moral realities:

> There are sins which it is not possible or desirable to treat as crimes, even if one had the kind of majority status that would permit making the laws. One major American experience in this respect was with prohibition. There are also voices today [this article was published in 1984] suggesting that drug abuse, like adult homosexuality and heterosexual adultery, like most of the other deadly sins (gluttony, sloth, avarice, pride . . .) could not properly be dealt with in the courts even if there were a majority to declare them worthy of civil punishment.[12]

I agree with Yoder here: Christians must do all we can to bring as much shalom as possible without trying to construct the New Jerusalem by ourselves. It is not enough to counter the false claim "You can't legislate morality" with the half-truth "Law is always legislated morality," much less with the might-makes-right retort of "Oh, yes, we can!" Yet these responses are typical of many Christians today, bent on wielding what cultural power they have left to conform society to their values to the extent that is still possible. We need to think about what law can and cannot do well in a liberal, pluralized, democratic situation in which we participate as disciples of Jesus and as neighbors to many fellow citizens who are not. Law is a minimum, not an ideal, that orders our life together, and it is a coarse instrument indeed to frame out a desirable pattern for that life together.

Yet law is not merely restrictive, not simply a necessary negative. Law is encoded, enforced discipline, and through discipline—properly devised and observed, of course—we learn how to live. In that light parents discipline children, teachers discipline students, coaches discipline teams, and society disciplines its members. Law is both regulative and pedagogical—indeed, it is regulative partly in order to be pedagogical. (Again, the Torah itself is both "law" and "instruction.") One learns beautiful improvisation only once one has learned the basics, through discipline. Law can provide us with a framework out of which we can learn how to live freely and well. Many laws in the real world are made badly, just as parents make mistakes, teachers are not all equally talented or motivated, coaches can be incompetent or corrupt, and so on. No human law, just like no human leader, short of Christ himself, will always do well. But for lack of perfection we hardly need to succumb to despair and see law—or any other form of discipline—solely as a grim restraint upon evil.

Still, we must seek law that is as consonant as possible with how God prefers to work in the world; in this era, that preference seems to entail law that provides as much justice and compassion as possible and as much social stability as is necessary, along with the maximum freedom possible for individuals and groups to live as they believe is best. Some might see this statement as a capitulation to secular modernity. I maintain, however, that the combination and the tension of each element with the others—justice, compassion, stability, and liberty—is Biblical. It is the way God works, and the way God wants us to work, this side of the New Jerusalem.

As we consider the intersection of liberty, order, justice, and compassion, we might ask, for example, whether wealthy countries have any moral obligation to help poorer countries improve upon their self-destructive economic practices. Before I answer, let me add that I do not believe that poorer countries are poor only because, or even primarily because, they have such practices. I am not trained in economics, nor do I have substantial knowledge of business life or of nations outside North America, so I will keep to very general terms in this example.

The International Monetary Fund and the World Bank do offer both financial and prudential help—the former kind of help usually depending on compliance with the latter. Many critics of these organizations see the IMF and the World Bank as perpetuating wealth for the minority and poverty for the majority. But those same critics usually suggest ways in which such organizations could provide better assistance of both sorts. They don't usually suggest that the IMF and World Bank should just go away. On the other hand, few suggest that the IMF and the World Bank simply take over troubled national economies, tempting as I expect this prospect is for some in those organizations who are convinced of the rightness of their recommendations. We generally acknowledge that nations, like individuals, are entitled to choose their own path—although they should be offered assistance to make the best of their situations.

We also ought to recognize that a nation is not simply a bloc. Nations and states are decidedly complex, with elites normally running the show and many, many people remaining poor both economically and politically. What, then, of any obligation on the part of the powerful elsewhere to intervene on behalf of the poor within a country whose government likely will bristle at any hint of interference with its sovereignty? The modern era offers a spectrum of options: diplomatic remonstrance with leaders of state; offers of financial and other assistance; promises of assistance tied to changes in policy or leadership; threats of political and economic harm in the absence of changes in policy or leadership; escalating political and economic coercion; and armed intervention.

In each of these cases, various principles must be weighed in the balance: the sovereignty of a state (and, by analogy, the relative sovereignty of each family, or corporation, or municipality); the self-interest of others; our own interests; as well as the sense among many people that neighbor-love requires us to care especially for the needy and vulnerable, both to benefit and to protect them—of which principle the Universal Declaration of Human Rights is but one articulation. Belief in the rightness of intervention on behalf of the oppressed does not automatically trump all other considerations. Those other principles are not merely realpolitik, but articulations of genuine goods. Some of us might object, for instance, to how the children are being treated in another nation, or school, or family, but we should consider carefully all the principles involved, and all the likely outcomes, before we march in and insist on what we believe are righteous changes. Coercion via intervention—the compromise of liberty—normally ought to be our last resort.

Too many of our neighbors today seem eager to impose their morality on the rest of us, whether in regard to environmental concerns (from a particular endangered species to forms of recycling that may or may not prove advantageous to the planet); bioethical controversies over abortion, contraception, and assisted suicide; sex and gender varieties and innovations; and so on. Freedom to dissent has rarely been a popular freedom to protect, and the landscape is strewn with blazing sites of resistance to this freedom, from roiling university campuses to demagogic political rallies to legislatures and courts eager to demonstrate that they are on the right side of history. We are going to have to think and work harder in the coming age to articulate and protect proper rights of conscience to dissent from what the majority has decided is right—and not just our own Christian dissent but the dissent of others with whom we deeply disagree. We need to recover the virtue of *tolerance*, abiding all the difference we possibly can in the name of liberty, or else succumb to the totalitarianism of whatever version of righteousness is held by the powerful of the moment—whether Christian, secularist, Islamic, or otherwise.

We must also keep recalling the ambiguities and limitations inherent in this present stage of the Christian story. Those of us with power have to decide how often, how much, and in what way to wield it, particularly on behalf of those who lack full human rights at home or abroad. Do we scatter our limited resources over every place where human rights are not fully honored? Do we pick a few places on which to focus our energies while leaving the others to languish? It is simply unrealistic to say, "Just do the right thing, fully and everywhere, and trust God to make it all come out right." The world we live in, under the mysterious providence of God and affected deeply by our sin, is a world of limits, ironies, and paradoxes, as well as opportunities. Making a way through this kaleidoscopic maze requires political wisdom informed by the highest principles and the best information. But even with all those advantages, that way is never guaranteed to be ultimately right and maximally productive of shalom, nor without its compromises and disappointments. Christian ethics often cannot provide a convenient conceptual sword with which we can simply cut through the Gordian knot of geopolitics—or of our relationship with an obnoxious neighbor or difficult family member. Sometimes obedience to the voice of Christ requires a patient picking away at an issue with the aim of accomplishing as much as possible on that occasion, however small the result might seem, with the resolve to return to work away at it again whenever the opportunity arises. We can hope only to fulfill what we discern to be God's particular calling on us in this place and at this time, recognizing that we can do only a little because we are little. But we are grateful that God calls and empowers us to accomplish genuine, if only ever partial, good.

We have glanced here at issues of deep complexity and recognized the tensions we confront in all our dealings with others—at home, in traffic, at school or work, at play, in politics, in church, and everywhere. Freedom is a complicated matter, and no simple slogan will suffice for our understanding of it and our negotiating the world in the light of it. As we shall now see, freedom is no less complicated when we turn to the Church itself.

UNITY AND DIVERSITY IN THE CHURCH

Traditionally, the question of unity and diversity in the Church has been resolved in one of two ways. The first is to assert that one form is correct and all others are more or less correct as they resemble and relate to that norm. The second is to assert the existence of a "mere Christianity" at the heart of every true form of the faith, which is then fleshed out according to different historical circumstances: fifth-century Mar Thoma churches in India, eleventh-century Orthodox churches in Russia, seventeenth-century Roman Catholic churches in New France, twenty-first-century house churches in China, and so on. Another possibility, however, is that no single form of Christianity can possibly image all the richness available in the Bible, whether in matters of social ethics (so that some Christians might obediently wage a war while others obediently advocate nonviolence) or worship (consider an African-American Baptist service versus a Greek Orthodox service versus a Taiwanese Presbyterian service).[13]

We do not have to choose just one of these options to govern our understanding of unity and diversity in the Church. We might well believe simultaneously that our denomination is the best of the extant choices, that it yet shares a more fundamental "mere Christianity" with lots of other groups, and that at least some of those other groups might have a better way of dealing with this or that question or challenge than we do. One can go even further, without lapsing into sheer relativism, by affirming that this denomination is the best *for me*, or *for me* to belong to *in this context*, or for *anyone* to belong to *in this context*, while holding on to the other recognitions as well.

We should see that denominational diversity is not the same as the existence of different attitudes and approaches toward culture. Every major Christian tradition in the world has had to deal with the disestablishment of ecclesiastical privilege and status—in the United States, Canada, Australia, and elsewhere. Traditions that began as small minorities have experienced the challenge of wielding cultural power as majorities in changed circumstances, whether Puritans in early modern England and New England, Mennonites in southern Manitoban villages, Baptists in most of the American South, Mormons in Utah, and so on. Richard Niebuhr's "Christ and Culture" typology defines various modes that churches and individual Christians can adopt depending on their situation, rather than being locked forever into a mode that used to define their tradition in a quite different cultural context. History shows us Catholics and Orthodox sometimes being "against" culture, Calvinists and Lutherans sometimes being "of culture," Baptists sometimes being "above" culture, and so on.[14]

Recognition of these different and changing responses to historical vicissitudes should have at least three salutary implications. First, an individual Christian or group of Christians should be open to reconsidering the position they have maintained heretofore in the name of tradition if the cultural situation has changed importantly. The sectarianism that made sense under persecution five centuries ago might make no sense in a free country today, while the hegemony that seemed to function well in the Middle Ages or in a colonial situation cannot work as well in the modern era. (There is a psychological parallel that might be instructive. "Coping mechanisms" that emerged understandably and usefully in the circumstances of one's childhood may no longer serve the teenager or middle-aged adult who now inhabits a quite different situation.)

Second, we should find grounds for ecumenical cooperation among those adopting the same posture toward their surrounding society. Many Christians are finding such grounds today, as they have in the past. Many more could do so. We do not have to agree with each other on everything. In fact, we need not agree on anything more than what is necessary in order to press for objective X. And if we agree that the cause of Christ will somehow be advanced by pressing for X in a particular mode of "Christ and culture," then why not band together with likeminded folk?

Third, we should be willing to at least consider affirming others who take different approaches from ours, even those at apparent cross-purposes to ours, as we recognize that Christ may have called such people to this apparently contradictory, but perhaps also complementary, stance. Maybe God is saying something through them that God cannot say through us, given the complexity of the situation. And we will be more willing to affirm them if we realize that our own tradition might end up "there" someday, or perhaps even has already been "there" in the past. To be sure, we might *not* affirm others if we believe the circumstances do not justify it. I am not commending either relativism or sentimentality. But we should be at least open to the possibility that our way is not identical with, or completely comprehensive of, all that God wants to do and show and say through all Christians in this situation.

At the "micro" levels of Christian families, churches, and special-purpose organizations, we ought to grant each other all the liberty we can. The only legitimate constraint on diversity should be whatever is *essential* to the *mission* of the (little) society to which we belong. Insistence on conformity of belief and practice too often merely serves the "comfort level" of insecure leaders. Creativity is not evidently in abundant supply in contemporary Western Christianity, and parents, pastors, and presidents who suppress difference on any matter that is not mission-critical are hurting, rather than helping, both themselves and those under their care.

Beyond all of this ecumenical openness, we recall that John Howard Yoder boldly affirmed that there is one best model for considering the questions of Church and culture. I think he is right that there is, but clearly I disagree with him on what particular model is best. To this last, comprehensive question, and to more of its implications, we turn in the next chapters.

MAKING THE BEST OF IT

DIETRICH BONHOEFFER POSED THE BASIC question of Christian discipleship: "Who is Jesus Christ, for us, today?"[1] The Christian religion centers on Jesus Christ: knowing him, proclaiming him, serving him, and enjoying him and all his blessings. Christian identity, orientation, and motivation arise from our answers to this question: How does each of us see Jesus Christ in our place and time?

In this book I have, in effect, posed the complementary question: *Who are we, for Jesus Christ, today?* Understanding and practicing Christian ethics is primarily about answering these questions: What sort of person am I, and what sort am I to be, for Jesus Christ, in this place and time? What sort of family, or congregation, or organization are we as Christians, and what sort are we to be, for Jesus Christ, today?

I have advocated a renewed Christian realism. "Realism" can be merely a euphemism for the cynical, jaded, clever, arrogant, manipulative, messianic, or self-serving. Any ethic that awards itself the title of "realism" had better be realistic about the dangers of hubris and condescension toward other views. I should also make clear that I do not mean merely to recover Reinhold Niebuhr's political theology, often identified as "Christian realism." I have learned a lot from Niebuhr, but I differ with him in crucial respects and my thought has been influenced even more by others, especially C. S. Lewis, Dietrich Bonhoeffer, David Martin, Glenn Tinder, and Martin Marty.[2] What I set out herein is called Christian realism because I cannot think of a better term for an ethic that tries to be true to the nature of things, to *reality:* true to the nature of the world, to the nature of God's revelation in Scripture, to the nature of the experience of God's people across several millennia, to the nature of our limitations and sinfulness, and especially to the nature of Jesus Christ as we know him, and hear his call, today.

This renewed Christian realism presents a crucial alternative to the two options most often offered to Christians today: (1) withdrawing from certain worldly institutions, or at least from sectors of those institutions that involve coercion and violence, into holy communities that bear witness to the alternative ethic of the Kingdom of God; and (2) wielding all the power available in the name of Christ to draw the world under the rule of the Kingdom of God. I certainly can see that there are circumstances so extremely dark that the Church must adopt a "Christ against culture" position. There are terrible societies in the world today, as there have been in every age. I also recognize that there might be a circumstance so promising that the Church might be tempted to think in terms of "Christ transforming culture." But I daresay that there are few cultures so bereft of the light of God that Christians must be entirely against them. I am even more convinced that there are, and will be, no cultures so open to the light of God that they are, or can be, conformed utterly to the way of Christ. Thus I think most of us need an alternative model for making our way in the world today.

To return to H. Richard Niebuhr's famous "Christ and culture" typology, let us consider a phrase now common in

Christian discussion of the Kingdom of God: "already, but not yet." Two of Niebuhr's types offer versions of an "already" motif: "Christ of culture" and "Christ above culture," while "not yet" is characteristic of "Christ against culture." Niebuhr's fifth type, "Christ transforming culture" does conform to the tension of "already, but not yet." But only Niebuhr's fourth type, "Christ in paradox with culture," retains the full tension of "already, but not yet"—itself literally a paradox. That paradox has sometimes devolved into acquiescence ("We cannot figure out what's going on, so let's just obey the authorities and lead comfortable, quiet lives") or been resolved by compartmentalization ("Caesar in this part of life, Christ in that"). I advocate what could be described as an *activist* version of the fourth type, acknowledging the paradoxes of life while trusting in the ongoing guidance of the Lord Jesus—or, if this makes more sense, a *chastened* version of the fifth model, "Christ transforming culture." (I freely make this allowance because I believe my views line up nicely with those of many Reformed friends, such as Richard Mouw and Nicholas Wolterstorff.[3])

Let us turn now to a lingering issue that must be clarified before we can conclude. I have cited John Yoder a number of times, largely because I think his will be, for many readers, the most attractive and provocative alternative to the model I offer. By now it should be obvious that I disagree with Yoder in a number of respects, even as I agree with him in others. It is time to state the heart of our agreement and disagreement.

I return to a passage I quoted early on:

> Some elements of culture the church categorically rejects (pornography, tyranny, cultic idolatry). Other dimensions of culture it accepts within clear limits (economic production,

commerce, the graphic arts, paying taxes for peacetime civil government). To still other dimensions of culture Christian faith gives a new motivation and coherence (agriculture, family life, literacy, conflict resolution, empowerment). Still others it strips of their claims to possess autonomous truth and value, and uses them as vehicles of communication (philosophy, language, Old Testament ritual, music). Still other forms of culture are *created* by the Christian churches (hospitals, service of the poor, generalized education, egalitarianism, abolitionism, feminism).[4]

Yoder does not advocate a simplistic "Christ against culture" model—neither do his latter-day epigones, such as Stanley Hauerwas and William Willimon. They are too intelligent and too Christian for that. I agree strongly with this passage of Yoder's. It is an excellent start at making the sorts of distinctions we all must make in terms of this or that element of culture, this or that pattern in culture, this or that institution of culture, and this or that opportunity or threat posed by culture.

My fundamental disagreement has to do with the cultural opportunities as well as the threats posed by societies whose dominant institutions are open to Christian participation. Most societies allow Christians to participate in their dominant institutions—so long as those Christians leave their distinctive convictions aside while assisting those societies toward their self-chosen goals. But I am thinking of societal openness to Christians participating *as Christians,* with their convictions properly and fully operative in what they think, say, and do. The Roman Empire in many respects was not open to such Christian participation, and that is the cultural context of the New Testament. But what is supposed to happen when the emperor not only opens a door to

Christians but welcomes them in, as Constantine did? Those who share Yoder's views see this as the Great Disaster, the co-optation of the Church by the world, which they never tire of identifying as the root of all sorts of evil. But what if we see the new era inaugurated by Constantine as an evangelistic success story, as simply the logical working out of the mission of God in the Roman Empire—with full recognition of all of the ambiguities, limitations, failures, *and blessings* that attend the mission of God being accomplished through human beings in the world?

Few readers of this book live in anything like "Christendom" today. Yet most of us have far more opportunity to participate in the life of our culture than did the first Christians—including participation in every institution of society. What are Christians supposed to do in this context? Keep acting like a repressed minority, when we are not repressed and not a minority? Yoder and his allies seem to suggest that it would have been best for Christians to retain that mentality.[5] As always, he makes an attractive case, as we stand many centuries downstream of Constantine's era and rue the entanglements of Christianity and culture that have occurred since his day.

Examples lie ready at hand. Touring the former papal palace at Avignon one hears of medieval popes who presented a golden rose to that year's favorite prince at Christmas and granted the privilege of kissing the pope's toe and then reading the third lesson at the mass. Generation after generation of American politicians have been heard to claim God for their side, ignoring the great wisdom of Abraham Lincoln, who grimly recognized that God might be judging *both* sides in the Civil War. One reads of widespread abuse of Native Canadian children in the mandatory residential schools established by federal governments and run by the major Christian denominations. Clerical blessing of colonial oppression of peasants and natives throughout the Americas, Christian support for the African slave trade and later for apartheid, repression of women's civil rights in the name of Christian order—all of these and more can be listed as wicked outcomes of Christian participation in the governing institutions of the world.

As attractive as the option to eschew power and glorify weakness may be—to maintain one's sanctity without compromise, and to denounce both worldly institutions and one's fellow Christians who participate in them—we must nevertheless return to these questions: Now that we are members of the imperial court, so to speak, who are we, for Jesus Christ, today? When we have the opportunity not only to purchase goods or services from a company but also to influence or even run that company by working in it or buying stock in it—who are we, for Jesus Christ, today? When we have the opportunity to vote or run for office and to share in the governance of cities and states—who are we, for Jesus Christ, today? When new forms of dissemination arise, and audiences emerge for art and entertainment shaped by Christian values—who are we, for Jesus Christ, today?

We are supposed to act like what we are: redeemed and reoriented human beings who have heard God's primeval call to make the best of it, using the resources providence has put to hand. That is how Christians reformed the excesses and debaucheries of the medieval church in both the Protestant and Catholic Reformations. That is how Abraham Lincoln provided saving—the adjective is not too strong—leadership to America in its greatest crisis. That is how Christians have sacrificed greatly to provide good schools, good farms, good water supplies, and many more forms of assistance around the world. That is how Christians have advocated for land reform, for the end of slavery and apartheid, for women's suffrage, and for universal human rights. Christians did all the things Yoder wanted them to do—pray, proclaim, form godly communities that modeled alternatives, serve society in various other positive respects—*and* they wielded power: the power of information media, the power of money, the power of politics, even (let us not be squeamish) the power of guns. And good things happened. Not unequivocally good things, which we should not expect before Christ returns. But better things happened than were apparently going to occur without the use of these kinds of power.

That, then, is the point. Are Christians to work with others to wield power—not only spiritual power through prayer and worship, not only moral power through holy living and charity, not only persuasive power in evangelism and advice, crucial as these are, but also the power of coercion, whether financial, political, or military? And are Christians who operate in the vortices of power to do what such people invariably must do: make deals, even compromises, in order to make the best of it? I believe that the cumulative testimony of the Bible—the *whole* Bible—and of Church history is that yes, we sometimes should.

If we are to adopt this dangerous stance—and dangerous it certainly is, for lurking everywhere are snares of pride, greed, lust, self-righteousness, and self-deception—we need a clear sense of mission and vocation. We need to shape our lives by gospel standards, and to respond with both obedience to Christ and resistance to forces that seek to misshape our lives, to optimize our participation in the mission of

God. How can we engage fully and properly in public life, as God grants us opportunity to do so?

We can look at the question of the shape of our lives in terms of three elements: (1) what we do to shape them, which I will call *construction*; (2) the situation in which we do that construction, which I will call *context*; and (3) the intermittent, interrupting, and sometimes interesting surprises that occur, which I will call *contingencies*. And I will look at how we shape our lives in three modes: individual, family, and church.

CONSTRUCTION

It may seem a truism that the shape of our lives should reflect God's mission and Christ's particular call upon us. But our lives often don't reflect those crucial realities. Because of evil in ourselves and in our surroundings, which is to say because of the confusion, and enticement, and oppression both within and around us, our lives often do not reflect what we profess about the mission of God and the vocation Christ has given us.

What would our priorities appear to be, based on an analysis of our bank accounts, credit card statements, homes, closets, garages, e-mail files, browser caches, and calendars? The Bible says plainly, "By their fruits ye shall know them" (Matt. 7:16). A basic obligation of discipleship is to shed whatever impedes it and acquire whatever improves it. One could profitably make time periodically to ask one simple question of each element of one's own life: "How does this help me be who I am supposed to be for Jesus Christ, today?" Families and churches can do the same: "How does this way of meeting, this schedule, this activity, this form of decision-making, this hierarchy, or this budget help us to be who we are supposed to be for Jesus Christ, today?"

Such an assessment obviously requires good theology, requires an appropriate understanding of the mission of God and the call of Christ on us, here and now. A deficient understanding of mission and vocation will prompt us to keep in or throw out the wrong things. It is crucial for individuals, families, and churches to educate ourselves theologically on these matters and to remind ourselves to keep *mission and vocation* in the foreground. We should keep asking, as our lives go on, "What do we need to learn *now* to be who we are supposed to be for Jesus Christ, *today*?"

In a wide-ranging study of major American denominations, the Search Institute of Minneapolis determined that the most important factor in producing a mature, well-balanced, and well-integrated Christian faith was not excellent preaching, worship, small-group fellowship, or anything else but *adult Christian education*.[6] And yet I daresay no element in contemporary church life in most areas of North American, the UK, or Down Under is more poorly served. A sermon and a home Bible study each week cannot possibly suffice to teach us all we need to know about the Christian tradition *and* how to apply it to contemporary challenges.

Consider this. A basic college or seminary course in New Testament introduction would take roughly 150 hours for most students to complete: lectures, discussions, readings, assignments, and examinations. At the pace of a thirty-minute sermon plus a one-hour Bible discussion plus one hour of individual preparation per week, it would take a little more than a year to put in the same amount of time. Allowing that eight to ten courses of this sort would add up to a single year of theological education, one is looking at a decade or more to gain anything like that single year's worth of full-time study. Add an hour of personal study to prepare for an hour of adult education, however, and now the timeline is cut almost in half.

We have got to take time to read, and read well. We have got to find ourselves teachers, ideally in person, whether every week at church or regularly at conferences and summer schools, in which the lively dynamic of personal encounter is richest. For people in remote places or in under-resourced churches, study may have to be online, and busy people can make time for distance education when in-person instruction is hard or impossible to schedule. We have got to make friends of Christians who are similarly serious about growing into spiritual maturity and devote time to study together. We have to move on from milk to meat, as the New Testament exhorts us (1 Cor. 3:1–3; Heb. 5:11–6:2).

Moreover, theological knowledge is crucial, but not itself sufficient:

> For this very reason, you must make every effort to support your faith with goodness, and goodness with knowledge, and knowledge with self-control, and self-control with endurance, and endurance with godliness, and godliness with mutual affection, and mutual affection with love. For if these things are yours and are increasing among you, they keep you from being ineffective and unfruitful in the knowledge of our Lord Jesus Christ. (2 Pet. 1:5–8)

To this discipline of study we must add the other holy habits of the normal Christian life, such as prayer, worship, charity, and the like. Our habits are the basic structures of our lives, so we need to scrutinize each one—our eating habits, our entertainment habits, our shopping habits, our thinking habits, our worrying habits, our friendship habits—to see, again, how each one helps us, or doesn't help us, participate in God's mission and fulfill our calling.

We must also consider how we have arranged these units in the overall shape of our lives. We must try to remove obvious contraries. Reading elevating literature in the morning and debasing literature at night won't get us far, just as exercising in the morning and overeating at night won't make us healthy. But we also must arrange things according to the priorities of God's mission and our calling. Exercise is good, but most of us would be neglecting our divine calling if we undertook all the rigors necessary to sculpt our bodies into athletic or aesthetic excellence. Bible study is good, too, of course. But I have known students so enthusiastic about their Bible study—whether alone or in groups—that they neglected their coursework and thus jeopardized the academic and professional careers to which God was calling them. Entertainment is good, but not at the expense of one's responsibilities at work or at home. And the opposites are true also, to be sure: family life and work must not crowd out the physical, spiritual, intellectual, aesthetic, emotional, social, and recreational dimensions of our lives.

Is the goal, then, the perfectly balanced life? Many Christians think it is, and seek the correct ratio of Bible study to prayer to work to leisure to sleep to exercise to . . . No, the goal is to be who we are meant to be here and now in order to grow in love for God and do God's work in the world. And, since the context keeps changing, so must the shape of our lives. Let's turn to consider that now.

CONTEXT

Earlier I discussed the crucial category of time in regard to our vocation. "To everything there is a season," Ecclesiastes reminds us, and each season of life includes its own limitations and opportunities. Just as it is foolish to try to educate a child at the level of a graduate student or to train a "weekend warrior" at the level of an elite athlete, so it is foolish to formulate a daily, weekly, or annual regimen for everyone to follow—or even for ourselves to follow in perpetuity.

The classics of Christian spirituality routinely refer to ladders, mountains, and other metaphors of upward progress. The progress, however, is not always simply upward. Sometimes we must move sideways, or even backward, to attend to parts of our selves and our lives that now should come to the foreground of our attention. Whereas we might have focused on particular habits, traits, and other "growth edges"—not exclusively, to be sure, since there are some things to which we always must attend—now the "curriculum" of our lives moves on to something else. God respects the fact that we cannot make progress on everything at once. So, under God's providence, the context of our lives undergoes shifts to provide us with fresh stimuli, challenges, blessings, and limitations.

We must not attempt to ignore a new situation and to maintain the same shape of life that worked well before. Some things do need to continue: prayer, Bible reading, fellowship, worship, mission, and so on. But even those should be reshaped by the altered environment of our lives—not merely capitulating to the demands of the world, of course (Rom. 12:2), but realistically ordering our spiritual disciplines and missional practices as healthily and effectively as possible in the current context. Some elements of our lives might be quite new: we studied then, we practice now; we were enthusiastic then, we persevere now; we were oblivious then, we comprehend now; we were childless then, we have children now; we were growing and healthy then, we are older and sicker now. We thus must squarely face both the limitations and the opportunities in the chapter of life we now live.

Realism is key here. Christians living under a repressive regime, for example, must reshape their practices accordingly. They must not abandon meeting, except in the most extreme instances (Heb. 10:25); they must not abandon prayer, as Daniel did not (Dn. 6); they must not remain silent about the gospel, as the apostles refused to do (Acts 4–5). But they must take into account the lack of dedicated meeting spaces like those available to Christians in freer countries, the lack of Bibles and other Christian literature, the lack of freedom of conversation, the lack of economic and professional opportunities for those refusing to kowtow to the state, and so on. As the earliest Christians made their way as best they could under the frowns of both Jerusalem and Rome, so Christians make their way as best they can in difficult situations today.

Life's difficulties come in different shapes. Recall the Christian businesspeople and professionals in Hong Kong who must work longer hours than they might think is best for a healthy family and church life because there simply are no jobs that allow one to work less than long days Monday to Friday and some part of Saturday as well. Farmers, factory workers, small-business owners, and many others around the world (who certainly cannot simply opt out of their societies) also generally work very long hours. Parents, especially of young children or of those with special needs, toil long and hard, day after day, year after year. What shall Christian leaders recommend to them regarding an appropriate balance of family life, personal devotional time, recreation, and so on? It is so easy, so absurd, and so offensive for those of us in North American professional comfort to prescribe the "normal Christian life" in terms that are simply impossible for others. Much better instead for communities of people in like contexts to encourage each other in the constraints peculiar to those situations—even as they do all they can to improve those contexts—which is another crucial reason for Christians to meet together regularly.

It helps greatly to see our context as only temporary and as given to us by God in order to get some good things accomplished in this world that cannot be accomplished any other (easier) way. Yes, our contexts are shaped by evil: the evil in individual leaders at every level, the systemic evil in institutions, the evil in traditions whose influence persists down the generations, and so on. Christianity encourages us to do what we can to resist evil and reshape these contexts toward shalom. But God rules above it all. And, paradoxically and dialectically, God works through and even sometimes in these elements to occasion opportunities for God's people to serve the divine purposes and to themselves be blessed—even as those opportunities often are accompanied by suffering and strain (Rom. 8:28).

Indeed, God rules above, and works through and even in, the interruptions, surprises, and "emergent-cies" of life.

CONTINGENCIES

The Book of Acts is full of interruptions. Christians are going about their business, presumably fulfilling their callings, when something odd occurs. A beggar accosts them and asks for money. Peter and John have none to give, and they heal him instead (Acts 3). Members of the church are donating money for various worthy causes—what can be more routine than "tithes and offerings"?—but one couple lies to the church and, as Peter makes clear, to the Holy Spirit, and they fall down dead (Acts 5). Preachers are arrested and jailed—a nasty kind of interruption—and then freed by divine intervention—a splendid kind of interruption (Acts 12, 16).

One such early Christian is Philip. Philip is a good man—a deacon, in fact—and an effective evangelist:

> Philip went down to the city of Samaria and proclaimed the Messiah to them. The crowds with one accord listened eagerly to what was said by Philip, hearing and seeing the signs that he did, for unclean spirits, crying with loud shrieks, came out of many who were possessed; and many others who were paralyzed or lame were cured. So there was great joy in that city. (Acts 8:5–8)

Some confusion breaks out, and Peter and John come down from Jerusalem to sort it out. But when they leave, does Philip resume his apparently very successful ministry? No, he does not. Instead of continuing this profitable work, he is suddenly ordered by the Holy Spirit to a strange place to encounter a strange man doing a strange thing:

> Then an angel of the Lord said to Philip, "Get up and go toward the south to the road that goes down from Jerusalem to Gaza." (This is a wilderness road.) So he got up and went.
> Now there was an Ethiopian eunuch, a court official of the Candace, queen of the Ethiopians, in charge of her entire treasury. He had come to Jerusalem to worship and

was returning home; seated in his chariot, he was reading the prophet Isaiah.

Then the Spirit said to Philip, "Go over to this chariot and join it." So Philip ran up to it and heard him reading the prophet Isaiah. He asked, "Do you understand what you are reading?"

He replied, "How can I, unless someone guides me?" And he invited Philip to get in and sit beside him.

Now the passage of the scripture that he was reading was this: "Like a sheep he was led to the slaughter, and like a lamb silent before its shearer, so he does not open his mouth. In his humiliation justice was denied him. Who can describe his generation? For his life is taken away from the earth."

The eunuch asked Philip, "About whom, may I ask you, does the prophet say this, about himself or about someone else?"

Then Philip began to speak, and starting with this scripture, he proclaimed to him the good news about Jesus.

As they were going along the road, they came to some water; and the eunuch said, "Look, here is water! What is to prevent me from being baptized?" He commanded the chariot to stop, and both of them, Philip and the eunuch, went down into the water, and Philip baptized him.

When they came up out of the water, the Spirit of the Lord snatched Philip away; the eunuch saw him no more, and went on his way rejoicing. But Philip found himself at Azotus, and as he was passing through the region, he proclaimed the good news to all the towns until he came to Caesarea. (Acts 8:26–40)

There is an intermingling of the amazingly supernatural and the entirely pragmatic in this story, a laconic intermingling that is characteristic of the Book of Acts. It is as if the Holy Spirit says, "Good, we've got this Samaria thing sorted out. Now I need a gifted evangelist to talk with this influential

Ethiopian who is about to leave the country. Philip, that's you. Go."

Philip goes, and he proves to be the right person for the job. The Ethiopian official is converted and, according to tradition, sets in motion the conversion of that entire nation—one of the two claimants (along with Armenia) to the title of "first Christian nation" in the world. It is an astonishingly strategic encounter, and it starts with the Holy Spirit telling Philip (How?) to go (How?) and Philip going—and then proceeds to depict Philip doing what he characteristically does, evangelizing, with wonderful results.

The story ends as strangely as it begins, with the Spirit snatching Philip away, redeploying him elsewhere until he comes to Caesarea—where the narrative leaves him for good, except for one small mention later in the Book of Acts: Philip the evangelist is residing in Caesarea now, with a Christian family (his four daughters are prophets), and hosting Paul, Luke, and others on their way to Jerusalem.

What is normal and what is supra-normal in this narrative? When Christians are living in the Spirit, there is no stark division between the one and the other. We should shape our lives today to be open to the radical, and even instant, reshaping that arrives in the form of interruptions, crises, opportunities, and even disasters. For, again, Christ is Lord of all *now*, and under his guidance the Church makes its way over the ever-shifting terrain of this troubled earth. Philip does not become someone he is not—indeed, it is because he is an evangelist that he is moved from one particular situation to another particular situation. But he could easily have misread these moves as distractions, as temptations, as removals from his true work. "Why leave Samaria, where crowds have been rejoicing, to stand by the side of this deserted road and talk to a single foreigner on a chariot heading home?"

To be sure, we must not see every interruption as a blessing in disguise to be seized at once. Particularly if we are not enjoying the current work to which God has called us, we may be quick indeed to interpret any opportunity to escape as the will of God. Interruptions sometimes are temptations to abandon obedience, to opt for the trivial and easy over the important and hard. Christians therefore must be as Philip was: *in the Spirit*, able to discern the Spirit's voice and then willing to do what God asks, whether it is to travel here and there from one exciting evangelistic encounter to the next, to make this apparently preposterous journey to encounter the Ethiopian eunuch, or to settle down in Caesarea, raise a family, and perform the same ministry but in yet another different mode. We need to know the Spirit so well—know the Bible (inspired by the Spirit), know the history of God's people (led by the Spirit), know the results of Christian discipleship (the fruit of the Spirit), and so on across the many resources the Holy Spirit has provided us—that we will recognize and respond well to a Spirit-ordained interruption when it arises.

In sum, we can retain the ideal of a "balanced life," but now in a way radically qualified by our understanding of mission and vocation. Balance in this case is not the balance of a dancer raised on one foot or even of a spinning top. It is much more dynamic: the balance of a runner traversing a broken-up and heaving landscape. To maintain the balance for this step and to prepare well for the next, the runner might have to lean way off center: to be deliberately off-balance in relation to any particular step, but properly balanced to progress in the journey. This metaphor rules out both the idea of a detailed template according to which every Christian life ought to be lived, on the one hand, and the utter confusion in which no option, no matter how extreme, can be judged as wrong, on the other. The proof is in the success of the journey. Missteps of either sort—trying to maintain a static, universal ideal or indulging in a capricious impulse—will result in a fall. The question is: Does the runner stay on the path and keep going toward the goal?

Realism requires constant renegotiation of changing contexts and contingencies. We must maintain the unchanging elements of any proper Christian living, and we also must adapt them to the features of the present occasion. It will not always be clear that we are, in fact, making the right choice. Once again, ambiguity cannot be avoided.

What we can try to avoid, however, is succumbing to either pride or sloth. Pride is the easier sin to spot: it's the excessive confidence that we are on the right side of history, we are doing the right things, and we are going to make it all right. This triumphalism is the besetting sin of all crusaders, however well intentioned. The Book of Revelation depicts the Lord's return to an earth in turmoil, a world badly in need of God's salvation, not to a planet brilliantly and beautifully arranged to which God need contribute nothing further. Wherever we go, there we are—and that means wherever we go, sin and inefficiency and conflict and unintended consequences show up, too. Pride must be resisted, even for Christians—in fact, especially for Christians who are convinced we are doing the will of God. Our theology, our worship, and our Spirit-guided consciences ought to keep hubris decisively in check.

Sloth lurks in the other ditch, a sin that is perhaps more in need of exposure today in a time of doubt, even despair, over the possibility of real, lasting, and beneficial transformation of ourselves or of the institutions in which we work. Reinhold Niebuhr warns us against sloth, not as laziness, but as what he calls "sensuality": "Sensuality represents an effort to escape from the freedom and the infinite possibilities of spirit by becoming lost in the detailed processes, activities and interests of existence, an effort which results inevitably in unlimited devotion to limited values."[7] Robin Lovin offers a brilliant and sensitive exposition of these twin themes of pride and sensuality/sloth. He warns us that sloth provides the false comfort of total absorption in work and play that examines no fundamental issues, of the complete preoccupation with the procedural and the trivial so as never to ask the hard questions of why we are doing this and who gets to decide such things. One can be very busy in such activity, even exhausted by it, but it is sloth nonetheless if one never stops to analyze the whole situation, let alone improve it:

> Those who find their work meaningless and who lack significant personal relationships will find much encouragement in a consumer-oriented society to devote themselves to new forms of gadgetry and to establish a firm decorative control over their limited personal environment. These evasions of freedom, along with the forms of indulgence more usually associated with "sensuality," must be seen as genuine forms of sin.
> ... We must also identify a form of institutional sin that elicits sensuality or sloth from persons by demanding commitments that preclude responsible attention to the range of choices and responsibilities that they ought to be attending to for themselves. The "up or out," "publish or perish" career trajectories imposed by businesses, law firms, and academic institutions provide familiar examples of this sort of pressure. ... Those who yield to these pressures are often pictured

as ambitious, "fast-track" achievers whose chief temptation would seem to be to emulate the pride of their seniors and superiors. In fact, however, their achievements are often expressions of sensuality and sloth. The rising executive or scholar abandons the difficult balancing of obligations that marks a life of freedom constrained by human finitude, and substitutes a single set of goals defined by outside authorities. . . . The over-achiever stills anxiety in precisely the way that Niebuhr describes the sensual evasion, "by finding a god in a person or process outside the self."[8]

This challenge to avoid both pride and sloth is so crucial that I want to emphasize it by quoting one more brilliant thinker on the question. David Martin warns of sloth in his distinctive way:

> The other danger is forgetfulness of promise, and immersion in the everyday. When that happens everything that *is* appears indefinitely prolonged. Material wants and satisfactions set the limit on desire and cut off the horizon of hope. People cease to hear any more this prophetic warning that God remains God and that the demands of righteousness and justice are not set aside.[9]

We must not assume that we can completely remake anything in our world. Nor may we assume that things must remain mostly as they are. Instead, we must make the best of them, neither in proud confidence nor in slothful acquiescence, but in hopeful faithfulness to, and in, the command and power of God.

When we do have opportunity, then, as most readers of this book will have, to engage public life in the furtherance of shalom, what can we do and say? That's what we'll discuss in our next chapter.

BEHAVING IN PUBLIC

GROUNDS FOR HOPE

It is easy for Christians in Europe, North America, Australia, and New Zealand to be discouraged about the future of Christianity in those places.[1] Many observers have tracked the decline of Christian influence over the past century or so, measured in references to Christian values and themes in public discourse, church attendance, the role of clergy in public events, the presence of Christian symbols in public places, and so on. Conversely, the trend toward greater secularity seems to proceed apace: Sundays treated as Saturdays in both commerce and recreation; liberalization of laws regarding sex, marriage, and family; religious people depicted in popular media as fanatics, buffoons, or hypocrites—the list goes on.

Yet, as we have noted, history does not proceed in single, straight lines indefinitely, and the trajectory of secularization or "de-Christianization" is one such non-single, non-straight line.[2] For one thing, many trends in contemporary life are more in keeping with Christian values than ever, particularly in the treatment of those who are not moneyed, white, Christian, and male. For another, the modern world has seen the rise of various forms of religion alternative to the polite

Christianity that dominated Western Europe and its colonial offspring, from evangelical Protestantism of various stripes to a manifold Islam, Asian religions, and new religious movements that fuse elements of different traditions. For yet another, Christianity itself has not gone away. In the United States, church attendance since World War II has remained at the highest level in American history. Canadian religious interest and observance seems to have stopped declining and shows signs of reviving. Evangelical Christianity, conservative Catholicism, Islam, and other faiths are burgeoning in Britain and elsewhere in Europe. All in all, religion clearly is not "over," even in these countries where so many obituaries for religion have been recited.[3] Philip Jenkins speaks of a perennial paradox in Church history:

> The best indicator that Christianity is about to experience a vast expansion is a widespread conviction that the religion is doomed or in its closing days. Arguably the worst single moment in the history of West European Christianity occurred around 1798, with the Catholic church under severe persecution in much of Europe and skeptical, deist, and Unitarian movements in the ascendant across the Atlantic world. That particular trough also turned into an excellent foundation, from which various groups built the great missionary movement of the 19th century, the second evangelical revival, and the Catholic devotional revolution. . . . Quite possibly, the current sense of doom surrounding European Christianity will drive a comparable movement in the near future.[4]

As Martin Marty has observed about America (and the same is true of other countries), there is rarely a simple "culture war" binary to sum up all that is going on.[5] The cultural landscape

230 | RESPONDING TO THE CALL OF JESUS

instead is crisscrossed with alliances traversing various religious and philosophical lines: over abortion, environmentalism, overseas wars, regulation of business, taxation, welfare reform, immigration, national security, sexual difference, and on and on. Today's enemy on one issue may be needed as tomorrow's ally on another one. So the battles are fought with relative civility—relative, that is, to the shooting wars fought under religious banners elsewhere in the world and in our own history. Recognition of the propriety of such political alliances has come slowly to some religious groups that have seen the world in binary terms and insisted that only the pure could stand with the pure. Here is the crucial significance of Jerry Falwell's Moral Majority in the 1980s, and of the new religious right in the United States ever since: even Christian fundamentalists could form alliances with other kinds of Christians and—*mirabile dictu*—people of other faiths with a view to achieving as much as possible of their vision of shalom in their nation and the world.

The political and social question for those who hold to other religious or philosophical traditions, and perhaps particularly those for whom territory (Islam) or ethnicity (Hinduism) are major elements, is whether those traditions can equip and inspire them to participate in democracy in this constructive way, or whether they are bound to persist in absolutist categories and strategies that will not rest short of total social domination. Not every religion or philosophy comports with pluralistic liberal democracy.

The question for the rest of us—Christian or otherwise— who are committed to liberal democracy, the Western legal tradition, and the like is how much anti-pluralist absolutism we can welcome and accommodate in our society—including ostensibly Christian forms of absolutism. As Charles Taylor warns, "Liberalism can't and shouldn't claim complete cultural neutrality. Liberalism is also a fighting creed. The hospitable variant I espouse, as well as the most rigid forms, has to draw the line."[6]

Our multicultural societies are only now realizing that we do need to draw such a line. At least since 7/7 and 9/11 we have begun to face the facts that we cannot tolerate, much less affirm, everything and everyone, and that we cannot continue to absorb heterogeneous and heteronomous elements into our societies indefinitely without peril.[7] We must not go back to the terrible old days that kept out everyone who was not "just like us," despite the increasing call, in Europe, North America, and Australasia, of revanchist voices. In particular, we must maintain hospitality for as many of the world's needy as we can help. Yet we will have to move beyond merely celebrating pluralism as diversity to what Martin Marty calls pluralism as "a polity and a framework for action," "a way of organizing life and encouraging an ethos to develop."[8]

There are grounds for caution, yes, but also for both gratitude and hope. Secularization is not an irresistible force. There is no evidence of an irreversible decline of Christianity in the West. As Jenkins has reminded us, it is too rarely acknowledged amid all the prognostications of spiritual doom that "un-Christian" and even "post-Christian" societies have been converted or revived time and again in Western history—whether during monastic revivals in the Middle Ages, the sixteenth-century Reformations, the Puritan and Pietist movements, the eighteenth-century evangelical revivals, the nineteenth-century renewal movements among Catholics and Protestants, and so on. There is no evident reason why such societies cannot be drawn to the gospel in our own time.

Even if our societies do not turn decisively to an authentic and healthy Christianity in our time, there are yet grounds for realistic engagement: for patience, strategy, compromise, and trust in God to work in and through our broken, but still useful, cultural institutions to produce a measure of shalom and a way for the gospel to reach still more people—as God does through us, broken but still useful.

We now should pause to ask ourselves a fundamental question: Is the imposition of a Christian regime in America, or Canada, or Britain, or elsewhere *desirable*, even if it were possible?

Let us recall instances from the modern past in which Christians did exercise comprehensive cultural control: the Christian "total cultures" of sixteenth-century Calvinist Geneva or Catholic Spain, of seventeenth-century Puritan England under Cromwell or Catholic France under the Sun King, eighteenth-century quasi-Puritan New England, the nineteenth-century American South or Orthodox and czarist Russia, or twentieth-century South Africa and Rhodesia. Each of these cases gives us serious pause. As grateful as we should be for the blessings God has given the world through Christian civilization, the record also shows that we Christians—who are, in Luther's phrase, *simul justus et peccator* (at the same time justified and yet sinners)—are capable of selfish mischief, let alone unintentional damage, when we wield unchecked power. We are, inevitably because of sin, *worldly* when we run the show.

I agree with Glenn Tinder's warning:

> The political meaning of Christianity, then, does not lie
> in the ideal of a Christian society for no such society can
> exist. . . . Society is the unity of human beings in subjection

to one another and to the worldly necessities underlying custom, law, and governance. The terms *Christian* and *society* cannot logically be joined.[9]

As Reinhold Niebuhr reminds us constantly, we are never in more danger of rationalizing our particular, sinful agendas than when we think we are acting simply and purely for the glory of God and doing simply and purely the will of God. Worse, when Christians govern in the name of God, according to what they sincerely believe, or even affect to believe, to be the precise will of God in each detail, there are no obvious grounds on which substantial dissent can be raised. (We Christians already have plenty of examples of small-scale political pathologies in our families and churches that feature those in authority styling themselves representatives of God's will and brooking no dissent.)

We must consider seriously the proposition that God does not want us to "take over America (or Britain, or Canada, or what-have-you) for Jesus" but instead to bring the goodness of Christian motivations, values, and insights to the God-ordained project of earth-keeping that we share with our non-Christian neighbors in a pluralized society. Even as we believe that authentic Christianity will improve any situation—and I do believe that—so we also should affirm that God works through others to advance justice and charity in the world, and to keep our own sin, and especially the sin that proceeds under the banner of Christian righteousness, in check.[10]

Those who write as I do sometimes are accused of prioritizing allegiance to liberal democracy over commitment to Christianity. And some might think I am somehow antipathetic to the happy circumstance in which a majority of citizens freely supports Christian values in a given society. Both of these charges are false. I am simply registering a Christian suspicion of all majority power, much less unchecked power, whether wielded by Christians or anyone else short of the Lord Jesus himself. And I thus recommend pluralism to help us in this penultimate era, an era of widespread and increasing pluralism, given the fallenness of everyone, including us, until God achieves God's ultimate purposes and we enjoy the immediate reign of Christ. We ought not to proceed in the hope that we will soon be able to "win (our country) for Christ," nor ought we remain disengaged from the messier aspects of cultural work and influence. We should remember that God is indeed sovereignly overseeing, ordaining, and guiding world history to good ends throughout *and through* the societies with which God currently has to work.

SHOW

The multitude of Christian congregations, denominations, and other organizations in the world today is itself an example of modern plurality. So how are we doing in modeling successful cooperation with other Christians? Can we give the idea of constructive pluralism some plausibility by our own actions? It's one thing to say, "Here's how we think it might work." It's a wonderfully different thing to say, "Here's how we actually *do* it."

At the local levels, let's ask again: How well do we handle diversity in our families, congregations, or denominations? How much do we seek not only *common* ground for our life together but also the flourishing of our complementary *differences* for the enrichment of each individual and of each other? Every society must insist on a certain amount of conformity of belief and activity, or nothing can be done together. But beyond what is necessary, our families and churches— like most groups—tend toward maximal conformity instead of maximal creativity. Cultivation of diversity can seem inefficient; it is, at least initially, more costly than uniformity in time, effort, and attention. But if we fail to provide places for different people to grow, and to grow together, we will alienate both our own "non-standard" brothers and sisters and also, in the case of churches and other Christian organizations, all those outside our company who might have wanted to join but now see that they would not be welcome *as themselves*. Such an attitude fosters a kind of social inbreeding that inevitably results in pathology. God has so arranged the world that we actually *need* a certain amount of diversity just to avoid going wrong, let alone to help us go more and more right.

We return to the metaphor of gardening. Are we deliberately planting diversity? Are we making room for it? Are we feeding it, nurturing it, inviting it? Or are we worried by it, fearful of it, and quick to discourage and uproot it? Leadership styles among parents or pastors are key to setting the tone for everyone else, and it takes a convinced, secure, and capable parent or pastor to actually welcome diversity while also enlisting it in the common good.

At the denominational level, how much effort do we make to consider what the Mennonites or the Anglicans, the Baptists or the Pentecostals, the Methodists or the Presbyterians have to say to the rest of us out of their *differences,* not just out of the affirmations we share in common with other Christians? Our patterns of ecumenical cooperation tend to bracket our differences rather than celebrate and capitalize on them. Finding common ground has been the necessary first step in ecumenical relations and activity, but the next step is to acknowledge and enjoy what God has done elsewhere in the Body of Christ. If at the congregational level we are willing to say, "I can't do everything myself, for I am an ear: I must consult with a hand or an eye on this matter," I suggest that we do the same among traditions. In fact, if we do *not* regularly and programmatically consult with each other, we are tacitly affirming that we have no need of each other, and that all the truth, beauty, and goodness we need has been given to us by God already. Not only is this doubtful in the extreme, but it presents a negative picture to the rest of society. Baptists, Presbyterians, and Roman Catholics failing to celebrate each other's diversity provide no positive examples to societies trying to understand how to celebrate diversity on larger scales and along other axes of difference.

At the same time, we must beware of what we might call "excessive diversity." Some factions within an organization really are at odds with each other on fundamental values intrinsic to the life of that organization. The global Anglican Communion, for example, has been in crisis on just this matter for a decade or more. It has prided itself on its vaunted capacity for inclusion. But, like any other organization, it can tolerate only so much diversity—theological, ethical, and political—before it becomes simply a weird association of individuals and groups who have not only differences but also opposing and mutually destructive views. The same thing is true of a country such as Germany, the United States, or New Zealand: a society can absorb, tolerate, and profit from only some limited amount of diversity before it disintegrates into warring sects. The Church has a long tradition of insisting on regulating core beliefs and practices, right back to the formulation of a "rule of faith" (*regula fidei*) in the earliest centuries. Yet it must be acknowledged that Church discipline is in a sad state in the West today—usually lax, occasionally domineering. Today we are challenged to be a light to the world by fostering maximum diversity while maintaining necessary and vital unity.

Finally, in Christian dealings with other religious believers, and with all of our neighbors, there is an opportunity to model a constructive and principled pluralism. We should affirm common concerns and participate in initiatives as part of our common human task of cultivating shalom: in artistic organizations, charities, youth groups, sports clubs, environmental societies, and everything else that promotes the flourishing of human beings and the planet given to us to tend.

(Some evangelistically minded Christians will point out that there is the secondary benefit of making friends among those who are not yet Christian in that we might draw them toward the faith. But I have taken pains to establish that this kind of civic activity is *good in itself* as obedience to the creation commandments of God, whether any direct evangelism takes place or not.)

Beyond affirmation and participation, there ought to be tolerance of different modes of life, including some that we are convinced are unhealthy but must be let alone in the name of the liberty God has already given us. "Tolerance" has to be recaptured nowadays as a genuinely good word. Of course, tolerating egregious *evils* is no virtue. But the very idea of tolerance is derided by many people today as a grudging thing because of the judgment it implies. After all, one *tolerates* that of which one does not, in fact, approve. Why, however, is that a bad thing? There is much in contemporary society, as there is much in the Church and even in myself, of which I do not approve. The same is true for you, and for everyone else, even if we disagree as to what belongs in the category of the "barely tolerable." So what? We can either tolerate these things, out of respect for the humanity of the other and for the liberty God gives us all, and in the hope of their eventual improvement, or we can *not* tolerate them. What none of us can coherently do, however, is what many voices nowadays tell us we must do to qualify as enlightened and commendable people: *affirm* everyone else's difference.

There are two problems with this latter agenda. The first is the absurd inconsistency that if one refuses to affirm A and B and C, one must then be condemned (note: not affirmed). The second problem is that to make *affirmation* the ideal means to marginalize or eliminate anything one does not affirm. And that means a much smaller set of things will be allowed to exist. Our three sons are grateful that we opted to allow into our home not only their girlfriends that we could affirm but also the wider circle of girlfriends that we could *tolerate*. Tolerance is the more expansive, more generous attitude.[11]

In our pluralized societies there will be disagreement over various means to the same end, and even over which ends are the best to pursue. Conflict is not to be feared as the great threat, however. Conflict is to be expected whenever thoughtful, creative people get together to consider any challenge that is not simple. Conflict should even be welcomed as an occasion to consider important differences and to find a better way forward than we might have found in a society

in which everyone thinks the same way.[12] I turn to no less an
authority than comedy writer John Cleese:

> Disagreement within a team, and the expression of diverse
> opinions is *creatively invaluable*. All the research shows that
> teams whose members share the same attitudes will enjoy
> the experience of working together, will have good opinions
> of the others in the team, and be keen to repeat the expe-
> rience; but creatively they will produce bugger-all. By con-
> trast, teams whose members view things differently from
> one another will argue, but this creative conflict produces
> innovation. You *want* creative conflict; what you don't want
> is personal conflict, because that will complicate proceedings
> and can result all too often in deadlock.[13]

It is with this critical but genuinely open attitude that
Christians should be participating in school boards, governments, and other forms of electoral politics, and also in
the courts as the conflicts of the day are worked out in that
mode. And civility ought to govern our participation in such
conflicts—literally, an attitude of common citizenship, a soli-
darity that comes from recognizing that together we bear the
image of God and share a common purpose in his service,
whether all our neighbors recognize that basis of civility or
not (as many won't).

Our world needs good ideas and good examples. The
challenge for the Christian Church is indeed to be a bright
city on a hill—a true city, a social organism of diversity in
unity, of individuality and cooperation, of creativity and
discipline, rather than an anarchy of self-centered and
small-minded individuals and factions. The further challenge of our times is for Christians to model true civility
within a world both troubled and blessed with increasing

pluralization of societies that were once perhaps more comfortably homogeneous.

The Christian hope is that God will eventually rule all nations. But God ought to rule first, and completely, each Christian individual and institution. We should be demonstrating what "the life of the world to come" looks like *now*.

TELL

Of course the most important message we have to tell is the gospel of Jesus Christ. That gospel is nested within the great story of all that God has done and said and all that God wants for us. So Christians will have much to say in the public sphere today.

- First, we ought to teach the values intrinsic to modern public life: democracy, the rule of law, human rights, self-worth, the worth of others, cooperation and competition, freedom and responsibility, and so on. These are the values that frame our common life in North America, Europe, and more and more of the rest of the world; they are not only compatible with, but even rooted in, the Christian religion. It is easy to be cynical about democracy and capitalism, and even law and government, as they work out so badly in actual life. But as disheartening as it is to witness waste, fraud, venality, and oppression, we must keep in view also the good things that emerge from these ideologies and systems, especially when compared not with the ideal state of the New Jerusalem but with the other existing, or likely, alternatives.

The supreme values of the Kingdom of God judge all of our efforts and programs and values. We must never directly equate anything we do with the Kingdom, but must instead conduct ourselves with the humility, faith, and openness to correction that such recognition entails. Yet we also must be realistic enough to strive to make the *best* of what we have to work with. And we must not discourage ourselves *or others* (Matt. 18:6) by indulging in a perpetual round of grumbling and finger-pointing, which fosters an attitude of pseudo-prophetic superiority coupled with self-indulgent Weltschmerz. If better values and systems are actually on offer, by all means let us embrace and commend them. We must not settle slothfully merely for what is. Nor must we abandon the defense of what good we have been able to attain just because we feel guilt for previous abuses and regret over continuing evil results—moral, aesthetic, economic, agricultural, political, or whatever—we have not been able to avoid.

Furthermore, we should hold our fellow citizens, our media, our public institutions, and our politicians to those values of modern public life. We may do so when we are injured by our neighbors' failure to behave toward us in accordance with those values. But we should do so especially when our own interests are not at stake, and especially on behalf of others who need assistance, representation, and defense—such as children, the undereducated, the mentally impaired, the ill, the newly arrived, and so on. Despite almost everyone's avowal of these values, they nonetheless are constantly under threat in matters great and small. Despite what almost all of us say we believe with respect to justice, let alone kindness and compassion, people in even the wealthiest and most free societies are constantly being treated as less than human, prejudice does run rampant, the strong perpetually oppress the weak—and Christians must vigilantly proclaim and champion the values everyone too easily and cheaply affirms.

- Second, we need to teach the sober fact that not everyone "wins" in democracy. Not all "values" are equally valued in our common life, nor should they be. Most of us frown on vigilantism, abuse, fraud, treason, bestiality, and child molestation. We do not believe that everyone and everything is entitled to equal affirmation or (and this is more controversial) even respect.

In a free society, we are entitled to disagree with each other on profound matters. Indeed, for a democratic society to work properly, we are at times positively *obliged* to argue with each other over such things, in order for the truth to have a chance to emerge and be embraced by everyone, or at least by more people than recognized it before. In some cases, we are obliged to work to impose behaviors on all citizens in the name of one set of values over another. That's what governments, courts, and police services properly do. As we have seen, toleration and respect for each other as human beings do not entail affirmation of every human preference or action—how could they?

It is, indeed, out of respect for you that when I deeply object to your behavior, I will not treat you as a mad dog or a virus, but as a human being who is thinking or doing something I think is both wrong and harmful. Most of the time I will tolerate your different choices, as you will tolerate mine. Sometimes, however, toleration must give way to intolerance: on behalf of your own good (as in an intervention), or on behalf of your victim, or on behalf of our common life.

Many people nowadays resist this grown-up idea, preferring a fantasy of everyone just leaving each other alone—or, better, everyone blessing everyone else with affirmation. But democracy is the best way we have yet found, short of the direct reign of God, to broker a common life together, to accommodate what minorities we can, and to leave the door open for further discussion. And in democratic discussion, there are usually winners and losers. Not everybody wins when there are intractable and irreconcilable differences. There is no way for everyone to win. And Christians need to join with others who are equally realistic to make this plain in the controversies of our day—to people in our own communities, as well as to the community as a whole.

One of the great things about democracy is that the way is always open for a defeated party to make its case again. That principle must be reaffirmed regularly, especially in the face of those who try to defend established positions very convenient to themselves with "We've already decided that" and "Let's move on." Beyond the core principles and practices that constitute the group and direct it toward its mission, nothing is settled forever, nothing is beyond reconsideration. Remembering this truth will pave the way for compromise in any dispute or at least grace in defeat. The losers can always give a little in the hopes of getting more tomorrow, or at least regroup to try again another day. If we believe that every single thing to be decided will be decided once and for all, then every issue is liable to become an absolute battle, with all the horrible implications of such binary opposition among fallible, fallen human beings.

Christians, in particular, who love to teach and defend the great truths of the gospel, have to guard against the sweet delusion that we are mostly right about almost everything else, too, and not merely swat away any challenge to our settled views. Moreover, if we practiced more humility and openness *within* our communities, we could have more integrity when we call upon our fellow citizens to be more humble and open regarding *their* conventions, prejudices, and preferences.

- Third, Christians can speak up to teach the public what Christians actually believe and do, rather than what various members of the public might think we believe and do. We should correct misstatements and caricatures in the media with better information and more accurate interpretations. As upsetting as it might be to see oneself and one's spiritual family distorted in public, we can also rejoice in these opportunities to proclaim the gospel message—opportunities that rarely arise otherwise than in a controversy provoked by someone else's mistake or attack. Mainstream media will never ask someone to set out the gospel—unless Christians are being criticized and a spokesperson is given the opportunity to reply with "Here's who we *actually* are..."
- Fourth, we can resist any form of ideological bullying, any insistence upon any single religion or worldview as if it alone were entirely true and all other viewpoints were entirely false. Christians should not be proponents of a restrictive orthodoxy of belief in which all diversity and novelty are feared and resisted, but defenders of genuine liberty in which ideas can emerge freely to then be rigorously tested.

For example, there is considerable confusion today about how to teach science. As Neil Postman pointed out decades ago, it is bad science education to present physics, chemistry, biology, or whatever as a collection of agreed facts and indubitable explanations.[14] The very nature of science is empirical, which directly entails that it is never certain, never *settled*, once for all. The theory of evolution, for example, was devised to explain the workings of the origin of species. It works with millions of facts, but it remains perpetually vulnerable to revision or replacement in the light of any of the following: (a) new facts; (b) old facts now shown to be wrong, wholly or partially; (c) better explanations for this or that subset of the facts; (d) an entirely new explanation that does a better job of the whole thing; or (e) some other development I haven't thought to list here.

We might pause briefly to note that "evolution is a theory that most scientists currently think is an explanatory scheme so helpful as to make an alternative seem highly implausible" has nothing directly to do with the truthfulness of evolution itself. It is a fact that most scientists do think this way about evolution, but this broad consensus doesn't establish evolution itself as a fact of nature. Most scientists used to believe in the "steady state" of the universe or the applicability of Newton's laws up and down the physical scale, neither of which beliefs anyone takes as a fact today. (One suspects that when scientists get doctrinaire, something other than science is at stake.)[15]

In the light of these basic traits of science, Postman makes the provocative suggestion that so-called creation science (for which he has no sympathy at all) should be taught alongside evolution precisely to show students how science works: in the contention of competing theories.[16] Now, some years after his essay was published, we might see Intelligent Design as even more useful in this regard, as its proponents are much more circumspect about scientific protocols than creation science advocates generally have been, and it clearly is not just creation science "dressed up," as some pundits (and jurists) have it. The classroom might come alive as students see how science in fact is the contest of interpretations, not the mere adding of factual bricks to a giant edifice.

Whether one accepts Postman's pedagogical suggestion, however, his epistemological and political point remains. Science is precisely *not* the discourse in which teachers should speak as if what happens to be in the textbooks in this particular edition is "just plain true," or for science museum curators to mount exhibits with captions written as if everything they say was settled fact, or for science magazines to pooh-pooh anyone who is not entirely convinced of whatever consensus happens to reign at the moment. This is not *science* but *bullying*, resorting to power to preclude any dissent. Christians provide a public service, we increase shalom, when we stand up against any oppression, including intellectual and cultural oppression, and particularly on behalf of the weak—in this case, children and the less informed.

To pick another example, Christians can help public discourse by resisting value judgments by public authorities and arbiters (such as schoolteachers, professors, and judges) that do not reflect the general consensus of our society, and for at least two reasons.

First, social science does not properly trade in value judgments, helping us pick out the heroes and villains on the social landscape. Consider the frequent depiction in history and anthropology of "good guys" and "bad guys" (e.g., good natives, on the one hand, and bad missionaries, traders, and soldiers, on the other), or the affirmation by public officials of various forms of sexual and gender diversity as perfectly healthy. I suggest that Christians equally should oppose any educator, textbook, or judge who says the opposite: natives are bad and missionaries are good, or that all divergence from heteronormativity is not normal but sinful. Properly circumspect social science does not deal in value judgments at all: like natural science, it aims to tell us only what *is* the case and *why*. We must then turn to our religions and life philosophies to tell us whether what *is* is good or bad. That is a distinction that tends to be forgotten. Some Christians resist all fact/value separation, but natural science, social science, and history rest on being able to do so in a disciplined— although, of course, never completely objective—way.

The second reason we should be wary, at least, of value judgments made by public officials and arbiters is that many such judgments have to be made according to values particular to constituent individuals or groups, rather than according to the basic values that frame our common life and upon which we all agree. (Examples of the latter values would be "legal due process is good" and "slavery is wrong.") Public institutions, such as schools, courts, or legislatures, should reflect the state of the *whole* society they represent and serve, including any important dissension on important matters within that society. Families, religious communities, and advocacy groups are communities within which judgments can be formed and promoted. But public officials must be carefully circumspect not to advocate values that are not held by the public at large and are endemic to our society's common commitments.

Teachers thus can report, accurately, that there were winners and losers in the story of Europeans coming to the New World, that promises were made and many were broken, that terror tactics were used by various groups in warfare, and so on. Such teachers do not have to render a moral judgment on these matters, however, for such a judgment will depend both on values that are not universally shared and on complicated matters of interpretation, such as the usefulness and genuineness of the missionary motive, the value to the native peoples of receiving modern technology willy-nilly, the relative difference in the treatment of natives by the Spanish, English, and French, and so on.

Likewise, teachers can report, accurately, that some people are attracted to members of the same sex such that they want to have romantic and even matrimonial relations with them. Teachers can report that most of the world's religious traditions disagree with this behavior, and that, nonetheless, many people think otherwise and that it is perfectly legal in some jurisdictions for such people to pursue their chosen affections. Children won't grasp all the nuances here—the difference, say, between what a society allows and what a society affirms—but the teachers are telling the truth now, and not adding the spin of their individual preference on an issue about which there is no complete public consensus. Furthermore, teaching this way can open up interesting and vital questions about pluralism, tolerance, respect, the law, and so on that are often smothered by the well-intentioned blanket of affirmation.

- Fifth, Christians should be in the vanguard of cultural change and stop fighting rearguard battles to maintain our diminishing cultural privileges in regard to religious events and symbols in schools, legislatures, courts, and other public institutions. Christians should protest any presentations of religion that move beyond *information* to encourage what amounts to liturgical *participation*, whether a native troupe at a school assembly inviting the room to chant a prayer to a tribal god, a "winter festival" (formerly a "Christmas concert") that proceeds to offer songs to a round of deities, or a teacher of "mindfulness" who teaches a version of meditation based on Buddhist principles.

We can protest such things with full integrity, of course, only as we cooperate in the cessation of our own practices being imposed on others, such as saying the Lord's Prayer, reciting the Ten Commandments, or singing Christmas carols. We can likewise suggest that Christian holy days should not be recognized above other religions' holy days in the public calendar. (It is not at all clear to me, for example, why Good Friday still should be celebrated as a national holiday in several British Commonwealth countries, including Canada, Australia, and New Zealand.) We thus both model and advocate a public life consistent toward everyone, neither privileging nor persecuting Christianity—or any other religion or philosophy that can be fairly practiced in the light of our culture's fundamental principles.

- Sixth, and related to this point, is the responsibility to practice a proper silence. In this discipline, we avoid taking advantage of authority in order to proselytize. Teachers and coaches, physicians and nurses, politicians and judges—none of us should seize on the vulnerability of a pupil, patient, client, or prisoner to advance our religious message. Everyone brings his or her personal values to their work, of course, and Christians are no exception. But evangelism is not the only Christian value because it is not the only calling upon Christians. Our values include doing our jobs well for their own sakes in obedience to the creation commandment to cultivate the world. And we Christians can expect other people to do their jobs with similar dedication, for earth-keeping and shalom-making are the human tasks as divinely ordained. It is vocationally unethical, however, to exploit authority in one role (teacher, physician, judge) to try to influence people in another—namely, as a religious advocate. Indeed, it is a betrayal of trust and brings shame upon one's religion to do so.

- Seventh, Christians can watch our language in public. We will be simply unintelligible to an increasing number of our fellow citizens if we use too much "in-house," Christian jargon. I daresay that this point is made often enough. But its complement is not—namely, that we must resist the cultural pressure to leave our religious identities and vocabularies at the door when we want to engage in public conversation. This pressure is a secularizing pressure, a pressure to use only the language of secular rationality, sense experience, and the ever-changing conventions of the au courant intelligentsia. And it is a merely dogmatic pressure—that is, not a principle actually justified by the common principles of our society.

The way forward is not to relegate explicitly religious values and categories to our private lives. That would be to succumb to ideological intimidation. Instead, we must get beyond the public/private distinction and look at what our Lord and the apostles did: They sought to be *persuasive*. If Peter was addressing Jews (Acts 2), he referred them to the

Old Testament and their common experience of Jesus' recent ministry and execution. If Paul was addressing Greek philosophers (Acts 17), he drew upon their own religious poetry and art. They made use of rhetorical materials that fit the task at hand.

In a democracy, public speakers ought to be free to refer to any source, any text, and any authority they like. If a speaker—whether a school board member, a legislator, a pundit, or a workmate in the cafeteria—wants to cite her favorite book, whether *The Communist Manifesto*, the Qur'an, or the *Bhagavad-Gita*, then she should be allowed to do so. The speaker is not committing any kind of public "sin" in doing so. She is explaining what she thinks and why she thinks it.

The practical question that follows is simply that of effectiveness: What will persuade a majority to agree? If she wants not only to announce her opinion but also win support, then she must consider whether she can persuade the most people by referring to the authority of Adam Smith or Martin Luther or the Dalai Lama or Albert Einstein. Nothing should be ruled out of bounds in advance. So Christians should campaign for Christian concerns today using whatever rhetoric in public they believe will do the job they want done. For, as postmodernists never tire of reminding us, there is no generically human philosophy to which we ought to conform our language and our activity. There are only particular societies, cultures, and conversations, each with their own distinctive qualities and limitations and characters. As Yoder puts it well, "There is no 'public' that is not just another particular province."[17]

In sum, we have to follow our Lord's advice to be as wise as serpents if we want to be heard on national networks or read in major periodicals. We have to learn what will and what won't be acceptable to the producers and editors of such media, and that means picking both our language and our issues carefully—again, in order to do as much good as possible. This sort of compromise is simply realistic. Major media won't let us preach the gospel, but they will let us offer pithy commentary on the day's events and issues if we can speak both intelligibly and attractively about them.[18]

To be sure, we may find that the filters are so thick against what we want to say that we have to abandon some of these media, at least in particular instances. And the medium itself may be problematic. Television news in particular is so terribly compressed—a "major" story can get all of three minutes—that some issues simply cannot, and should not, be discussed in that medium. Television is much too limited to discuss, say, the providence of God in a natural disaster, the reasons for and against same-sex marriage, or the issues involved in churches offering sanctuary to refugees. And the pressure to entertain, even in the news, is relentless and over-whelming. In the age of the Internet, social media, and other communication revolutions, Christians can recognize that there are lots of other forms of public discussion in the world today that we can both provide and access, and we should make use of those that can do a particular job well.

When we do speak up, moreover, we should not apolo-gize for being who we are as Christians, just as most of our neighbors don't expect Jews or LGBTQ+ people or feminists or native peoples to apologize for who they are and to adopt some kind of generic, neutral, and depersonalizing language just to be heard in public. Glenn Tinder observes,

> While Christians can sometimes put their understanding of things in secular terms . . . they cannot do invariably. They

cannot leave out distinctive Christian terms entirely and still speak as Christians. Hence to forbid Christians to use Christian terms in the public realm is tantamount to excluding them from the public realm.[19]

Yes, in some modern societies, or at least in some sectors of some societies, there is still a backlash against Christians in particular—the understandable, if regrettable, resentment that lingers in the wake of our former cultural dominance. Particularly in Britain, Canada, and Australasia, but also in parts of the United States that have "cooled" in regard to Christianity (e.g., New England and the Pacific Northwest), Christianity is often treated differently from all other outlooks because the cultural position of Christianity is unique and, for many, uniquely implicated in what they dislike about their culture.[20] Thus the commonly observed double standard in these regions by which Christians are treated worse than any others. (Having lived in Texas and the American Midwest, I can appreciate that readers in those areas and the South might find the foregoing surprising, to say the least.)

Such treatment is to be expected as a pendulum swing, and we Christians simply have to weather this storm until it abates. Increasingly, however, our neighbors are recognizing that we, too, deserve the same respect as anyone else in the name of multiculturalism, diversity, and the like. The decline of Christianity has this silver lining: it has allowed many people—again, especially outside the United States, where the cultural influence of Christianity is still particularly strong—to lower their guard and let Christians say their particular things along with everyone else in the forum of public opinion.

Quite practically, I believe our Christian preachers, teachers, writers, broadcasters, and activists need to learn true "*public* speaking" that will get them heard by the public at large and by key publics such as the courts, the legislatures, the news media, the entertainment media, and the schools. And then they can model such discourse for the rest of us as we go about our vocations, seeking to speak a good word wherever and whenever we can.[21]

- Eighth, our Christian theology can help us help society think through difficult questions and solve difficult problems by offering creative alternatives.[22] In attempting to resolve aboriginal land claims, for example, or to deal with the legacy of slavery and racism, or to respond to corporate misbehavior, we can join the call for justice. But we will not remain stuck on justice, so to speak, as so many have remained stuck, with some disputes locked indefinitely in mutual accusation and fury. Christians can draw from our repertoire of ethical options to advocate forgiveness. Some issues cannot be resolved by trying to revert everything and everyone to "first position." Nor is it always possible to calculate, let alone afford, full recompense for damage done. If we insist only and ever on justice, we will remain frustrated by unconquerable realities. Forgiveness helps us cut the chains of history that perpetually hamper us from moving ahead into a good future.[23]

Christians will affirm that forgiveness entails naming what happened as exactly what it was. Forgiveness does not mean hiding or whitewashing the past. Quite the contrary, it means to be totally clear-eyed about what was done by whom to whom. Moreover, genuine forgiveness is not just exhorting people to "move on" and "get over it," as if they are being self-indulgently recalcitrant. Such condescension would be to victimize them a second time. No, genuine injury must be dealt with adequately, not merely "moved on from."

Ideally, forgiveness would be rendered after the offenders—and those who have benefited from the offense—both own up to what happened and then do their part: confession of offense if appropriate; restitution if possible; and then whatever else is necessary to make things as right as can be. The cause of justice ought to be firmly pressed. But forgiveness can be tendered even if the perpetrators refuse to repent. Forgiveness empowers victims to free themselves from perpetual victimization by the offenders, to draw a line and leave the past in the past. *Without* the option of forgiveness, victims remain dependent on the good behavior of their oppressors. She can't go on with her life until he repents. So forgiveness can be a gift to the guilty, yes, but also can bless those who grant it.

Forgiveness thus takes us beyond vengeance or sentimentality, and even beyond the requirements of justice. Sometimes justice cannot fully be done. Sometimes it simply *won't* be done. Forgiveness provides another constructive option. The realistic imperative here is to *make the best of it*. Otherwise the cycle of injustice and anger continues indefinitely.

Christians can bring hopeful practicality to the table out of a Christian view of things. Because of our theological understanding of human nature, we can remind those who need to hear it that disputes are often about more than mere money and power but about personal and spiritual matters as well—and thus awarding mere money and power to the victimized won't be enough to heal the wounds. We can remind others that goodwill and wishful thinking are badly insufficient to remedy situations that do indeed have important economic and political dimensions. Some problems *will* be solved by throwing money at them, not mere words. Christians take all of these human realities seriously in our theology, and we can help our societies think and behave in a way that pays proper tribute to each element of this complex of healing and renewal, however approximate it will always be.

- Ninth, part of good telling is good *listening*. There is a place for arguing over things that matter. But argument need not, and must not, be our primary mode of discourse with our neighbors: *conversation* must be. And conversation involves listening, learning, and enjoying each other as much as possible, in the cooperative mode rather than the competitive or calculating. As Martin Marty puts it, "One does not hear claims such as 'I sure won *that* conversation!' And conversation is especially appealing because it invites in on equal terms host and guest, belonger and stranger, the committed and the less committed, the informed and the less informed."[24]

Indeed, how can we really know who our neighbors are and how we can love them best if we do not spend considerable time and effort in listening to them—and particularly to those who are on the margins and who thus are not accustomed to being listened to? For that matter, we can hardly be said to love our enemies if we listen to them only to immediately refute and defeat them, and we never attend to the underlying fears and aspirations that motivate them, with which we might have some sympathy and with which we need, at least, to reckon.[25]

- Finally, the image of conversation reminds us of the apostolic injunction to speak the truth *in love* (Eph. 4:15). This has both formal and material dimensions. Formally, we simply have to speak the truth in love because most of our neighbors will not listen with genuine openness to someone who doesn't seem to care about them, who doesn't assure them that this message is coming with their best interests at heart. And if we don't honestly love our neighbors, then we should keep quiet.

Materially, we must speak the truth in love because, to put it starkly, God cares about people even more than God cares about mere principles or propositions—about "truth" in that restricted sense. To speak truth without caring about whether it actually touches and helps our audiences—and fear and anger particularly can blind us to the needs of our audiences— is merely to indulge oneself, perhaps scoring points on one's tally of duty and accomplishment but failing to please God at all. We are to *make shalom*, to help things get *better*—which orientation is toward the *other*—rather than merely discharge a duty—which orientation is toward *ourselves*.

CAMPAIGN

Finally, let's turn to the particular question of advocacy, of campaigning for what we think is right and good for the common life of our schools, neighborhoods, municipalities, regions, and countries. Let's consider, in turn, which Christians should do it, in what modes we should do it, and how we should do it.

In our discussion of vocation we concluded that not everyone is responsible to take part in public advocacy in any major way, and some perhaps should avoid it—except to support others with prayer and perhaps money or other logistical help. Some Christians clearly are called to various kinds of campaigning and are thus equipped with wise speech, political authority, personal networks, technical expertise, and so on. Others may not feel so gifted, but providence thrusts them into advocacy through experience and therefore opportunity: Mothers Against Drunk Driving, for example. We recall the principle that just because a particular form of service, in this case advocacy, is good, that doesn't entail that everyone should be involved in it. *All* kinds of service are good, but no one is called to undertake all of them. At the same time, in an era of widespread disillusionment with public institutions, small numbers of well-positioned people can make a big difference. Each of us, then, and each institution should periodically consider whether this season and circumstance of life is one in which Jesus is calling me, or us, to this particular mode of service, whether to fight the incursion of gambling in our town, support refugees, resist rapacious development, or encourage civic beautification.

Pastors (and other religious professionals, such as leaders of Christian organizations and theological professors) particularly must have a clear sense of what they can and cannot do well. Christian politicians and political scientists usually will have the clearest and most helpful advice about politics; Christian educators, social scientists, parents, and students will think most critically and creatively about schools; Christian physicians, nurses, other medical professionals, administrators, chaplains, and patients will have the most to offer regarding healthcare; and so on.[26] Pastors serve such Christians well in three modes: helping them become sound, solid Christians; teaching them about the fundamental principles of Christian engagement (such as the nature of Christian mission, vocation, and the like); and exhorting them to pursue their particular callings.

It is the unusual pastor who has the expertise, insight, and opportunity to enter another realm—such as politics, education, or healthcare—and do or say something better than his fellow Christians who already work in that realm. Indeed, pastors and politicians work not only in different categories but also, to a considerable extent, in mutually exclusive ones. Pastors emphasize purity, loyalty, clarity, and totality, while politicians must work with mixedness, expedience, ambiguity, and compromise. When pastors insist on speaking out of their depth, they risk undermining their credibility and usefulness in their primary calling, causing people to doubt them when they speak about what pastors really *do* know.

Finally, pastors who engage directly in party politics particularly risk alienating those of different political opinions— and few topics promote alienation more readily and deeply than electoral politics. Worse, by taking sides, pastors forfeit their rightful position as prophets who should subject to godly criticism whoever is in charge, now or later. Worst of all, by supporting particular candidates, programs, and parties, pastors will be implicated in, and thus discredited by, the sin and failure that inevitably result in every regime.

One can think of exceptions, of course. Church history includes many pastors who became fruitfully involved in politics, from Gregory the Great to Bartolomé de las Casas, from John Calvin to Mary Slessor, and from Tommy Douglas to Martin Luther King, Jr. In general, however, if pastors long for Christian voices to be raised and Christian hands to be employed in this or that cultural challenge, they must be clear that the pastoral calling per se is not to leap into it themselves but to "equip the saints for the work of ministry" (Eph. 4:12).

The Christian Church can be deployed in a wide range of modes in order to accomplish a wide range of actions. We can act as an individual, as a family, as a congregation, as a denomination, as an ecumenical fellowship, as a Christian special-purpose group, as an interfaith coalition—and also within secular political parties and other secular channels: a neighborhood association, a charity, a labor union, or an advocacy group. Again, pastors, congregations, denominations, and ecumenical fellowships—what we normally, and too narrowly, tend to call "the Church"—need to consider what each individual and group can do well and what other individuals and groups can do better.

On vexed issues, there is rarely a particular policy that is "just plain Christian," that simply flows directly out of the Bible and Christian tradition. Sometimes, to be sure, we do face such an issue: campaigns for the care of children or for the end of religious persecution can be such causes. Protecting the Jews was one such cause in Bonhoeffer's time, and so he termed such an issue a *status confessionis*—a basic matter of Christian conviction.[27] But in most cases, people of equal fidelity and competence can disagree about what is to be done in a given circumstance. Pastors, congregations, denominations, and ecumenical fellowships—those officers and organizations that represent what we might call "the Church in general"—need to carefully distinguish between proclaiming principles to guide such decision-making (which can be a vital ministry) and advocating particular decisions themselves (which may confuse the situation and impede the work of those Christians with more pertinent competence).

It would be far better, I submit, for pastors, congregations, denominations, and ecumenical fellowships to encourage each Christian to work with other Christians and with other citizens of goodwill as best he or she can in whatever organizations best suit the purpose. Yes, that will often mean that members of the same family or church or congregation will end up in different parties or otherwise advocate different recommendations as to what is to be done. But that's fine. These organizations represent and foster creative and constructive diversity. They let us focus our energies in particular and diverse ways, as no single, uniting organization (such as a congregation or denomination) can do. Our congregations, denominations, and ecumenical fellowships then would be left to represent Christian unity as they "maintain the bonds of peace" among us around our common life in Christ: sacraments, preaching, liturgy, mutual service, and so on.

Therefore, when someone looks at a current controversy or area of need and asks, "Where is the Church? Is it involved?," the answer is not to be couched solely in terms of the actions of ecclesiastical elements: clergy, congregations, denominations, and so on, as if Christ deploys his Church only in these modes. The answer instead should be, "Here, and here, and here. Indeed, look at all the instances of significant, useful action by Christians on behalf of shalom."

Finally, a few words about how Christians ought to participate in public contention, reiterating themes I expect are now familiar to the reader. Christian individuals and

Christian organizations should aim to do whatever they can that, so far as they know, will result in the most shalom that seems possible in the situation. Again, Christians can and should pray for miracles, for what does *not* seem possible in the situation. God may choose this particular time to intervene in a dramatic way, and we will be glad if God does so. Meanwhile, however, God does not ask us to lay aside everything we have learned about how the world normally works and how to participate most effectively in that normal world so that instead we can just pray and God can do all the rest. That is not what God told us to do in the cultural mandate nor in any of the other commandments. That is not why we're here. *Ora et labora,* as the medieval monastic motto had it: Pray and work.

So we must form partnerships, compose strategies, make compromises, and otherwise do the best we can to cultivate the earth and make disciples. In doing so we will join with a changing cast of allies on this or that issue, and it is important to underscore that our allies will change depending on the issue. It therefore does not make sense to say, as a number of religious conservatives have been saying, that the new line of division in society lies between "people of faith" and secularists. The Bible approves no such thing as "faith in general" or "people of faith." Moreover, many secularists are *particular kinds* of secularists, namely, secularized Christians or Jews, and thus they retain many values similar to ours. (Consider, by contrast, secularized post-communists in China or Russia, or secularized post-imperialists in Japan. Many of their values diverge sharply from those held by people who have been raised in a post-Christian culture.) Indeed, many of our secular neighbors will agree with Christians about retaining monogamy as a societal norm, for instance, versus the preference for plural marriage among many observant Muslims and a small but conspicuous minority of Mormons—"people of faith" most definitely. To pick another example, one that actually separates Christians from each other, many Protestants—even evangelicals—will agree with secularists on strategies to deal with HIV/AIDS that might dismay their conservative Roman Catholic neighbors (allies of those Protestants in the pro-life struggle) because many Catholics want nothing to do with artificial contraception.[28] Part of Christian realism, then, is a willingness to cast about for the most and best allies possible in each particular campaign. It also means to beware easy, dangerous "culture war" categories of "us versus them" or "red versus blue" or "good versus evil," as if everyone and every issue sorts itself nicely into one category or another, and as if we ourselves were always both coherent and correct about everything.

As we campaign, then, we must also trust God to guide us along the way. If God prefers us to take a path we are not planning to choose, we will depend on God to tell us so, and we will joyfully, faithfully take it. But until God does direct us in such a clear way, we ought to act like the responsible adults God created us to be and simply make things better—in recognition of our finitude and fallibility; of the certainty that we will not accomplish every possible good and that evil will accompany whatever good we do accomplish; of the likelihood of unintended consequences that we will then have to deal with; and so on. We seek half a loaf if a whole loaf seems unavailable. We will even abandon particular battles if the war can be fought better in doing so. We recall that God doesn't proceed on all fronts simultaneously with *us*. We remember that some things matter more than others. We keep our main ends in view, with due regard for the

particular situation, with its constituent opportunities, limitations, and temptations. We think strategically, tactically,
and logistically, trying to be faithfully effective. And then we
act to make the best of it.

I recognize once more that this recommendation is
fraught with ambiguity, ambivalence, paradox, irony, and
danger. How easy it would be to invoke this ethic to promote
the merely convenient, let alone the positively self-serving.
How tempting it would be to call this theology to the aid of
one's self-deception and one's manipulation of others. I haven't
said much about the devil in this book because I think the
Bible basically tells us to trust and obey God, and Satan will
be kept at bay. But here is where the Deceiver's mischief lies
closest to hand: in rationalization and ideology, in dressing
up both our ruthless voracity and our lazy conformity in the
guise of "Christian realism." So we must be vigilant against
this constant peril.

Yet, as I have argued, the options of total purity or total
conquest seem to be not only inconsistent with the (whole)
Bible's teaching but also simply impossible short of the return
of Jesus in power and glory. We live in the meanwhile, and
we must be prepared to work as God works: glad for today's
gains, however meager or magnificent; sad or even angry
about today's setbacks, however great or small; certain of
the ultimate end of perfect peace; and therefore persistently
faithful in the tasks at hand to make things better.

TURN THE TABLES

The fundamental move is quite simple: to turn the tables, to
put the shoe on the other foot, to ask, "How would you feel

if it happened to you?" For instance, Christians might view the imposition of "bubble zones" against pro-life protesters at abortion clinics more sympathetically if we imagined loud antagonists being kept away from the entrances to our churches. Christians might refrain from proselytizing in the workplace if they imagined a zealous Jehovah's Witness or Muslim doing the same thing.

It is in this light that I question why God should be invoked in national anthems (Canadian and British), or cited in the Pledge of Allegiance (American), or be prominent in other such national symbols? Sadly, the word "God" is just specific enough to marginalize those citizens who are not monotheists while not being specific enough to indicate which deity is being referenced: Yhwh? The God and Father of our Lord Jesus Christ? Allah? Vishnu? If our country required monotheism as a qualification of citizenship, then using "God" in this way makes sense. But since it does not, then I respectfully suggest that we should not encode it in our national symbols, to which only some of the body of legitimate citizens can subscribe.

Let's get clear that simply because a majority of us believes in God does not mean we should be putting the word "God" in national symbols, for national symbols in the nature of the case are binary and universal: here is who we are and here is who we are not. You can't be "mostly" British or "85%" American. Therefore the opinions of majorities, no matter how large or passionate, must not determine such basic issues. Otherwise we have the farcical situation of citizens being conscience-bound to opt out of this or that clause of a national anthem or pledge, singing or saying two or three out of six or eight lines—which is exactly the opposite of the intent of such unifying, general symbols.

Some might follow this logic and then ask, should religious organizations in general be stripped of any privileges or government assistance? Churches and other religious institutions do perform functions, I believe, that the contemporary pluralized state can recognize as worth supporting through tax breaks and other means. A case can be made for clergy in this respect as well. Let me make the case briefly here.

First, religious groups provide many social services to their communities. Someone has a new baby? Religious groups provide meals, run errands, and help with childcare for frazzled new parents. Someone's getting married? Religious groups provide celebrations, yes, so that everyone feels honored—not just those who can afford to fête themselves. But they also provide food, household items, and time-honored wisdom to help give new unions a good start. Someone's lost a loved one? Religious groups gather around to mourn, to console, and to provide.

Beyond rites of passage, moreover, religious groups provide considerable social capital. They provide information centers and friendship networks for lonely and disoriented newcomers. They constitute safe meeting places for singles looking for mates. They offer companionship and recreation for the unemployed or retired. And they educate people in life skills, from parenting teenagers to coping with divorce to financial planning. Beyond community, furthermore, religious groups mobilize volunteers in a bewildering range of publicly helpful activities: running blood drives, cleaning up beaches and roadsides, offering daycare and summer camps—and all of this before we even start talking about typical charities: shelters, food banks, educational services, AA meetings, and more.

Indeed, on the sheerly pragmatic level, many religious groups stretch tax dollars a long way by adding many of their own. A small grant to a soup kitchen can make the difference between it surviving or shutting down—but the main funding and the main volunteer work are rendered by religious people freely contributing their charity to the needy. Religious schools likewise are run at a fraction of the cost of public institutions because of the contributions of religious supporters.

Second, and this point is often overlooked, religious groups provide places for people to stop, think, and talk about the Big Questions. Where else in our society do people get to pull their noses away from the grindstone, step off the treadmill, escape the rat race, and consider the meaning of life? Book clubs? Maybe. Universities? If you take the right courses. . . . Bars? Well, yes, bars. But perhaps the quality of reflection isn't quite adequate to the subject matter in such conditions.

Religious groups, however, are all about these issues. What is the true nature of things? What constitutes the well-lived life? What are the grounds for morality, and what does it mean to be truly good? What is it all about, really? Surely the public good is advanced by making sure that there are institutions—and vital, well-funded institutions—in which such conversation takes place in communities of respect and freedom.

And that last phrase brings me to an important qualification: Not all religious groups are characterized by respect and freedom. Not all of them advance the public good in any discernible way. Some, in fact, are utterly inward. A few are positively dangerous. So not all religious groups deserve tax support, that's for sure. But many, even most, clearly do. And those who subscribe to such religions, or who at least value the work they do, will need to make such a case in the face of not only antagonism by militant opponents of religion but also sheer unawareness on the part of increasingly large sectors of the population.

Clearly, then, I do not intend to encourage a secularist evacuation of all religious institutions, symbols, values, and personnel from public life—not at all. Instead, we Christians should be taking the initiative to surrender those privileges that no longer make sense in a post- or semi-Christian society. And we ought to use our shrinking cultural power to establish new relations of religion–society and church–state that will benefit all participants, including religious communities and state institutions, without unjustly penalizing or privileging any. Indeed, we should use what influence we have left to help construct the sort of society in which we ourselves would like to live once our power to effect it has disappeared. And we can be guided in part by our "tribal heritage" of being a minority at the beginning of our religion and in various societies ever since. How unseemly it is for Christians to fight in the courts and legislatures for what remains of the dubious honors and advantages of Christendom! There is no more prudent time to do unto others as we would have them do unto us.

Let's conclude this section by considering Christian cultural participation in three illustrative jobs: teacher, chaplain, and politician.

As we have already noted, the Christian teacher in a public school must not see his job as primarily an opportunity for proselytizing his students or his colleagues. C. S. Lewis, a lifelong teacher, made this point sharply: "I do not mean that a Christian should take money for supplying one thing (culture) and use the opportunity thus gained to supply a quite different thing (homiletics and apologetics). That is stealing."[29] Nor must he see it primarily as an opportunity for impressing his pupils with his own particular values. Instead, he must see public education on its own terms as worthwhile from a Christian perspective and undertake it in that spirit. Thus he will count it a good day's work, or a good year's work, or a good career's work even if no child under his care and no colleague within his acquaintance ever professes a conversion experience because of his example or teaching. He will wish it were otherwise, of course, since he longs for every one of those children and workmates to be reconciled to God. Nonetheless, the task of public education must be viewed as worthwhile in itself. That's why he's there as a human being obeying God's creation commandment to cultivate shalom. He's there to teach.

A Christian who teaches with passion, skill, sympathy, and prudence will shine such that colleagues may well ask him to discuss his motivation and values, which might result in spiritual conversation. And as he naturally shares his life with students in the course of teaching, he will unselfconsciously drop clues (such as mentioning church or prayer or God) that will connect him with his religion and thus add luster to students' opinion of that religion. Again, all of this good work as a teacher, as a properly functioning human being, also conduces to the furtherance of his specifically Christian objective: to win and grow disciples of Christ. But two conclusions follow.

First, the success of the Christian teacher is to be measured by his *teaching*, not by some other activity, such as evangelism. Second, the Christian teacher must always remain just as circumspect about his faith as he would want the Scientologist teacher in the next classroom and the Buddhist teacher down the hall to be as well. None of them should hide who they are. None of them should be shy about answering the sorts of questions that anyone can be asked in the workplace. But none of them should take advantage of their teaching position to do something else—even something as otherwise commendable as proselytizing. For the will of God is for public education to be conducted well by everyone involved, just as it is the will of God for Christians to evangelize—without the two activities interfering with each other.

In the second case, the Christian chaplain—let's say in a hospital, but the same principles stand in a prison, the armed forces, or some other public institution—cannot be other than who she is (Christian), and no system should ask her to be other than that. In particular, she should not be expected to become "generically religious" or "spiritual" or to become a religious chameleon who can be Hindu to Hindus, Jewish to Jews, and Wiccan to Wiccans. Such transformation is impossible, so no chaplain should be asked to perform it. (I am aware that chaplains are often *expected* and even *instructed* to behave this way by well-meaning people, but those good intentions do not make such an impossibility possible.)

Instead, chaplains need to be clear about their role in such an institution. That may take some doing for, as in public school teaching, there is no unanimity about all that the institution should be trying to accomplish, and thus how a chaplain ought to contribute to the institution's mission. But what *can* be done by chaplains is to offer a measure of care that takes spiritual things seriously in an environment (hospital, prison, military base) that otherwise rarely does so. And chaplains can offer that spiritual care to people in the measure and in the style *in which the chaplain can serve with integrity* and *in which the people they serve will consent to be helped*. To do so is to love your neighbor as you love yourself, and to do to others as you would have them do to you.

So a Christian chaplain who naturally cannot pray with a Hindu to Vishnu (or Shiva, or Kali, or whomever) can yet sit with that Hindu while he prays to his god, find a Hindu to pray with him, listen to him discuss his spiritual concerns, or secure Hindu books for him to read while he convalesces. The chaplain can also gladly offer what wisdom and encouragement she can from her own tradition, as much as her patient wants to hear. And the Hindu chaplain can do the same for his Christian charges. Thus there is much that a chaplain can do for a broad public without being asked to compromise his or her distinctive religious commitments. The key is to keep turning the tables: If you're a Christian, imagine a Hindu chaplain coming to care for you. What would you expect and want from such a person in such a role?

In the third case, the issue of personal faith and political decision-making breaks out into two questions: (1) Should a politician take her faith into account when she is considering an issue? (2) Should a politician make policy strictly according to the dictates of her religion?

The answer seems easy if we are true to the form of government we have. Canadians, Americans, and others around the world have chosen representative democracy over direct democracy. We elect people to represent us in political decisions. They are to gather the information, listen to all sides, and then decide on our behalf. They are, in short, to do this complex work for the rest of us who are too busy, uninformed, or unskilled to do the job ourselves. And if we are sufficiently unhappy with what they decide, we replace them in the next election. Our choice on election day, that is, is for people who will go on to decide on our behalf, not people who will simply survey our collective opinions and then vote. That would be direct, not representative, democracy—the sort of politics that is meant when we complain of "government by polling" rather than "government by principle."

The confusion comes right in the word "representative." Are our legislators supposed to represent simply the current collective opinion among their constituents (54 percent in favor, 30 percent against, 16 percent undecided—at least until tomorrow's poll)? Or have they been elected by the majority to be entrusted with the task of thinking through the issues and then offering their best judgment as to what is right for the riding/district/territory and the country? If we really want the former sort of decision-making, then we don't need representatives at all anymore. Now we can govern directly via the Internet, and we can all log on every day and cast our own votes and make laws directly. Some days, granted, that option looks pretty good. But I doubt we really want what amounts to mob rule. We have chosen instead to elect a small group of people to be equipped with staff and technologies and personal expertise, and to be guided (and restrained) by precedent, other institutions, constitutions, and the like, to do our deciding for us.

Since we have so chosen, then we should be thinking hard about just whom we are placing in office to decide for us. Such a person is, after all, a particular combination of upbringing, education, job experience, family life, and religious commitment—understanding "religious" to denote whatever is most basic to his or her philosophy of life. When our representative is deciding about an issue, we should expect her to bring everything pertinent about herself to bear on that decision. Indeed, why should she be expected to pretend she doesn't know something that she thinks she does know—such as what the Bible says as the Word of God on this matter? If we have elected a traditional Christian, we should expect her to decide as one. And if we elect someone else, say, a secular humanist, or a liberal Muslim, or an observant Jew, then we should expect him or her to decide accordingly.

A Christian politician is thus both a Christian and a politician. She should decide what she thinks is right according to her best, Christianity-informed judgment. But that decision is more complex than it might sound at first.

In considering the vexed issue of government recognition of same-sex marriage, for instance, she might agree that marriage really is best defined just the way traditional Christianity says it is. But that's not the end of the matter. She then must act as a politician, which means trying to broker the best arrangement for all concerned—and *that* is how she represents everyone in her constituency, on behalf of the common good. (She cannot possibly act in a way that is 56 percent one thing, 34 percent another thing, and 10 percent undecided!) As she looks at the options available to her, she might well decide among various possibilities and not just automatically try to impose traditional Christian teaching about marriage on a very varied population. Thus she might vote for the state to call same-sex unions "marriages"—again, whatever her own views about marriage might be—while preserving the rights of religious groups to reserve their own marriage ceremonies only for those unions they can conscientiously bless. Or she might move to take the word "marriage" out of the state's vocabulary entirely and endorse "civil unions" or "registered domestic partnerships" instead.

Or she might well decide that traditional Christian teaching about marriage is exactly what is needed in her society, and so she votes that way. *All* of these are legitimate options for her, consistent with the creation commandment to produce as much shalom as possible. That's why she's there.

If her constituents don't like the way she makes up her mind about such things, they are free to replace her. But the crucial thing worth repeating is that she has done her job properly in *any* of those three ways: she has voted according to what she felt was politically the most realistic way to secure the most shalom for her home constituency and her country—no matter what the current polls show her constituents think about the issue. To be sure, she should not ignore polls, for she must remain in office to get certain things done, and sensitivity to her constituents' preferences is also a legitimate and important part of political office. It just is not the only one—or else we don't need a representative at all.[30]

Some religious and philosophical outlooks, however, and that includes some Christian ones, cannot accommodate such a view of politics. They think they know what is right, and they believe that everything must be exactly their way or not at all, since their way is God's way and God brooks no compromise.[31] One observer ruefully lumped together communist, Islamic, and Christian fanaticism in regard to Osama bin Laden's second in command in al Qaeda, Ayman al-Zawahiri: "Like a good Marxist or Leninist, al-Zawahiri was interested in 'building the Kingdom of God on earth.'"[32] But I have been suggesting that as we Christians read our Bibles, we find God working in mysterious, patient, and piecemeal ways to bless—blessings that anticipate the final and full coming of the Kingdom that only God can bring. So we should commend good politicians also, of whatever stripe, for doing the best they can, step by step, to bring whatever measure of shalom they can.

Such, then, is a formal view of the work of such Christians in public settings. Before we leave them, let us say a word about the content of their participation. Beyond the generic concern for shalom-making, at least two particular concerns will be on their agenda. The first will arise out of their theologically informed anthropology, their view of human nature, to preserve a sense of the importance of the spiritual and to resist the pressure to reduce matters to the merely economic, or psychological, or hedonic. Faithful teachers, chaplains, and politicians will model, as well as espouse, such a view of humanity that includes a dimension of transcendence, and will help others at least to respect their fellows who do so, so that important public matters do not get squeezed down under the low ceiling of secularism. Spiritual things matter, too.

The second abiding concern will be to defend free space specifically for the Christian Church. Not only the "spiritual in general" but also the gospel in particular must be protected, else society loses a crucial voice—not only about the world to come but also about the here and now. The Church is not the sole valuable voice on religious questions, but Christian teachers, chaplains, politicians, and others in public life will be especially appreciative of the Church's mission and will therefore do what they can to help others appreciate it and thus maintain its liberty. As governments and developers increasingly view church property through the lens of economic growth; as institutions find it increasingly inconvenient to oblige religious concerns in the workplace or in leisure activities; and as society at large increasingly wants the public schools to produce the next generation of compliant and productive citizens without any irksome religious odd-ity, let alone resistance, Christians must work to maintain freedom for the Church to bring its distinctive message and perform its distinctive service to the world.

Of course, "freedom" does not mean "privilege." And Christians must be clear about the difference or else we risk losing both—or gaining both at the cost of sacrificing the respect of our neighbors and any claim we might make to love them as we love ourselves.

CONCLUSION

Final Formulas

AMBIGUITY AND AMBIVALENCE HAVE RECURRED often in our discussion. We walk by faith, not by sight. But many themes—themes of the Christian story, the mission of God, our vocation, and our hope—are clear, not shadowy, and give our lives firmness and direction, enabling us to make the critical daily decisions necessary to follow Jesus.

As we conclude, we must be careful to distinguish the fundamental concern for shalom-making from mere utilitarianism, which is at best half right. Yes, we seek the greatest good possible, but not just for the greatest number. Moreover, what counts as "good" is not to be calculated merely along an axis of pleasure and pain, and certainly not according only to the pleasure of the powerful (whether an elite or a majority) at the expense of others. Instead, what is good is defined for us by the Bible—and in a way much richer than I have been able to set out in this volume as we have looked at shalom, the flourishing of God's creation.

So let's simplify some of the larger themes of our conversation to contrast them sharply with the dangers that lurk around any careless or half-understood version of this way of being Christian. I use the title "final formulas" somewhat ironically, since our fundamental concern is *not* to devise pat answers but to attend constantly to the voice of Christ who guides us daily into greater and deeper and broader and finer love for God, for each other, and for the world. But we can recall only small units of wisdom at a time, so I will suggest some "portable" phrases to help us situate ourselves properly, in a critical and creative tension, as we strive to listen to Jesus.

ENGAGEMENT WITH CULTURE WITHOUT CAPITULATION TO CULTURE

Each of us engages our culture whether we want to or not. I simply *am* a Canadian, an Anglo-Canadian, a Canadian who studied and taught in the United States, and a Canadian from northern Ontario who has lived in Britain, on the Canadian prairies, and on both of Canada's coasts. These are geographical statements, and they are statements about who I am: the shape of the land and the shape of the human societies on that land have shaped me. As Jesus prayed, we are given to him by the Father from the population of this world . . . and then we remain in this world—*sent into* it, in fact, as Jesus was—in order to perform our calling. That's why we're here (John 17).

Therefore, we are to engage daily in an ongoing conversation with the world; a give-and-take, a symbiosis, a dialectic. We were originally created this way, out of the very earth itself, enlivened by the breath of God (Gen. 2), and commissioned by God to garden this gorgeous globe. As we fell, we dragged the world down with us. Now we participate with

God in redeeming the world, in lifting it up again here and there, in remaking what cannot be salvaged, and in waiting for the full restoration that only God can bring at the end of this time.

I have not defined "we" or "world" here, because I think whatever definition we attach—"we" as generically human or specifically Christian, or "world" as planet or as human community—the relationship and the vocation remain the same. We simply *are* engaged with the world. There is no available option of either complete withdrawal or complete domination. So we make the best of it.

Making the best of it means, among other principles, refusing to capitulate to the world. This is not merely a Christian imperative, but also a human one. We human beings were put in charge of the world to cultivate it—indeed, to "subdue" it. We are not to succumb to the lure of "natural rhythms," of letting things be, however beautiful they are and however ashamed we feel about our previous mismanagement. We are to garden the world, to take its potential and improve it. We are not to abandon our dignity and responsibility, however intimidating the task may seem and however unnerved we are by our recognition of past failures. We are to make shalom, to make things even better.

In this crucial sense, then, the Christian is not called to something fundamentally different from that to which anyone else is called. The command to work with God in the redemption of humanity serves the larger purpose of helping humanity to fulfill the creation commandments and renew the world. As Christians live out all of these mandates, we bear witness to what it means to be generically human, not peculiarly Christian—for to be Christian, in this fundamental sense, means to follow the Son of Man, "the Human One," the very image of God (Col. 1:15), in the work of generic humanity: loving God above all, loving one's neighbor as oneself, and loving the earth. It is the destiny of the whole earth to follow that one Lord. The peculiarity of Christianity and its temporary salvation commandment will fade away as "every knee shall bow . . . and every tongue confess that Jesus Christ is Lord, to the glory of God the Father" (Phil. 2:10–11).

If no human being should capitulate to the "wild" of the natural world, the not-yet-cultivated spaces of it, no one likewise should capitulate to the limitations, much less the evil, of the current world system. We must beware—not categorically avoid, but beware—any alliance with the powers: powers of government, powers of commerce, powers of ideology, powers of entertainment. Such alliances always will tend to draw us away from the Lordship of Christ and toward idolatry. Ultimately, we cannot serve two masters, and we must be vigilant against any alluring inclination to think we can. We must cooperate with the powers as far as such cooperation produces shalom and avoids worse evil. But we must also simply expect "tribulation" in the world (John 16:33) from those powers, because our ultimate loyalties are elsewhere and higher, and conflict is therefore inevitable.

Christian apologists throughout history have claimed that Christians make good citizens, good employees, and good neighbors. That claim has been true when Christians have observed the instructions of Scripture. It has been true, however, only up to the point at which the powers demand from us what we, as disciples of Christ, will not give them: whether it be the cessation of our evangelism, our complicity in their wrongdoing, our silence in the face of injustice, and our basic allegiance above all. When that conflict comes, then Christians must once again be the prophetic subversives we have always been when we have had our priorities straight. And the powers seem to know, better sometimes than we do ourselves, that we are, at least potentially, such dangerous people—which is why the powers never stop suspecting the Church and trying to keep it under control, one way or another.[1]

Christians also must live alertly in the interplay of the responsible individual and the Church. We love the Church and esteem it as our primary group, our new "family" that transcends all other social allegiances. We recognize that the Church one day will become the splendid community of peace depicted in Biblical prophecy. In the light of that prophecy, however, we should recognize that the Church as it exists today can only approximate that golden future. We therefore will be on guard against social forces in congregations, denominations, special purpose groups, and even home fellowships that compromise Christian ideals and harm the individuals involved. We will not be shocked and discouraged at sin and stupidity in the Church. Rather, we will expect it, plan for it, deal with it, forgive it, and carry on. And we will also be grateful for the Church's patience with each of us, as we sometimes dilatorily, sometimes dogmatically, and sometimes overzealously participate in it.

Each of us belongs to society and to the Church, and we participate in them both as faithfully as we can as disciples of Jesus Christ who has lovingly and wisely placed us in both contexts to work for shalom. We remain, however, fully beholden neither to society nor to the Church, but only to Christ, even as we long for that day in which the distinction between society and Church forever disappears.

Full engagement with culture—which entails patience, compromise, and persistence in the face of setbacks and no more than partial success—must never succumb to the sloth of capitulation or any kind of hopeless resignation of "Oh, well, what can you do?" What you can do, what we all can do, is the will of God: to cultivate as much shalom as we can in every situation. We will not give up, nor will we expect to fully triumph. Thus we will maintain a constant, creative pressure on every situation toward its improvement, while also maintaining a "holy discontent" (John R. W. Stott) with every outcome until the New Jerusalem descends (Rev. 21).

TRANSFORMATION OF CULTURE WITHOUT CONQUEST OF CULTURE

This impetus to garden the world, and the specifically Christian impetus to recover and redeem the world, must be tempered by the recognition of our own limits and sinfulness. We may hope to reign with Christ someday; we dare not presume to reign *for* Christ *now*. One certainly can sympathize with Ian Frazier's rueful warning that "history may be useful to know, but when people start thinking of themselves in terms of history with a capital 'H,' look out."[2] We Christians, who *should* think of ourselves, and everyone else, and the whole planet, in terms of the Christian story, are reminded by our own story of how susceptible we are to the lure of power justified by self-righteousness.

Furthermore, any inclination toward domination must be tempered by the recognition of the genuine humanity of our neighbors. They, too, are gardening the world. God has broadcast blessings on everyone to further the divine purposes everywhere. So this worshiper of a false god over here nonetheless has an extraordinary gift of art, and this follower of a misdirected philosophy over there nonetheless has an extraordinary gift of analytical acuity, and this community of another faith nonetheless has an extraordinary gift of compassion, and so on. We can rejoice, and we ought to rejoice, in goodness discovered anywhere, since all goodness comes from the same fountain.[3] And we must be both humble and careful not to pull up the good that God has placed here or there in our rush to weed out whatever errors we find. "Transformation" rarely, if ever, ought to mean "total eradication and then rebuilding from the ground up," nor should it mean "our way is identical with God's way, so we shall brook neither dissent nor compromise," although it has often meant exactly that in the history of Christian imperialism.[4]

Lesslie Newbigin is eloquent on this point:

> All human traditions, institutions, and structures are prone to evil—including religion and including Christianity and the Church. They are all part of this present age. They are all prone to make absolutist claims. They are all ambiguous. There are always good reasons for attacking them. But human life is impossible without them, and God in his mercy preserves them in order to give time for the Church to fulfill its calling to make manifest to them the wisdom of God.... We are not conservatives who regard the structures as part of the unalterable order of creation, as part of the world of what we call "hard facts" beyond the range of the gospel, and who therefore suppose that the gospel is only relevant to the issues of personal and private life. Nor are we anarchists who seek to destroy the structures. We are rather patient revolutionaries who know that the whole creation, with all its given structures, is groaning in the travail of a new birth, and that we

share this groaning and travail, this struggling and wrestling, but do so in hope because we have already received, in the Spirit, the firstfruit [*sic*] of the new world (Rom. 8:19–25).[5]

ACCEPTANCE OF PLURALITY WITHOUT ENDORSEMENT OF RELATIVISM

Even as we recognize that our non-Christian neighbors contribute to the generic human program of earth-keeping, so we ought to recognize that our various Christian siblings make distinctive contributions to the specifically Christian work of salvation. Rather than insisting that every Christian sing from the same song sheets, preach from the same texts, teach the same formulations of doctrine, practice the same modes of piety, undertake the same kinds of service, and evangelize in the same ways, we should endorse a plurality of missional modes, each accomplishing something particular and good, and a plurality of missional messages, each articulating something particular and good.

Such a principle is easy to articulate, but it is often hard to practice, particularly if one is passionate about one's own perspective on, and proposed solution to, a keenly felt problem, whether retaining the religious interest of distracted young people, caring for increasing numbers of homeless people, or responding to a controversial governmental proposal. But humility about one's own limitations and gracious recognition of our Christian siblings' dignity should persuade us of the likelihood that we do not have all truth and that they, too, have something good to contribute to this matter.

Indeed, we must go beyond a benign tolerance of such differences—a kind of "comity" arrangement (as held in various missionary situations) that lets the Presbyterians do their thing there while we Methodists do our thing here, so that now we let the environmentalists do their thing there while the evangelists do their thing over here. That "staying out of each other's way" is fine as far as it goes. But if we would respectfully and expectantly pay closer attention to our differences, we might learn how to be better versions of ourselves. Environmentalists might become excited to see that their work, important on its own terms according to the creation commandments, is also truly evangelistic, as ecologically concerned neighbors connect and work together with Christians to protect the land. Meanwhile, evangelists might rejoice to proclaim the much-expanded (and much more attractive) message of a God who loves the whole earth, not just human souls.

Here again we encounter one of the more provocative implications of the line of thinking presented in this book. We must allow that in complex situations equally faithful Christians may end up saying and doing not just different but also apparently contrary things. Sometimes we might understand why God paradoxically calls Christians to opposing positions and efforts. Some non-Christians, perhaps, will resonate with these kinds of Christians and be repelled by those, while for other non-Christians the opposite will be true. Some Christians can articulate and manifest this part of God's complex truth on a matter while some other Christians can represent another part. God deploys different kinds of Christians to connect with different kinds of neighbors. But sometimes we won't understand what's going on, and we should remain open to the idea that God calls different sorts of people to different sorts of tasks to get different things done in God's unfathomably complex plan of winning as much of the world as possible—including the sanctioning of apparently contradictory and even antagonistic beliefs and behaviors. Affirming plurality, however, does not mean surrendering to relativism. Not all options advocated by anyone at all who claims to be Christian can be, or should be, affirmed or even tolerated. All sorts of horrors have been justified by certain professed Christians in the name of their religion, from chattel slavery to genocide to cultural annihilation to spousal abuse to child molestation. If we have no qualms about simply pronouncing these things wrong, and I trust we have none, then we are poised similarly to flatly disagree with other bad options offered in the name of Christ. Humble openness to honor God and each other in the recognition of authentic plurality must remain in tension with the humble willingness to honor God and each other in the recognition of genuine error and sin. Although there *may* be more than one commendable option in this situation, there may equally *not* be.

No one can be certain of striking a perfect balance here, of course, because no one but God can be certain of perfect judgment on *anything* beyond the simple or trivial. What I write today I may well want to modify or even retract tomorrow—indeed, I almost certainly will want to do so; this book is not a finding handed down from some pinnacle of final wisdom but rather a report from one pilgrim on the journey on which we all are embarked. Still, life requires us to make determinations and decisions—some of them important—and all we can do is strive to be as open as we can be to goodness, while also as resistant as we can be to all that is not good. We listen hard, then, for the voice of Jesus, rather than settling for an easy embrace or curt exclusion.

CONFIDENCE IN OUR CONVICTIONS WITHOUT DELUSIONS OF INFALLIBILITY

We walk with confidence in Christ because we have the conviction that Jesus really is Lord, that he really has called us into his company, and that he really has assigned us a mission—the distinctive Christian mission of salvation—along with our generic human "standing orders" of cultivating the earth. These are the convictions that shape and dignify everything we do, everywhere, at every moment. This is why we're here. Thus we must be both patient and persistent. We will be patient because of our understanding of the ways of God's providence, including the understanding that we yet do not fully understand God's providence—and can trust God anyway. We will be persistent because we have heard God's call and strive to obey it as the very words of life. We walk by faith, not by sight—but we do walk, trusting God to guide us, equip us, correct us, forgive us, bless us, and use us.

Strong in these convictions, we yet must avoid hubris. We cannot succeed by ourselves. We need our particular Christian communities, we need the support and wisdom of other Christian communities, we need the cooperation and gifts of other human beings, in countless ways we need our fellow creatures, and we fundamentally need God: ever, always, now. We also have to recognize daily that we may well be wrong about quite a lot, and we are undoubtedly wrong about some things—unless we presume to claim a correctness that is justified neither by the Scriptures nor the history of the Church. We must further recognize that even our best-intentioned, best-conceived, and best-executed work will rarely entirely succeed, nor will it always result exclusively in good consequences. We must go on from these sobering reflections to recognize that very little of our work meets that high standard (best-intentioned, best-conceived, and best-executed), leaving us to expect that the rest of what we do is even more likely to issue in far less than optimal outcomes. We should speak, therefore, with humility. And the same humility should likewise characterize our actions, our relationships, and our self-esteem.

Christian humility is not at all the same thing as luke-warmness, or cowardice, or laziness. Christian humility is, fundamentally, submitting gladly to God the Father and fol-lowing joyfully his Son in the power of the Spirit. The world needs bold, enterprising, passionate, and persistent disciples of Christ who will see it for what it is, who will love it as God does, and who will care for it with creativity, realism, and hope. The whole world—God's world, our world—is at stake, and we must make the best of it.

That's why we're here.
That's why you're here.

NOTES

Introduction

1. Quoted in George Marsden, *Fundamentalism and American Culture: The Shaping of Twentieth-Century Evangelicalism, 1870–1925* (New York: Oxford University Press, 1980), 38.
2. This phrase has been popularized by James Davison Hunter, *To Change the World: The Irony, Tragedy, and Possibility of Christianity in the Late Modern World* (New York and Oxford: Oxford University Press, 2010). As I shall endeavor to make clear in what follows, "faithful presence" can be commended if it issues in effective influence, in a constant critical and constructive pressure upon the world in God's name. Anything less than that, however, amounts merely to quietism.
3. *Making the Best of It: Following Christ in the Real World* (New York and Oxford: Oxford University Press, 2008).
4. *Need to Know: Vocation as the Heart of Christian Epistemology* (New York and Oxford: Oxford University Press, 2014).

Chapter 1

1. Mircea Eliade, *The Myth of the Eternal Return or, Cosmos and History*, trans. Willard R. Trask. (Princeton, NJ: Princeton

University Press, 1954); Herbert Butterfield, *The Origins of History* (New York: Basic Books, 1981).

2. I might pause to make clear that I am not implying anything pro or con regarding family planning, contraception, and the like. The command to "be fruitful and multiply" was given to our first parents as part of the general command to care for the earth *by all of humanity*. For *humanity* to stop reproducing, thereby letting the earth languish without its gardeners, would be wrong. But individuals have different particular callings— such as single people, whom God, as the rest of the Bible makes clear, does *not* call to reproduce. Thus it would be a simplistic inference from the text to advocate that everyone, everywhere, reproduce, let alone reproduce a lot.

3. Dallas Willard, *The Divine Conspiracy: Rediscovering Our Hidden Life in God* (San Francisco: Harper, 1998), 378.

4. Lynn White, Jr., "The Historical Roots of Our Ecological Crisis," *Science* 155 (1967): 1203–7.

5. *Unabridged Merriam-Webster Dictionary*, s.v. "dominion"; http://unabridged.merriam-webster.com/cgi-bin/unabridged? va=dominion&x=0&y=0; accessed December 22, 2006.

6. I recognize that "dominion" has more than one meaning and that, indeed, it has changed meanings over the course of history. Canada, for example, is no longer under the "British monarch" but recognizes Queen Elizabeth II as the Queen of *Canada*, while also acknowledging that she happens to rule over other realms as well, such as, for one example, the United Kingdom.

7. John Paul II, *Centesimus Annus, Encyclical Letter on the Hundredth Anniversary of Rerum Novarum* (Boston: St. Paul Books, 1991), 54; quoted in Jean Bethke Elshtain, *Who Are We? Critical Reflections and Hopeful Possibilities* (Grand Rapids, MI: Eerdmans, 2000), 53.

8. Andy Crouch, "Feeling Green," *Books and Culture* (March/April 2007): 33.

9. I am not going to engage in a discussion of "natural law," "common grace," and so on, since I have not yet found the longstanding debates around them to have delivered solid, useful categories for the present project.

10. This critically appreciative perspective is shared by David Fergusson, *Faith and Its Critics* (Oxford: Oxford University Press, 2009).

11. Irenaeus, *Against Heresies*, IV.20.vii (my translation); Philip Schaff and David S. Schaff, eds., *The Creeds of Christendom*, 6th ed. (Grand Rapids, MI: Baker, 1931), 676.

12. Jonathan Edwards is particularly helpful on this question, finding, as he does, that "a man's loving what is grateful [agreeable] or pleasing to him, and being averse to what is disagreeable . . . is the same thing as a man's having a faculty of will" (*The Nature of True Virtue*, in *Jonathan Edwards: Ethical Writings*, ed. Paul Ramsey [New Haven, CT: Yale University Press, 1989], 575–76).

13. Mark Buchanan, *Your God Is Too Safe: Rediscovering the Wonder of a God You Can't Control* (Portland, OR: Multnomah, 2001), 108–9. I recognize that E. P. Sanders and others have rehabilitated some Christian stereotypes regarding the Pharisees, but I think Buchanan's characterization stands—especially given the way Jesus addresses them and the issues over which they contend with him.

14. David Martin, *Christian Language in the Secular City* (Aldershot, UK: Ashgate, 2002), 185.

15. See Robin Lovin, *Reinhold Niebuhr and Christian Realism* (Cambridge: Cambridge University Press, 1995).

16. There is even evidence that Christian values can assist in a matter that gets as close to Realpolitik as can be imagined, namely, the interrogation of prisoners. US Marine Major Sherwood F. Moran applied techniques of care and respect for his subjects during World War II and was much more successful than anyone else at his job. The counterintuitive story of his interrogation manual is told in Stephen Budiansky, "Truth Extraction," *Atlantic Monthly* (June 2005): 32–35.

17. To be sure, sometimes, if all too rarely, we human beings are capable of genuine self-sacrifice in the interests of justice and the welfare of others. Rodney Stark sums up the research of many others to observe that the abolition of slavery was advanced in America, Britain, and France to the immediate, lasting, and considerable cost of individuals and of those

societies in general (*For the Glory of God: How Monotheism Led to Reformations, Science, Witch-Hunts, and the End of Slavery* [Princeton, NJ: Princeton University Press, 2003], 358–59).

18. Ronald J. Sider combines these virtues in his presentation of "Seven Short Principles for a Political Philosophy," namely, "Everybody should have power, not just a few"; "The poor deserve special care"; "Every person should have the capital to earn a decent living"; "Maintain the balance between freedom and justice"; "Always think globally"; "Protect the separation of church and state"; and "Understand the limits of politics" (*Living Like Jesus: Eleven Essentials for Growing a Genuine Faith* [Grand Rapids, MI: Baker, 1996], 130–37).

19. When I think of contemporary Christian pacifists, I am reminded of Oliver O'Donovan's vivid phrasing: "The prophet is not allowed the luxury of perpetual subversion. After Ahab, Elijah must anoint some Hazael, some Jehu" (*The Desire of the Nations: Rediscovering the Roots of Political Thought* [Cambridge: Cambridge University Press, 1996], 12).

20. Wendell Berry, "Christianity and the Survival of Creation," in *Sex, Economy, Freedom, and Community* (New York: Pantheon, 1992); quoted in Brian J. Walsh and Sylvia C. Keesmaat, *Colossians Remixed* (Downers Grove, IL: InterVarsity, 2004), 168.

21. Paul Marshall, *Heaven Is Not My Home: Living in the Now of God's Creation* (Nashville, TN: Word, 1998). See also Richard J. Mouw's excellent exposition of Isaiah along these lines: *When the Kings Come Marching In: Isaiah and the New Jerusalem* (Grand Rapids, MI: Eerdmans, 1983); and J. Richard Middleton, *A New Heaven and a New Earth: Reclaiming Biblical Eschatology* (Grand Rapids, MI: Baker Academic, 2014).

22. Anna Fels, *Necessary Dreams: Ambition in Women's Changing Lives* (New York: Pantheon, 2004); see also Barry A. Harvey, "What We've Got Here Is a Failure to Imagine: The Church-Based University in the Tournament of Competing Visions," *Christian Scholar's Review* 34, no. 2 (2005): 201–15.

23. Among the best descriptions I have encountered of shalom is the one provided by Nicholas Wolterstorff in *Until Justice and Peace Embrace* (Grand Rapids, MI: Eerdmans, 1983), 69–72.

Chapter 2

1. The best Christian treatment of alienating work I know of is Miroslav Volf, *Work in the Spirit: Toward a Theology of Work* (Oxford: Oxford University Press, 1991), ch. 6.
2. Nicholas Wolterstorff, "More on Vocation," *The Reformed Journal* 29 (1979): 23.
3. Charles Taylor uses Hall's phrase as a chapter title in *Sources of the Self: The Making of the Modern Identity* (Cambridge: Cambridge University Press, 1989), 221.
4. Jeff Haanen, "Investments for the Kingdom," *Christianity Today* (November 23, 2016): http://www.christianitytoday.com/ct/2016/december/investments-for-kingdom.html; accessed January 13, 2017.
5. James Fallows, "How America Is Putting Itself Back Together," *The Atlantic* (March 2016): http://www.theatlantic.com/magazine/archive/2016/03/how-america-is-putting-itself-back-together/426882/; accessed January 13, 2017.
6. Derek Johnson, "A World without Work?" *The Atlantic* (March 2015): https://www.theatlantic.com/magazine/archive/2015/07/world-without-work/395294/; accessed January 13, 2017; Paul Collier, *The Bottom Billion: Why the Poorest Countries Are Failing and What Can Be Done about It* (Oxford: Oxford University Press, 2007).
7. Again, just to be clear: I am not against distance education in every form. After all, this book itself is a technology of "distance education." I also applaud innovations in techniques and technology that have brought educational opportunities to people who otherwise cannot access them. I am here railing against those who think that there is no important difference between in-person and distance education such that the former is not worth the cost and needs to be phased out in the dawning of a glorious new technological age. To whimsically attack this notion using its own jargon, I would say that too much of the signal is degraded or lost when put through the pipelines of distance education, and I would urge those in the early throes of excitement about the purported economies and efficiencies of distance education and instructional technologies to read the

likes of Michael Polanyi (on the value of "tacit knowledge" and "apprenticeship") and Parker Palmer (on the importance of the personal qualities of the teacher and of the student in their interaction) before they go any further.

8. Perhaps a straw in the wind is the decision by some major grocery stores to remove self-serve lanes: Nancy Luna, "Albertsons, Vons Getting Rid of Most Self-Checkout Lanes at Southern California Stores," *Orange County Register* (November 29, 2016): http://www.ocregister.com/articles/self-736860-service-checkout.html; accessed January 13, 2017.

9. Reinhold Niebuhr, *Moral Man and Immoral Society: A Study in Ethics and Politics* (New York: Charles Scribner's Sons, 1960 [1932]).

10. David Martin, *Tongues of Fire: The Explosion of Protestantism in Latin America* (Oxford: Blackwell, 1990); Martin, *Pentecostalism: The World Their Parish* (Oxford: Blackwell, 2002).

11. I am deliberately avoiding the Kuyperian language of "sphere sovereignty" here—not because I am ungrateful for this way of thinking, to which I am deeply indebted, but because the term itself can convey to some the idea of mutually exclusive jurisdictions, which, of course, as the example of educating children demonstrates, is often not the case.

12. Percy Bysshe Shelley, "Ozmandias," *The Examiner: A Sunday Paper, on Politics, Domestic Economy and Theatricals for the Year 1818* (London: John Hunt, 1818), 24.

13. C. S. Lewis, *The Weight of Glory and Other Addresses* (Grand Rapids, MI: Eerdmans, 1949), 14–15.

Chapter 3

1. Jacques Ellul is, of course, a careful and penetrating thinker about many things, but on the subject of the city, he is prone to gloomy oversimplification. See his *The Meaning of the City* (Grand Rapids, MI: Eerdmans, 1970). A helpful alternative viewpoint to Ellul's is found in Eric Jacobsen, *The Space Between: A Christian Engagement with the Built Environment* (Grand Rapids, MI: Baker Academic, 2012).

2. Charles M. Sheldon, *In His Steps: What Would Jesus Do?* (New York and Toronto: Revell, 1897).

3. I tend to hold to the traditional ascriptions of authorship in the New Testament, including the conviction that the same author, John, wrote the Gospel and the Epistles that bear his name. But my point stands even if one doesn't hold to this position.

4. This, to me, is one of the most fundamental mistakes typically made in the Anabaptist tradition and by important exemplars of it such as John Howard Yoder: "For the radical Protestant there will always be a canon within the canon; namely, that recorded experience of practical moral reasoning in genuine human form that bears the name of Jesus" (*The Priestly Kingdom: Social Ethics as Gospel* [Notre Dame, IN: University of Notre Dame Press, 1985], 37). I believe that Christian thinking should be Christological and Christocentric, but, as I argue here, that means neither that the earthly career of Jesus is normative in Yoder's sense nor that the Gospels themselves are privileged above other Biblical literature. For an explanation of how Christ *ought* to figure in theology, see my "Evangelical Theology Should Be Evangelical," in John G. Stackhouse, Jr., ed., *Evangelical Futures: A Conversation on Theological Method* (Grand Rapids, MI: Baker Academic, 2000), 39–58.

5. Richard Bauckham, *The Bible in Politics: How to Read the Bible Politically* (Louisville, KY: Westminster/John Knox Press, 1989), 3–4.

6. Oliver O'Donovan, *The Desire of the Nations: Rediscovering the Roots of Political Thought* (Cambridge: Cambridge University Press, 1996), 219.

7. Harold Mattingly, *Christianity in the Roman Empire* (New York: Norton, 1967), 49. For more on the debate over soldiers in the early Church, see John F. Shean, *Soldiering for God: Christianity and the Roman Army* (Boston: Brill, 2010); Ronald J. Sider, *The Early Church on Killing: A Comprehensive Sourcebook on War, Abortion, and Capital Punishment* (Grand Rapids, MI: Baker Academic, 2012); George Kalantzis, *Caesar and the Lamb: Early Christian Attitudes on War and Military Service* (Eugene, OR: Cascade, 2012); and Despina Iosif, *Early Christian Attitudes to War, Violence, and Military Service* (Piscataway, NJ: Gorgias, 2013).

8. Mark Allan Powell reminds us that "people do not have to die and go to heaven to live in a realm of power ruled by God. Already, in this life, Jesus says, God is ready and willing to rule our lives. And this, he adds, is 'good news' (Mark 1:14–15)" (*Giving to God: The Bible's Good News about Living a Generous Life* [Grand Rapids, MI: Eerdmans, 2006], 37).

9. Darrell L. Guder, ed., *Missional Church: A Vision for the Sending of the Church in North America* (Grand Rapids, MI: Eerdmans, 1998).

10. Dietrich Bonhoeffer, *Letters and Papers from Prison*, ed. Eberhard Bethge, trans. Reginald Fuller, Frank Clarke, and John Bowden (New York: Macmillan, 1962 [1953]), 286.

11. Martin, *Christian Language*, 24–25.

12. The phrase is Robert Jenson's, from his "The Church's Responsibility for the World," in Carl E. Braaten and Robert W. Jenson, eds., *The Two Cities of God: The Church's Responsibility for the Earthly City* (Grand Rapids, MI: Eerdmans, 1997), 4.

Chapter 4

1. Richard Bauckham, *Bible and Mission: Christian Witness in a Postmodern World* (Grand Rapids, MI: Eerdmans, 2003), 99.

2. Robert L. Wilken remarks that "to defend the existence of God, Christian thinkers in early modern times excluded all appeals to Christian behavior or practices, the very things that give Christianity its power and have been its most compelling testimony to the reality of God" (*Remembering the Christian Past* [Grand Rapids, MI: Eerdmans, 1995], 52). For further reflection on the ways in which Christians can exemplify the faith, please see my *Humble Apologetics: Defending the Faith Today* (New York: Oxford University Press, 2002), ch. 11.

3. "Theology must be political if it is to be evangelical [by which O'Donovan means, I think, both "of the gospel" and "evangelistic"]. Rule out the political questions and you cut short the proclamation of God's saving power; you leave people enslaved where they ought to be set free from sin—their own sin and others" (Oliver O'Donovan, *The Desire of the Nations: Rediscovering the*

Roots of Political Thought [Cambridge: Cambridge University Press, 1996], 3).

4. One might make a similar case for so-called pure research, construing scholarship that investigates the world God made as a form of worship, of taking so seriously and appreciatively what God has done, and what God's creatures have done, that we devote time and money to tracing it out. I assert, that is, that not all research has to "pay off" in some way, in some clear practical application improving human life or the life of other creatures. "This research grant could have been sold and the money given to the poor."

Or perhaps such research yet does "pay off." For research that opens up God's work and ways, and helps us to see God's creation better, is "paying off" indeed: "in wonder, love, and praise." Any version of Christianity that fails to support such God-honoring work is a truncated one.

5. For some helpful reflections on a Christian appreciation of art, see Leland Ryken, *Culture in Christian Perspective: A Door to Understanding and Enjoying the Arts* (Portland, OR: Multnomah, 1986); Nicholas Wolterstorff, *Art in Action* (Grand Rapids, MI: Eerdmans, 1980); Makoto Fujimura, *Culture Care* (Salem, MA: Deschamps, 2014); and Abigail Woolley, "Art's Claim on Resources: Sabbath Ethics as a Framework for Value," *Journal of Scriptural Reasoning* 16 (forthcoming, 2017).

6. Robert Wuthnow, *The Restructuring of American Religion: Society and Faith Since World War II* (Princeton, NJ: Princeton University Press, 1988), ch. 6.

7. I have said more about parachurch organizations, both in affirmation and in warning, in "The Parachurch: Promise and Peril," in *Evangelical Landscapes: Facing Critical Issues of the Day* (Grand Rapids, MI: Baker Academic, 2002), 25–36.

8. John Howard Yoder, *The Priestly Kingdom: Social Ethics as Gospel* (Notre Dame, IN: University of Notre Dame Press, 1985), 81.

9. Paul Griffiths, *An Apology for Apologetics: A Study in the Logic of Interreligious Dialogue* (Maryknoll, NY: Orbis, 1991), xi–xii.

10. Yoder, *The Priestly Kingdom*, 97.

11. Mark Buchanan, *Your God Is Too Safe: Rediscovering the Wonder of a God You Can't Control* (Portland, OR: Multnomah, 2001), 101–2.
12. Quoted without reference in David Martin, *Christian Language in the Secular City* (Aldershot, UK: Ashgate, 2002), 141; italics in original.
13. Quoted in George Marsden, *Fundamentalism and American Culture: The Shaping of Twentieth-Century Evangelicalism, 1870–1925* (New York: Oxford University Press, 1980), 38.
14. Epigraph to Alan Jacobs, *A Visit to Vanity Fair: Moral Essays on the Present Age* (Grand Rapids, MI: Brazos, 2001).

Chapter 5

1. Along with sources mentioned below, I recommend Robert Benne's teaching from an American Lutheran perspective. For an introduction to his thought that goes well beyond the "economic life" of the title, see his "The Calling of the Church in Economic Life," in Carl E. Braaten and Robert W. Jenson, eds., *The Two Cities of God: The Church's Responsibility for the Earthly City* (Grand Rapids, MI: Eerdmans, 1997), 95–116. Then see his *The Paradoxical Vision: A Public Theology for the Twenty-First Century* (Minneapolis: Fortress, 1995).
2. The phrasing is Oliver O'Donovan's (*The Desire of the Nations: Rediscovering the Roots of Political Thought* [Cambridge: Cambridge University Press, 1996], 202; citing Epistle 189).
3. As Glenn Tinder remarks (in an echo of Lord Acton's dictum): "Steeped in violence and power, the state is morally impure at its best. And it is never at its best. State power is rarely in the hands of people who are morally very good. This is partly because few such people exist. And it is partly because high positions in the state are nearly irresistible incitements to pride. The leaders of states enjoy privileges, pleasures, and adulation to a degree that can leave only the most extraordinary personalities undefiled" (Glenn Tinder, *The Fabric of Hope: An Essay* [Atlanta: Scholars Press, 1999], 168).
4. An example of such realism is Jonathan Rauch, "What's Ailing American Politics?" *The Atlantic* (July 2016): 51–63.

5. This distinction between the ultimate and penultimate I owe to Dietrich Bonhoeffer's reflections in his *Ethics*, ed. Clifford J. Green, trans. Charles C. West Reinhard Krauss, and Douglas W. Stott (Minneapolis, MN: Augsburg Fortress, 2005 [1949]), 146–70.

6. C. S. Lewis's discussion of this subject has not been bettered: *Miracles* (San Francisco: HarperSanFrancisco, 2001 [1947]). See also, however, a more recent *tour de force*: Craig S. Keener, *Miracles: The Credibility of the New Testament Accounts*, 2 vols. (Grand Rapids, MI: Baker Academic, 2011).

7. These aphorisms have been variously attributed.

8. David Martin, *Reflections on Sociology and Theology* (Oxford: Clarendon, 1997), 62–63. The previous paragraph of mine is inspired by Martin's use of geological and hydrological metaphors throughout his work.

Chapter 6

1. Oliver O'Donovan, *The Desire of the Nations: Rediscovering the Roots of Political Thought* (Cambridge: Cambridge University Press, 1996), 195.

2. I say "with all of its attending challenges" to sharply distinguish my view from the effusions of Eusebius of Caesarea, notorious celebrant of Constantine (see particularly the "panegyric" in his *Ecclesiastical History*, Book X, chapter 4). For a classic account of the early challenges, see Charles Norris Cochrane, *Christianity and Classical Culture: A Study of Thought and Action from Augustus to Augustine*, rev. ed. (Oxford: Oxford University Press, 1980 [1940, 1944]).

3. Kenneth Scott Latourette, *A History of the Expansion of Christianity*, vol. 1: *The First Five Centuries* (New York: Harper and Brothers, 1937), 154.

4. The *oeuvre* of Rodney Stark offers large-scale portraits of this theme, beginning with *One True God: The Historical Consequences of Monotheism* (Princeton, NJ: Princeton University Press, 2001).

5. Robert Wilken echoes this point as he discusses the matter from Augustine's point of view: "For Christians who lived

during the first three centuries the task of running the cities and the empire seemed to be someone else's responsibility.... . By Augustine's time, however, Christians did not enjoy such luxury. Without the participation of Christians the cities would lack qualified people to serve as magistrates, judges, civic officials, teachers, and soldiers" (Robert L. Wilken, "Augustine's City of God Today," in Carl E. Braaten and Robert W. Jenson, eds., *The Two Cities of God: The Church's Responsibility for the Earthly City* [Grand Rapids, MI: Eerdmans, 1997], 35).

6. James Davison Hunter, *To Change the World: The Irony, Tragedy, and Possibility of Christianity in the Late Modern World* (New York and Oxford: Oxford University Press, 2010).

7. This is not the place for a full apologetic on behalf of divinely mandated genocide, particularly since it is an open question in Biblical studies as to just how extensive—or how hyperbolic—these commands really were. But I do not find this command of God immediately implausible. A society that has become so evil that it sacrifices its own children to its gods, as the Canaanites were known to do, could well be a culture that is irretrievably wicked and harmful—indeed, lethally harmful even to its own children. The eradication of such a society might well have been in everyone's interest, particularly from a Christian point of view that takes resurrection seriously and believes in a merciful God who would be generous in the next life to any innocents killed in such a way. All I want to say here is that such Old Testament accounts should not be immediately set aside as unworthy of God but read as Scripture in the hopes of better understanding God and God's ways.

8. A related semantic muddle afflicts this discourse regarding the word "power." Being "for" or "against" power is like being for or against light, or fire, electricity, or momentum—all, not coincidentally, forms of power. For some refreshing Christian reflections on power, see Andy Crouch, *Playing God: Redeeming the Gift of Power* (Downers Grove, IL: InterVarsity Press, 2013).

9. See Nigel Biggar, *In Defence of War* (Oxford: Oxford University Press, 2013).

10. "Why the Christian Church Is Not Pacifist," anthologized in Reinhold Niebuhr, *The Essential Reinhold Niebuhr: Selected Essays and Addresses*, ed. Robert McAfee Brown (New Haven, CT, and London: Yale University Press, 1986), 118.

11. I wonder how someone in the Two-Thirds World, groaning under one or another form of tyranny, would hear North American or British ethicists telling them to eschew violence and rebellion in the cause of justice. Isn't it just a trifle suspect for those of us who enjoy positions of safety and prosperity won through violence to tell others not to use it?

12. David F. Ford, *The Shape of Living* (London: HarperCollins, 1997), 69.

13. Yoder offers a powerful challenge:

> How do we know that violence will be effective toward the ends which are posited? Has a long enough time frame been allowed? Has there been attention to the possibility that social changes imposed by superior forces are less stable, or that the people living under unfreedom are less productive than when social change is achieved without violence? Has really serious legal process or really serious social science analysis been invested in testing whether the violence one is ready to resort to is really the last resort, and whether there would be no nonviolent alternatives offering a comparable percentage of probability of achieving comparable results? (*The Politics of Jesus* [Grand Rapids, MI: Eerdmans, 1972], 115)

We differ in our answers to these rhetorical questions. He presumes that nonviolence can be shown to be at least as effective as violence, although he doesn't actually attempt any such demonstration himself. I don't think so and have advanced some instances to the contrary in this discussion and also here: "A Dash of Cold Water for Christian Anarchism," *Geez* (Winter 2012): 38–39.

14. Dietrich Bonhoeffer challenges us thus:

> Who stands fast? Only the man whose final standard is not his reason, his principles, his conscience, his freedom, or his virtue, but who is ready to sacrifice all this when he is called to obedient and responsible action in faith and in exclusive allegiance to God—the responsible man, who tries to make his whole life an answer to the question and call of God. . . .
>
> Free responsibility . . . depends on a God who demands responsible action in a bold venture of faith, and who promises forgiveness and consolation to the man who becomes a sinner in that venture. . . .
>
> The ultimate question for a responsible man to ask is not how he is to extricate himself heroically from the affair, but how the coming generation is to live. (*Letters and Papers from Prison*, ed. Eberhard Bethge [New York: Macmillan, 1971 (1953)], 5-7.)

Chapter 7

1. Mark Buchanan, *Your God Is Too Safe: Rediscovering the Wonder of a God You Can't Control* (Portland, OR: Multnomah, 2001), 228.
2. Thus Frederick Buechner asks, "What about sin itself as a means of grace?" (*The Sacred Journey: A Memoir of Early Days* [San Francisco: HarperSanFrancisco, 1982], 3).
3. I altered NRSV's "trustworthy" to the traditional, synonymous "faithful."
4. Some will notice that I am paraphrasing Paul Tillich, *Systematic Theology*, vol. 1 (Chicago: University of Chicago Press, 1951), 7.
5. We might round out the Gospel picture by referring to John 20:21: "As the Father has sent me, so I send you." One sends someone somewhere to do something. Jesus was sent to get certain things done (one of his last words was, "It is accomplished" (John 19:30). So he sends his disciples into the world to do "greater works than these" (John 14:12).

6. Glenn Tinder, *The Political Meaning of Christianity: An Interpretation* (Baton Rouge: Louisiana State University Press, 1989), 131.
7. On this theme, see ibid. and Glenn Tinder, *The Fabric of Hope: An Essay* (Atlanta, GA: Scholars Press, 1999).
8. Martin Luther, "The Freedom of a Christian," anthologized in *Martin Luther: Selections from His Writings*, ed. John Dillenberger (Garden City, NY: Anchor, 1961), 52–85.
9. Irshad Manji enquires into her own Islamic tradition to investigate why some Islamic regimes have been tolerant, even welcoming, of "others." She attributes this openness partly to "the concept of a future," to an Islamic confidence that all is unfolding as God wants it to: "Accumulating military victories meant that Arabs felt they had an appreciable and secured future. Which, in turn, meant that Islam didn't need to be thoroughly rigid or in-your-face.... . When Arab Muslims lost their empire, they also forfeited the balance between past and future, tribalism and tolerance" (*The Trouble with Islam Today: A Wake-Up Call for Honesty and Change* [Toronto: Random House Canada, 2003], 157). Those Christians who believe Jesus is Lord, the Kingdom of God is here and expanding, and Christ will come again—that is, all Christians worthy of the name—ought to be especially willing to accommodate others and to cooperate with the often nonlinear, apparently meandering, and usually pluriform providence of God.
10. The terms "accepting love" and "transforming love" are attributed to William F. May in Michael J. Sandel, "The Case Against Perfection: What's Wrong with Designer Children, Bionic Athletes, and Genetic Engineering," *Atlantic Monthly* (April 2004): 57.
11. Tinder, *The Political Meaning of Christianity*, 106. Tinder has much to say on this theme of liberty; see the chapter by that name in ibid., 101–49; and also his *Liberty: Rethinking an Imperiled Ideal* (Grand Rapids, MI: Eerdmans, 2007).
12. John Howard Yoder, *The Priestly Kingdom: Social Ethics as Gospel* (Notre Dame, IN: University of Notre Dame Press, 1985), 100-1.

13. Richard Mouw affirms this viewpoint in *He Shines in All That's Fair: Culture and Common Grace* (Grand Rapids, MI: Eerdmans, 2001), 79–80.

14. See H. Richard Niebuhr, *Christ and Culture* (New York: Harper & Row, 1951). I defend the abiding relevance of Niebuhr's typology in chapter 1 of *Making the Best of It: Following Christ in the Real World* (New York and Oxford: Oxford University Press, 2008).

Chapter 8

1. Only Bonhoeffer aficionados will care, but I will observe that this question does not actually appear where it is always said to appear, namely, in Bonhoeffer's famous letter to Eberhard Bethge of April 30, 1944 (*Letters and Papers from Prison*, ed. Eberhard Bethge, trans. Reginald Fuller, Frank Clarke, and John Bowden [New York: Macmillan, 1962 (1953)], 279). Bonhoeffer, in fact, writes thus: "What is bothering me incessantly is the question what Christianity really is, or indeed who Christ really is, for us today."

2. My debts to each of these thinkers are more evident in *Making the Best of It: Following Christ in the Real World* (New York and Oxford: Oxford University Press, 2008).

3. See, for example, Richard J. Mouw, *He Shines in All That's Fair: Culture and Common Grace* (Grand Rapids, MI: Eerdmans, 2001); Nicholas Wolterstorff, *Justice in Love* (Grand Rapids, MI: Eerdmans, 2015).

4. John Howard Yoder, "How H. Richard Niebuhr Reasoned: A Critique of *Christ and Culture*," in Glenn H. Stassen, D. M. Yeager, and John Howard Yoder, eds., *Authentic Transformation: A New Vision of Christ and Culture* (Nashville, TN: Abingdon, 1996), 69.

5. John Howard Yoder, "The Kingdom as Social Ethic," in *The Priestly Kingdom: Social Ethics as Gospel* (Notre Dame, IN: University of Notre Dame Press, 1985), 80–101.

6. Eugene C. Roehlkepartain, "What Makes Faith Mature?" *The Christian Century* (May 9, 1990): 496–499; Peter L. Benson and Carolyn H. Eklin, *Effective Christian Education: A National*

Study of Protestant Congregations: A Summary Report on Faith, Loyalty, and Congregational Life (Minneapolis, MN: Search Institute, 1990).

7. Reinhold Niebuhr, *The Nature and Destiny of Man: A Christian Interpretation*, repr. ed., 2 vols. (New York: Charles Scribner's Sons, 1964 [1941]), 1:185.

8. Robin W. Lovin, *Reinhold Niebuhr and Christian Realism* (Cambridge: Cambridge University Press, 1995), 150. See Niebuhr, *Nature and Destiny*, 1:228–40.

9. David Martin, *Christian Language in the Secular City* (Aldershot, UK: Ashgate, 2002), 120.

Chapter 9

1. I might mention, out of a concern for both clarity and courtesy, that I have been using this phrase "behaving in public" for some time in lectures on these matters and in my previous book on these questions, *Making the Best of It: Following Christ in the Real World* (New York and Oxford: Oxford University Press, 2008). I want to acknowledge also, however, the book by this title on similar concerns more recently authored by Nigel Biggar: *Behaving in Public: How to Do Christian Ethics* (Grand Rapids, MI: Eerdmans, 2011).

2. The most trenchant critic, and for half a century, of simplistic secularization theories and accounts has been David Martin. Among many other works, see David Martin, *On Secularization: Towards a Revised General Theory* (Burlington, VT: Ashgate, 2005).

3. A key early account of the multifarious forms religion has been taking in contemporary societies is José Casanova, *Public Religions in the Modern World* (Chicago: University of Chicago Press, 1994).

4. Philip Jenkins, "Downward, Outward, Later," *Books and Culture* (September 2006): 15. Jenkins is well aware, of course, that churches have also disappeared, whether in North Africa, the Near East, and elsewhere, and that the same destiny might indeed await European Christianity—as he notes on the same page from which this quotation comes.

5. Martin E. Marty makes this theme of shifting alliances a key category in his study of *Modern American Religion*, vol. 1: *The Irony of It All, 1893–1919* (Chicago: University of Chicago Press, 1986). For an introduction to this theme, see Martin E. Marty, "Cross-Multicultures in the Crossfire: The Humanities and Political Interests," in David A. Hoekema and Bobby Fong, eds., *Christianity and Culture in the Crossfire* (Grand Rapids, MI: Eerdmans, 1997), 15–27.

6. Charles Taylor, "The Politics of Recognition," in Charles Taylor et al., *Multiculturalism*, ed. Amy Gutmann (Princeton, NJ: Princeton University Press, 1984), 62.

7. Jürgen Habermas issues warnings precisely along these lines: "Struggles for Recognition in the Democratic Constitutional State," in Taylor et al., *Multiculturalism*, 125–142. In fact, in *Making the Best of It*, published in 2008, I said the following in this context, only to have intervening events already overtake this sentence: "The next decades of political argument will deal largely with where we will draw the line and why."

8. Martin E. Marty, *When Faiths Collide* (Oxford: Blackwell, 2005), 69–70. See also his *Building Cultures of Trust* (Grand Rapids, MI: Eerdmans, 2010).

9. Glenn Tinder, *The Political Meaning of Christianity: An Interpretation* (Baton Rouge: Louisiana State University Press, 1989), 61. Tinder's point recalls the classic distinction between *Gemeinschaft* (community) and *Gesellschaft* (society) made in 1887 by Ferdinand Tönnies (*Community and Society*, trans. Charles P. Loomis [Mineola, NY: Dover, 2002]).

10. Oliver O'Donovan pushes beyond considerations of the modern individual state to rebuke any larger ideal of Christian political aspiration as well. He avers that the Old Testament stands against empire, even a righteous one, and that "divine providence is ready to protect other national traditions besides the sacred one" (*The Desire of the Nations: Rediscovering the Roots of Political Thought* [Cambridge: Cambridge University Press, 1996], 73). He concludes that "Yhwh's world order was plurally constituted. World-empire was a bestial deformation. . . . *The appropriate unifying element in international*

order is law rather than government" (72). And, finally, "the titanic temptation which besets collectives needs the check of a perpetual plurality at the universal level. There are always 'others,' those not of our fold whom we must respect and encounter" (73). These passages, by the way, show how facile it is to construe O'Donovan as merely an apologist for Christendom.

11. Amy Gutmann helpfully distinguishes further between views that one can disagree with but respect, and views that one might tolerate but not respect, such as "misogyny, racial or ethnic hatred, or rationalizations of self-interest or group interest parading as historical or scientific knowledge." See her introduction to Taylor et al., *Multiculturalism*, 22.

12. John Feikens, "Conflict: Its Resolution and the Completion of Creation," in *Seeking Understanding: The Stob Lectures 1986– 1998* (Grand Rapids, MI: Eerdmans, 2001), 343–371.

13. John Cleese, *So, Anyway . . .* (Toronto: Anchor Canada, 2014), 369–70; emphasis in original.

14. Neil Postman, "Scientism," in *Technopoly: The Surrender of Culture to Technology* (New York: Vintage, 1992), 144–163.

15. In a huge field, see the work of scientists-cum-theologians John Polkinghorne (e.g., *Belief in God in an Age of Science* [New Haven, CT: Yale University Press, 1998]) and Alister E. McGrath (e.g., *The Foundations of Dialogue in Science and Religion* [Oxford: Blackwell, 1998]). See also J. Wentzel van Huyssteen, *Duet or Duel? Theology and Science in a Postmodern World* (Harrisburg, PA: Trinity, 1998).

16. Neil Postman, *Conscientious Objections: Stirring Up Trouble about Language, Technology, and Education* (New York: Vintage, 1988), 128–135.

17. John Howard Yoder, *The Priestly Kingdom: Social Ethics as Gospel* (Notre Dame, IN: University of Notre Dame Press, 1985), 40.

18. Some Christians seem to think that to use the word "values" is to concede entirely to relativism, as if the word "values" means simply subjective preferences while the word "virtues" refers to objective realities. Alas, this is a distinction not supported by any dictionary I consulted.

Calling one's own values "virtues" in this context thus can appear to mean that one considers one's values to be objectively grounded—to be true to the nature of things, to be *facts*. To think so is perfectly fine, of course, and is arguably the default position of human beings. I myself am such a moral realist—I do think that child molestation or the indifferent despoliation of the earth is just wrong, everywhere and always, and that it is therefore virtuous to recognize such moral facts. Such terminology, however, doesn't solve the challenge of convincing other people to come around to one's point of view, especially since such usage might well imply that "*we* have virtues (we are right) while *you* have mere values (and thus are wrong)."

19. Glenn Tinder, *The Fabric of Hope: An Essay* (Atlanta: Scholars Press, 1999), 7.

20. Sociologist Rodney Stark remarks: "Recently, the local media expressed approval when the chief of police of Seattle prohibited his officers from wearing their uniforms to take part in a 'March for Jesus.' The media were equally agreeable when, the *next day*, the chief wore his uniform to march in the 'Lesbian Gay Bisexual Transgender Parade.' In similar fashion, protest vigils against capital punishment held outside prisons when an execution is scheduled are invariably treated with respect, but vigils outside abortion clinics are not. When animal rights activists berate and abuse women in public for wearing furs, their media treatment is favorable in comparison to that given demonstrations against clubs featuring women wearing nothing. . . . Indeed, the media could not even report the death of Mother Teresa without providing 'balance' by soliciting nasty attacks on her sincerity and merit from various professional atheists" (Rodney Stark, *One True God: Historical Consequences of Monotheism* [Princeton, NJ: Princeton University Press, 2001], 251–252).

21. See my "Speaking in Tongues: Communicating the Gospel Today," chapter in *Evangelical Landscapes: Facing Critical Issues of the Day* (Grand Rapids, MI: Baker Academic, 2002), 185–204. I would point to the work of the Centre for Public Christianity in Sydney, Australia, as an extraordinarily good example of such discourse: https://publicchristianity.org.

22. An influential book in this respect is Luke Bretherton, *Christianity and Contemporary Politics: The Conditions and Possibilities of Faithful Witness* (Oxford: Wiley-Blackwell, 2009).

23. For reflections that bear the marks of the author's own Croatian experience, see Miroslav Volf, *Exclusion and Embrace: A Theological Exploration of Identity, Otherness, and Reconciliation* (Nashville, TN: Abingdon, 1996); and Miroslav Volf, *Free of Charge: Giving and Forgiving in a Culture Stripped of Grace* (Grand Rapids, MI: Zondervan, 2005).

24. Marty, *When Faiths Collide*, 91.

25. An admirable example of listening and responding, in this case to postmodernists, is J. Richard and Brian J. Walsh Middleton, *Truth Is Stranger than It Used to Be: Biblical Faith in a Postmodern Age* (Downers Grove, IL: InterVarsity, 1995).

26. C. S. Lewis is rather direct on this point: "The application of Christian principles, say, to trade unionism or education, must come from Christian trade unionists and Christian schoolmasters: just as Christian literature comes from Christian novelists and dramatists—not from the bench of bishops getting together and trying to write plays and novels in their spare time" (*Mere Christianity* [Glasgow: Collins/Fount, 1977 (1952)], 75).

27. Bonhoeffer used this term, which has roots in the Reformation, in his famous essay on "The Church and the Jewish Question" (April 1933).

28. One notes that Pope Benedict XVI allowed for the use of condoms to prevent the spread of AIDS: http://www.nytimes.com/2010/11/24/world/europe/24pope.html; accessed February 2, 2017.

29. "Christianity and Culture," in C. S. Lewis, *Christian Reflections*, ed. Walter Hooper (Grand Rapids, MI: Eerdmans, 1997 [1967]), 21.

30. David Martin offers trenchant reflections for politicians—and for academicians—that have informed this discussion in his "The Christian, the Political, and the Academic," in *On Secularization*, 185–99.

31. One advance reader of *Making the Best of It* asked me, "Are you not convinced by the argument that marriage *cannot* be

subject to human construction?" I reply, first, that it is simply a matter of fact that marriage *has* been subject to human (re-) construction, notably in polygamy, in the taking of concubines and mistresses, in the serial monogamy typical of modern societies, in common-law marriages, and so on. Second, I think the reader means instead that, however we human beings have altered marriage to suit our wishes, marriage is in fact a divine institution, per Genesis 2, and therefore has just one actual, legitimate form. With that, I do agree. But the fact that I think so doesn't mean that I might not see, as a politician, that the best decision I can make in a given situation might be to cast a vote for the redefinition of the word "marriage" so as to preserve what can be preserved in the face of malign or confused social forces that otherwise would score an even bigger victory against what I believe to be the best— that is, divinely instituted—values of human relationship. The fact that I believe there is only one proper understanding of marriage doesn't mean I could not vote for the legal accommodation of more than one understanding in the law of a plural society, just as I might vote for the legal accommodation of more than one expression of sexuality, despite my traditional views to the contrary. It all depends on what political options happen to be available, among which I have to choose that which I trust will produce the most shalom in a situation deeply compromised by sin and confusion.

32. Thomas Friedman, quoting his friend Abdallah Schliefer, in *The World Is Flat: A Brief History of the Twenty-First Century* (New York: Farrar, Straus and Giroux, 2005), 396.

Conclusion

1. Oliver O'Donovan indicates a crucial difference in the political realm between the Christian understanding of society versus rulers: "Society and rulers have different destinies: the former is to be transformed, shaped in conformity to God's purpose; the latter are to disappear, renouncing their sovereignty in the face of his.... Christ has conquered the rulers from below, by drawing their subjects out from under their authority"—and,

as I say above, I think many rulers, as well as other sorts of powers, sense that fact, fear it, and resent it (*The Desire of the Nations: Rediscovering the Roots of Political Thought* [Cambridge: Cambridge University Press, 1996], 193).

2. Ian Frazier, "Invaders," *The New Yorker* (April 25, 2005): 54.

3. John Calvin, *Institutes*, I.i.2; cf. James 1:17 and Augustine, *City of God*, 10.3.

4. Nicholas Wolterstorff refers to an anonymous "seventeenth-century English writer" who testified, "I had rather see coming toward me a whole regiment with drawn swords, than one lone Calvinist convinced that he is doing the will of God" (*Until Justice and Peace Embrace* [Grand Rapids, MI: Eerdmans, 1983], 9). Wolterstorff does so, I think, with playful approbation. But the quotation works the other way, too. The regiment might yet be reasoned with, bargained with, or even bought off, if necessary. But the "lone Calvinist" convinced of the identity of his cause with God's will, will be relentless and implacable—which will be entirely in order if the gospel itself is at stake, but not if anything else is.

5. Lesslie Newbigin, *The Gospel in a Pluralist Society* (Grand Rapids, MI: Eerdmans, 1989), 209.

INDEX